A Review of Good Practice in Deaf Education

Stephen Powers, Susan Gregory, Wendy Lynas, Wendy McCracken, Linda Watson, Angela Boulton and Dot Harris

The Universities of Birmingham and Manchester

RNID gratefully acknowledges the support provided by the Trusthouse Charitable Foundation and the Equitable Charitable Trust towards this research.

Published by RNID
19-23 Featherstone Street
London EC1Y 8SL

ISBN 0 900634 71 5

First published in 1999

Contents

Page

Acknowledgements

The research team would like to thank The Royal National Institute for Deaf People (RNID) for funding this project and Carol Gray from DfEE for being a member of the advisory group. We would also like to thank Hilary Sutherland for acting as deaf consultant and Mary Griggs who helped with organising and facilitating the focus groups of FE students. We are grateful to all those who helped with the distribution of questionnaires and/or set up focus groups.

Finally, and in particular, we would like to thank all those colleagues who became involved in the case studies and who supported this project by giving their time so generously.

Chapter 1

Executive Summary

Executive Summary

Introduction

This investigation into reported good practice in the education of deaf children and young people was commissioned by The Royal National Institute for Deaf People (RNID). It acts on the belief that substantial evidence about good practice in deaf education is available through the experience of those most directly involved in the process, but that this evidence is not routinely represented in academic papers and professional journals. This report presents a review of good practice as reported by teachers, parents and other participants. For RNID, the *Good Practice Review* is part of a larger Guidelines Project which aims to improve educational opportunity for deaf children by informing and improving the educational practice of professionals.

There were three main aims in the *Good Practice Review:*

1.   to survey the views of teachers, parents, the major deaf organisations and others on what constitutes good practice; to ask for named examples of schools, services, resource bases, colleges and individual teachers and to provide well-documented case studies of reported good practice

2.   to identify common threads in reported examples of good practice

3.   to provide clear definitions and descriptions of systems and approaches used in the education of deaf children in the UK

Individual teachers, parents and others, and the major deaf organisations were asked through questionnaires to give their views on what they think constitutes good practice in the education of deaf children and young people and to name and describe examples of good practice. There were 628 replies to the questionnaire with the largest category of responses coming from parents. A selection was made from the named examples in order to conduct a number of case studies across a range of educational approach and placement. Fifteen case studies were selected, each conducted over a period of one to three days.

Key findings are as follows:

The notion of good practice:
Deaf organisations and questionnaire responses (Chapter 3)

- The notion of good practice is complex and at times paradoxical.

- There is significant consensus on what should be the aims of deaf education although parents, teachers and deaf adults vary in the priority which should be given to them.

- It has not been difficult to arrive at a number of themes which need to be addressed in a consideration of good practice.

- There are differences on how the aims of deaf education should be realised.

- Parents do not find the debates between professionals helpful, and disagreements between professionals are seen as destructive.

Leadership and management (section 4.1)

- Effective leadership is a key component of good practice.

- Heads who have strong commitment and high expectations, who also value the contributions of individuals and allow professional autonomy are well regarded by their staff.

- Many of the schools and services we visited have a strong sense of team spirit.

- Clear and detailed documentation can ensure that a shared vision and philosophy is translated into a consistent approach.

- A joint approach to self-reflection and evaluation is a common feature of good practice.

- There is no one model of organisation to suit all services; factors such as size and geography play a role.

Ethos (section 4.2)

- The ethos of a school or service derives from and is inextricably linked with the features of its leadership and management and its underlying philosophy of deaf education.

- School life provides many opportunities for occasions to reflect on and reinforce core values which can help maintain a strong ethos.

- An important feature of ethos is valuing individuals, and staff-pupil relationships which reflect mutual respect.

Professional development (section 4.3)

- Regular team meetings which specifically evaluate the service or school, consider areas for development and share expertise across the team are seen as vital.

- Heads of schools and services emphasise the importance of employing teachers who hold the mandatory qualification to teach deaf children.

- A comprehensive audit of all staff skills is helpful which includes all areas of expertise together with a clear plan for development of the individual to enhance service delivery.

- A proactive head of school or service can ensure funding opportunities are put to maximum use.

Inclusion (section 4.4)

- There is a universal support for the goals of inclusion among providers whether mainstream or special school.

- The goal of inclusion is supported not undermined by a component of separate, discrete specialist provision for deaf pupils.

- Welcoming attitudes and a commitment to inclusion on the part of the receiving school contribute greatly to the perceived success of the practice of inclusion.

- Teachers of the deaf are seen to play a significant role in overall school improvement and in promoting whole-school policies.

- The practice of inclusion is perceived by some providers as underpinning the natural aural approach.

- Deaf adults are increasingly playing a role in the education of deaf children and young people and this is seen as a positive step towards inclusion and equal opportunities.

Support in mainstream schools (section 4.5)

- In most cases a mixed approach is taken where support is offered in class, in tutorial sessions and in reverse integration groups.

- Teachers of the deaf adopt an approach where they seek to work collaboratively with mainstream teachers and learning support assistants, sharing the responsibility for the deaf pupils. The teacher of the deaf often takes on the coordinating role.

- Increasing emphasis is being placed on the need for joint planning between teachers of the deaf and mainstream teachers even where there are constraints.

- Some services involve parents and pupils in decisions about the amount and type of support provided.

- There is widespread awareness of the need to constantly monitor and evaluate levels of support.

- There is a strong emphasis on INSET for mainstream teachers which makes significant and specific requirements of teachers of the deaf.

Audiological management (section 4.6)

- A positive working relationship with health service providers, early identification and early access to services for deaf children are key features of good practice.

- Access to appropriately fitted amplification and high quality earmoulds is essential.

- Teachers of the deaf should be audiologically competent and enable other adults and the child to become proficient audiological managers.

- Teachers of the deaf need to be fully conversant with the potential effects of room acoustics and the importance of daily access to an acoustically friendly area.

- There should be regular assessment of changing audiological needs in conjunction with an educational audiologist.

- A clear developmental programme to monitor and encourage optimum use of amplification is needed.

Spoken language development (section 4.7)

- A great deal of importance is placed on the development of spoken language. This is true regardless of setting or communication approach.

- It may be regarded as the main channel of communication or as one of a range of options.

- In oral settings spoken language development is seen as building on audition, with speech intelligibility receiving emphasis.

- Where it is one of a range of communication options the emphasis is on 'live' English to facilitate communication with hearing people.

- In all settings on-going detailed assessment and monitoring of progress are essential.

Literacy (section 4.8)

- Great emphasis is placed on the promotion of literacy skills in all settings.

- Teachers working with deaf children in oral settings draw heavily on work with hearing children, based on spoken language development.

- Sign bilingual and Total Communication settings have developed their own distinct ways of developing literacy skills.

- An important feature of good practice is a continuing focus on pupils' reading development at the secondary stage.

- In all settings creative use is being made of the Literacy Hour to enhance learning for deaf pupils.

Personal and social development (section 4.9)

- Concern with the personal and social development of deaf children is much in evidence with particular attention given to developing high self-esteem, independence, a positive sense of identity and appropriate social skills.
- Many see a strong link between the development of personal and social skills and academic achievement.
- Deaf adults and deaf peers play key roles in a range of contexts.
- Identity is a complex issue for deaf young people, families and educators.

Deaf children with disabilities (section 4.10)

- A key worker is needed to coordinate services for deaf children with disabilities.
- Assessments should focus on the whole child and inform intervention.
- Very small steps in learning need to be recorded and built upon.
- Teachers and other professionals should have expectations which do not underestimate the child.
- All children with a degree of hearing loss which has implications for learning are entitled to sensitive support from a teacher of the deaf.

Work with families and young children (section 4.11)

- Many services we visited stress the need for very early visiting after diagnosis with a target time written into policy.
- Regular support and advice during preschool years with provision for school holidays is seen as vital.
- Schools and services should make a number of resources and opportunities available to parents including the opportunity for visits, information packs, parent groups, signing classes, audiological support and links with national organisations.
- There should be a continuing partnership between schools and services and families during the school years.
- Good practice is also characterised by the constructive use of Individual Education Plans (IEPs), annual reviews and advice on provision in working with parents.

Work with children and families from minority ethnic backgrounds (section 4.12)

- It is vital that support for families should include a native speaker of their own language.
- Families from minority ethnic backgrounds, particularly mothers, derive great benefit from a support group. This can help with developing children's language and communication and managing their behaviour.
- Schools and services need to facilitate access to a range of services such as providing free transport to parent support groups.

Further education (section 4.13)

- Information on courses and careers is important for students and their families.
- The provision of adequate support in lectures requires careful initial assessment and the monitoring of provision.
- Professional development of staff is a key feature of provision.

Issues around the language and mode of communication (section 5.1)

- The issue of approaches to language and communication in deaf education is a complex one.
- While there may be some consensus on the aims of deaf education, there are differences in people's views on how best these aims are realised.
- Different priorities in deaf education have led to different approaches, particularly in the area of language and communication, some of which differ from each other in major and significant ways, while others seem to be variations on a theme.
- Issues in approaches are confounded by the lack of clarity about definitions.
- The choice of terminology to describe the approaches has linguistic, social, historical and political roots.

The oral aural approach (section 5.2)

- The target in all oral/aural approaches is the promotion of spoken language.
- Fundamental to all oral/aural approaches is the belief that residual hearing should be exploited to the full.
- Early diagnosis is seen as highly desirable, followed as soon as possible by hearing aid fitting and the promotion of listening skills.
- Spoken language is promoted through conversational interaction. In natural aural approaches this is seen as the primary means, but other oral approaches may supplement this with more structured language teaching.
- Speech intelligibility is given priority in oral/aural approaches. This is promoted through the use of residual hearing, supplemented in some approaches by speech intervention work.

The sign bilingual approach (section 5.3)

- Crucial to sign bilingualism is the systematic and separate use of two languages, British Sign Language (BSL) and English.
- The use of BSL requires tuition and assessment of sign language for all involved – children, parents, teachers and other staff.
- The approach has implications for staffing including the increased participation of deaf people and communication support workers.
- Sign bilingualism is a relatively new approach to the education of deaf children and thus is still evolving.

Chapter 2

Introduction

Introduction

Background

This investigation into reported good practice in the education of deaf children and young people was commissioned by The Royal National Institute for Deaf People (RNID). It follows and builds on a literature review in the same area which was commissioned by DfEE in 1998 [1].

The Good Practice Review and DfEE Literature Review are complementary data collection exercises. Their common aim is to inform and improve educational practice with deaf children and young people. The Good Practice Review acts on the belief that substantial evidence about good practice in deaf education is available through the experience of those most directly involved in the process, but that this evidence is not routinely represented in academic papers and professional journals. This report presents a review of good practice as reported by teachers, parents and other participants. The main aim of the exercise is to provide a synthesis of accumulated wisdom and experience that has not until now been available in published form.

The participation of DfEE as a member of the advisory group steering the Good Practice Review provided welcome continuity with the Literature Review from 1998. For RNID, the Good Practice Review is free-standing, but also part of a larger Guidelines Project. The aim of this project is to improve educational opportunity for deaf children by informing and improving the educational practice of professionals. The dissemination of information about reported good practice has an important role to play within this broader agenda. Guidelines materials for teachers using the information from this report and from other sources will be produced in collaboration with a range of agencies and service providers in 2000.

It is important to say at the outset what this report is *not*. First, it does not claim to be a *comprehensive* account of current good practice – otherwise it would be several times longer. There are many nominated examples of good practice which we were unable to investigate and therefore are unable to report. This review presents only a sample of reported cases. Second, this review is not a 'how to do it' manual. It does not seek to provide a set of prescriptions or strategies for others to directly copy. Rather it seeks to provide a wealth of detailed description relevant and useful to individual teachers which we hope will cause them to reflect on and improve their practice. Third, this review does not aim to make its own recommendations for good practice. Rather it

---

[1] Powers, S., Gregory, S. Thoutenhoofd, E.D. (1998) *The Educational Achievements of Deaf Children. DfEE Research Report RR65.* London: DfEE

aims to characterise good practice by reporting the views of others. We investigated good practice *as reported by teachers, parents and others,* not good practice identified by ourselves. We did not impose any objective measures and in fact such objective measures do not exist.

The reader will find that often there are alternative approaches described and sometimes these are contrasting. That they appear together in a review of reported good practice is partly a reflection of the different more general views there are on how deaf children are best educated, itself linked to the different views there are on the *aims* of deaf education. This theme is discussed in more detail in chapter 3.

Aims

There were three main aims in the Good Practice Review:

1.   to survey the views of teachers, parents, the major deaf organisations and others on what constitutes good practice; to ask for named examples of schools, services, resource bases, colleges and individual teachers and to provide well documented case studies of reported good practice

2.   to identify common threads in reported examples of good practice

3.   to provide clear definitions and descriptions of systems and approaches used in the education of deaf children in the UK

Coverage (populations, sectors and themes)

We did not set out to look at any particular group of deaf children, that is to *exclude* any group. Our brief was to look at deaf children in general and in doing this we aimed our coverage to be as comprehensive as possible. However, in reviewing our case study material it is clear that most of the discussion relates to children with more severe degrees of hearing loss rather than those with mild or even moderate deafness. This is a reflection of the role that teachers of the deaf are asked to perform. We need to acknowledge this as a gap in the report, that children with mild hearing losses are given only small consideration in the discussion that follows.

The focus of this Review is firmly on the school, preschool and further education sectors. Higher education has not been included as it was considered beyond the scope of the study. Teacher of the deaf training is also not included. While an interesting and important area it is actually quite separate – in fact rather than including teacher training as a good practice topic the final report should *inform* the training of teachers of the deaf.

Our aim was to report under a number of themes or topics (for example literacy, working with parents), but rather than choosing these topics at the outset they were allowed to emerge from the research itself. We anticipated that there were some topics that *would* and *should* evolve, not least because of how the project sought views on what constitutes good practice. Also, we expected that the major themes of the government Green Paper [2] would be likely to develop as main topics (for example preschool support, inclusion, organisation of services, and the efficient use of resources).

Design of the research

Phase one
Individual teachers, parents and others, and the major deaf organisations were asked to give their views on what they think constitutes good practice in the education of deaf children and young people and to name and describe examples of good practice. The deaf organisations were also asked to name and define the terms they use and the approach(es) they seek to support or promote.

Also, a brief literature search was conducted to identify material in the professional press relevant to this project which might have fallen outside the scope of the 1998 DfEE Literature Review.

Phase two
A selection was made from the named examples of reported good practice in phase one in order to conduct a number of case studies across a range of educational approach and placement. It was anticipated that about fifteen case studies would be selected, each conducted over a period of one to three days.

Methods

Phase one
The main method in phase one was a questionnaire survey. The questionnaire (Appendix 1) was compiled in two parts and respondents were invited to complete either or both parts. Part one asked respondents to nominate a school, service, college or individual teacher as an example of good practice and to state for which aspects of work the nomination was made. The following list of items was included as a prompt:

> Teaching reading and writing
> Working with parents
> The use of hearing aids

---

[2] DfEE (1997) *Excellence for All Children: Meeting Special Educational Needs.* London: The Stationery Office.

The language/communication approach used
The choice of schools for parents
Exam results of deaf children
The work of classroom assistants
Developing children's signing skills
Supporting deaf pupils in ordinary schools
Developing children's spoken language skills
In-service training for teachers of the deaf
Helping children develop independence
Helping children develop their identity
Work with deaf children with disabilities
Work with very young children
Further education
Other (please specify)

This list was compiled to be relevant to all phases of education, to all placements and all communication approaches, as well as making reference to non-academic as well as academic concerns. It was carefully worded to be readable to as wide an audience as possible. It was not meant to be a comprehensive list, but instead was meant to present some examples of aspects of work which might be mentioned. A box was added for further comment.

Part two of the questionnaire asked for more general views on good practice as well as views on what are the most important aims of deaf education.

The questionnaire was distributed to a wide range of people with an interest in the education of deaf children, including parents, teachers and lecturers, deaf adults, speech and language therapists, educational psychologists, and deaf organisations. Most questionnaires were sent as flyers in magazines, distributed at conferences or sent individually. We were not aiming to obtain a randomised sample of returns, but rather used a blanket approach to reach as many people as possible. The questionnaire was circulated as follows:

BATOD Annual General Meeting
BATOD *Magazine*
British Deaf News (including video newsletter)
Colleges of FE (listed in the NDCS directory)
Deaf Nation conference
Deafview page on Teletext
DELTA newsletter
Ewing Foundation

Heads of Schools and Services for Deaf and Hearing Impaired Children
Heads of Schools and Services conference pack
Information Exchange magazine
LASERBEAM magazine
NATED newsletter
NDCS branches
NDCS *TALK* magazine
RNID *One in Seven* magazine
SENSE magazine
Speech and Language Therapists mailing list

More than 25,000 questionnaires were circulated, but due to wastage in the distribution of some magazines and that some people received multiple copies we estimate that considerably fewer than this number of people received a copy. The reader is referred to chapter 3 for a discussion of the returns.

A further method in phase one was focus groups. We organised a number of meetings where deaf students in further education could discuss their recent experiences of school, the aim of this being to inform the case studies. These focus groups are reported later in this chapter.

Other methods used in phase one were manual searches of the literature, telephone interviews and document analysis.

Phase two

The case studies used multiple sources of evidence including interviews (the main research method), observation and document analysis.

Views were sought from a wide range of participants including heads of schools, heads of services, teachers of the deaf, parents, present pupils, learning support assistants, teachers in mainstream schools, educational audiologists and educational psychologists. They were interviewed on a number of topics, or themes, for which the case study had been nominated and were also invited to provide detailed examples of strategies that worked well for them.

Schedules for interviews and classroom observation were devised, each comprising a short list of what we judged to be key issues to be addressed under a particular theme. In compiling these schedules we made use of the collective broad experience of the research team. However, our aim was to report practice according to the constructs and terms used by the participants themselves, therefore the schedules were used in a semi-structured way where on some occasions questions or items were omitted or others added. This approach allowed us to follow up interesting points immediately. Our main interest was to know from participants what from their point of view worked well and what was most important to good practice, and if possible for them to provide examples.

Selecting themes

The following themes are reported in chapter 4:

> Leadership and management
> Ethos
> Professional development
> Inclusion
> Support in mainstream schools
> Audiological management
> Spoken language development
> Literacy
> Personal and social development
> Deaf children with disabilities
> Work with families and young children
> Work with children and families from minority ethnic backgrounds
> Further education

These themes are largely ones that emerged from the questionnaire although some arose from the case studies themselves, notably leadership and professional development. Some themes, or areas of work, were nominated in only a handful of places – it was particularly disappointing that there was not more mention of work with deaf children with disabilities and those from minority ethnic backgrounds. Clearly, we did not tap into these groups well enough.

One of the main themes addressed in this report is that of spoken language development, an issue for all case studies regardless of their approach to language and communication. It might thus be thought that there would be a parallel section on sign language development. However, while we have some information on this topic, which is discussed in various places including the section on sign bilingualism, we did not have the range of information to justify its inclusion as a theme. It is worth noting in this context the recent emergence of sign language as a language for education and the fact that only recently has there been any standard way of assessing sign language development in children (cf. Herman 1998 [3]).

[3] Herman, R. (1998) The need for an assessment of deaf children's signing skills. *Deafness and Education*, 22, 3, 3-8

Selecting case studies

There are different ideas on what constitutes good practice and it was important to include all of these in our selection of case studies. However, we do not claim that the examples chosen are representative of their type. The approach taken is illuminative case study based on selective sampling.

The case studies were selected according to the following criteria:

1. the number of nominations received
2. that there were nominations from different groups (parents, teachers etc.)
3. the need to reflect the range of provision made for deaf pupils regarding educational placement and language and communication approach
4. the need to include a wide range of different aspects of work (or topics)

The following factors were considered in sampling across the range of provision to select the case studies:

(i)   Type of educational programme:
- preschool
- primary resourced school (unit)
- secondary resourced school (unit)
- individual integration programme in primary
- individual integration programme in secondary
- day special school for deaf children
- residential special school for deaf children
- other special school
- further education

(ii)   Language and communication approach used (e.g. oral, bimodal, sign bilingual)

(iii)   Other factors:
- inner city vs rural
- large minority ethnic population
- advantaged vs disadvantaged areas
- deaf children with complex needs

We aimed to include at least one example from the main different approaches, one FE college and one programme for deaf children with additional difficulties.

According to the criteria for selection not all the schools, services or colleges that were strongly nominated were chosen as case studies. Also, in the ones that were chosen the aspects of work selected for investigation are not the only ones for which the school, service or college was nominated. While aiming to investigate each area of work at least two or three times we also decided to restrict the number of aspects of work investigated in any one case study to allow greater depth.

It should be emphasised again that in selecting case studies we were not guided in our own views about what are good schools, services or colleges. We did not include or reject any recommendation on the basis of our own experiences, nor did we refer to Ofsted reports. We regard one of the strengths of this project is that it was not the 'experts' making the choices of what is 'good', rather it offered the practitioners an opportunity to have their say.

According to the procedure just described it was not difficult to agree on the selection of case studies. Final decisions were made after consultation with the advisory group representatives from RNID and DfEE. Fifteen case studies were chosen, five three-day studies, five two-day studies and five one-day studies – the length of the study determined by the number of aspects of work to be investigated. Brief descriptions of the 15 case studies appear at the end of this chapter.

The schools, services and college selected for study were initially contacted by telephone to explain the purpose of study including mention of the aspects of work we wished to investigate. A briefing document was also sent at this stage and the establishments were asked to consider whether they wished to participate in the study. All agreed. Each case study was conducted by a team of two, comprising one of the principal researchers and one research officer. We did not go in with a prescribed agenda, rather the details for each visit were negotiated with establishments beforehand including opportunities for interviewing and observation. There was also an invitation to send documents before the visit, although we did not specifically request information on pupil achievement because a report on this topic was not intrinsic to the study.

Each case study was written up as a report and a copy was sent to establishments to allow factual errors to be corrected. Some quotations and 'vignettes' are taken directly from the case study reports in which case they are attributed in the Review to 'case study X' rather than to any individual. Where a quote is from an individual or taken from a document this is stated.

The individual case studies are not identified in this report.

The views of recent consumers

As part of the process of developing the study, it was decided to tap the views of recent consumers of the education system by talking to deaf students in further education. Visits to four different locations for further education (FE) were made by members of the research team. The aim in each case was to seek the views of deaf students, particularly their perceptions of good practice in their former schools and their present experiences in college. The four provisions included a large specialist college supporting students in a number of mainstream FE colleges, a specialist college providing a range of courses and some support in a mainstream college, a specialist unit within a mainstream college, and an LEA service providing support to students in mainstream colleges and university. Students in these four settings had originally come from a wide range of educational settings – mainstream, unit provision and school for the deaf – and used different languages and communication modes. The diversity of courses that the students were undertaking were indicative of a wide range of ability. Overall over 65 students were consulted.

Discussions took two main types; large group discussions chaired by a deaf facilitator with a sign language interpreter or notetaker as appropriate, and small group work where members of the team worked with individual students, based on communication preference. Although the focus of the discussion was on positive aspects of education, it was noticeable that in many cases students needed to get their negative experiences 'out of the way' first. The views mentioned below were those held by several people – however, it should be noted that students had a range of different perspectives on the issues under consideration and there was not always consensus.

Communication

A very wide range of views were expressed by the students about communication, and many expressed the view that communication is the most important element of deaf education. Some stressed the importance of speech, some sign. Some wanted more specific instruction in speech, others said that having to try and speak when they found it difficult was stressful. Others expressed a belief in the importance of lipreading skills in interactions with hearing people. Signing was believed by some to greatly increase confidence.

At school, positive factors contributing to good communication were said to be speech and language therapy and the use of hearing aids and radio aids. At college, students appreciate positive encouragement to use their preferred communication mode. On the negative side, students reported a wide range of difficulties in communication. They spoke of their own inability to comprehend, which in turn was because of a number of factors, for example teachers who spoke too fast and for too long. Teachers who were unable to sign or signed inadequately were criticised by some.

Teachers and staff

The students felt they benefited from teachers who gave clear explanations and used appropriate communication strategies for example turning before speaking, explaining video content. They appreciated a number of positive features of teachers including patience, a 'caring manner', being understanding and having an understanding of deafness. There was a view that teachers in schools for the deaf 'break things down more', but have lower expectations for pupils. They were also perceived to be too lenient by one student. A few problems relating to mainstream teachers were also expressed including the fact that some had no prior experience with deaf children, did not appreciate the importance of radio aids and became angry when the pupil did not understand. Some embarrassment was expressed over the presence of the notetaker/communication support. The presence of deaf adults in the educational setting was seen as advantageous.

Inclusion/support

Two advantages of receiving a mainstream education were mentioned; first an exposure to a pattern of speech which contributed to the development of spoken and written language, and second increased achievement. Problems included the lack of support in the classroom and limited deaf awareness on the part of mainstream staff. A number of students expressed difficulties in accessing the curriculum and learning, with much material going 'over the head'. Students also had criticisms of the curriculum they had been offered at school. Some felt that it had been too narrow, whilst others saw it as insufficiently demanding.

Personal/social issues

Friendships were important and in mainstream schools some spoke of having supportive hearing friends while others valued the opportunity to meet deaf friends at break time. Pupils in special settings enjoyed having all deaf peers, and a number benefited from a good social life at residential schools. Particularly depressing were tales of bullying and teasing by hearing children, mentioned by many former mainstream pupils. Bullying by deaf children also occurred. Even if children were not bullied, they feared it and some felt isolated, lonely and fearful.

Conclusion

Due to the range of opinions expressed by the students we spoke to and the specific nature of their views, it was not possible to use them as topics to inform the Good Practice case studies. Nevertheless, they provided useful valuable background information. It is not possible to draw any firm conclusions from such a range of views, often contradictory, of people with such diverse backgrounds. One or two general points emerge, however. Even allowing for the elapse of a number of years and developments within them, the amount of disquiet relating to the primary and secondary years is salutary. The importance of language and communication is significant and comments relating to bullying are perhaps of particular concern.

Literature search

In seeking to identify good practice, the main emphasis throughout this research has been on the work of the practitioner. Therefore, it was appropriate to seek out articles written by those working directly in the field and in which they describe their practice. In this country the journal of the British Association of Teachers of the Deaf and the Association *Magazine* serve as important forums for the sharing of practice among those working in the profession. Therefore, the contents of these publications from 1979-1999 were examined for relevant texts relating to the themes. A small selection from this brief search of the literature is reported as 'further reading' at the end of each theme in chapter 3. Most of those chosen were written by teachers of the deaf or other professionals working with deaf children and young people. Some articles written by researchers have also been included, especially where the research relates to the effectiveness of particular educational approaches and methods. Some key books relating to the themes are also included.

Terminology

The choice of terminology throughout this review reflects that used in the schools, services and colleges we visited. So for example the reader will find reference to both 'deaf' children and 'hearing impaired' children, 'units' as well as 'resourced schools', 'classroom assistants' as well as 'special needs assistants'. This usage reflects the lack of consensus on what terms are best. Our own preference, based on convenience, is to use the term 'deaf' to refer to all children with a significant hearing loss.

We have used the term 'inclusion' with care, recognising the different ways the term has been used in the literature. In one sense it appears perfectly logical to talk about 'including' deaf children in ordinary classes referring to no more than their physical placement. This usage we have adopted. At the same time we do not describe this practice as 'inclusion' or 'inclusive education', terms which have been accorded a particular import in recent times.

The reader wanting further discussion on the issue of terminology is referred to the recent DfEE report on *The Educational Achievements of Deaf Children* (Powers *et al.,* 1998, p14ff and p137ff op cit) and Powers (1996) [4].

Organisation

The next chapter, Chapter 3, discusses the notion of good practice in deaf education. It presents the views reported to us by deaf organisations, parents, teachers and deaf adults and in doing so demonstrates the complexity of the notion.

---

[4] Powers, S. (1996) Inclusion is an attitude not a place: Part 1. *Journal of the British Association of Teachers of the Deaf* **20** (2) 35-41.

Chapter 4 presents the main findings of the case studies under a number of themes. Although these do not lend themselves easily to grouping, we have ordered them according to three main categories – management themes, general pedagogical themes and themes relating to specific groups of children or young people.

Chapter 5 is our response to the third main aim of the study relating to descriptions of language and communication approaches to the education of deaf children.

Chapter 6 presents the main conclusions.

Chapter 3 and all the sections in Chapters 4 and 5 end with a summary of the main findings presented as a number of bullet points. These are brought together in the executive summary in chapter 1.

Finally, it is not intended that the reader starts at the beginning of this report and reads through to the end. The sections in chapter 4 to a large extent stand alone, although there are strong links between some sections and this has been indicated in the text. We hope we have presented our findings in a way that allows the reader to dip in wherever interest takes him or her.

The case studies: brief descriptions

Fifteen case studies were chosen, five three-day studies, five two-day studies and five one-day studies – the length of the study determined by the number of aspects of work to be investigated. Most of the case studies were from England, but one was from Scotland and one from Northern Ireland.

(i) The three day case studies

Case study A

A Deaf and Hearing Impaired Support Service which is LEA maintained and centrally funded and is based about a mile from the centre of a large city said to incorporate the fourth poorest and the fourth wealthiest ward in the country. It also incorporates a large and diverse minority ethnic population. The service has a sign bilingual policy.

Case study B

An LEA Service for Sensory Impaired Children in a rural county. A natural aural approach is used. Out of county provision is made in some cases.

Case study C

A non-maintained residential special school for deaf pupils of primary and secondary age. The school is an oral school and uses the 'maternal reflective method' (MRM) to develop spoken language skills.

Case study D

An LEA Educational Service for the Hearing Impaired in a compact, socially mixed metropolitan borough in a large conurbation. The majority of deaf pupils are supported in their local schools with a natural aural approach. A sign bilingual approach is offered in the two resource-based schools.

Case study E

An LEA Service for Hearing Impaired Children in a large rural county. The service has a broadly oral/aural approach.

(ii) The two-day case studies

Case study F

An Educational Audiology Service in a rural area that includes some remote and isolated communities. The approach of the service is auditory oral.

Case study G

An LEA controlled special school for deaf children of primary age. There is a separate secondary department situated in a mainstream school one mile away. Residential accommodation is offered. The school itself has a Total Communication policy.

Case study H

An LEA Service to Hearing Impaired Children in a large rural county with a dispersed population. The approach of the service is auditory oral, explicitly differentiated from the natural aural approach.

Case study J

A non-maintained residential special school for secondary aged pupils on the edge of a large town. The communication approach is natural aural.

Case study K

An LEA Service for Hearing Impaired Children in a rural county. A natural aural approach is used.

Case study L

A further education department of a non-maintained residential school and college for deaf children and students in an urban area. An eclectic communication approach is taken according to the needs of students.

(iii) The one-day case studies

Case study M

A nursery provision for hearing impaired children within a mainstream primary school in the outskirts of a large city. Children 'out of authority' can attend. A natural aural approach is used.

Case study N

An LEA controlled resource base in a one class entry infant-junior school in a large urban LEA. It operates under the system of Total Communication.

Case study P

An LEA controlled day school for primary aged children in an urban area which has a nursery class for deaf and hearing children of preschool age. Work with very young deaf children from the age of diagnosis is also based at the school. The communication approach offers parallel provision in oral and Total Communication (Sign Supported English) classes.

Case study Q

An LEA controlled Service for the Hearing Impaired in a large city which provides for a large minority ethnic population. An eclectic communication approach is taken including the use of sign.

Chapter 3

The notion of good practice: deaf organisations and questionnaire responses

The notion of good practice: deaf organisations and questionnaire responses

General remarks

While the focus of this report is good practice, and a major aim to seek out and describe examples of good practice, the notion itself is complex. Within education in general the notion of good practice is a contested category. Although there are areas of agreement, there is no clear consensus on how it is characterised and how it is constituted. The debates about National Curriculum tests and league tables, about the role of sport or citizenship in the curriculum, are indications of this.

Within deaf education views can be even more varied. Because deafness impacts on the language acquisition process and access to spoken language, educational policy has to take account of language and mode as well as other factors and the nature of the understanding of good practice reflects this.

The notion of good practice underpins this project. It was decided from very early on that good practice should be defined by interested parties rather than by the research team and to this end the questionnaire described in chapter 2 was sent out. This allowed for the identification of case studies. However, the questionnaire also yielded more data on the perception of good practice by the various groups of respondents and this information was supplemented by a review of the stated views of good practice by the major deaf organisations.

This chapter considers the notion of good practice from a number of sources and discusses the challenges this brought for the research team. While the choice of case studies was unproblematic, the research team found that it had to review notions of good practice in a more complex way in considering how to present the information gained from the case studies. The various areas are considered below.

Views from deaf organisations

All the major deaf organisations were contacted and asked for their views on good practice in deaf education. Many responded by sending their policy statements. This gave us a great deal of information – that on good practice is included in this chapter, and a detailed account of the information supplied is included in Appendix 2. It should be noted that we have categorised the responses for comparison purposes but that not all the organisations supplied responses which cover every category.

Common objectives of all the organisations are equality of opportunity for deaf children and young people and the chance for them to reach their maximum potential. Whilst recognising that 'deaf children and young people are not all the same; they have differing needs and requirements' they acknowledge that 'deaf children and young people have the same potential for language and learning as their hearing peers' (BATOD National Policy) and 'should be expected to achieve the same levels of educational attainment, social responsibility, employment and citizenship' (BDA *The Right to be Equal*). Another shared emphasis is on the right to a language, literacy skills and means of effective communication, together with the ability to find a place in society. The organisations differ, however, in how they interpret these aims and in how they believe they can be achieved. Their conceptions of 'good practice' are, therefore, determined by their particular perspective on these topics.

Obvious points of difference which emerge concern choice of language or communication mode and educational placement, particularly the practice of 'inclusion' or 'integration' of deaf children in mainstream schools. Ostensibly the differences relate to methodology, but closer inspection of the views of the organisations reveals that these alternative pedagogical practices derive from different philosophies. The organisations diverge in their conception of the purposes and necessary outcomes of deaf education which in turn relate to more fundamental conceptions of what deafness is and what being deaf means. Whilst many documents mention the right to be accepted as what they are – a deaf person – what this means, and thus what constitutes good practice, will vary according to the basic philosophy of the particular organisation.

A distinction can be drawn between those deaf organisations that represent a broad constituency such as the main organisations for teachers of the deaf (BATOD) or the major organisation representing families of deaf children (NDCS) and those organisations that comprise groups of people with shared views of an aspect of deaf education. DELTA, DEX, LASER, and the EWING Foundation came about because of a commitment to a particular approach to deaf education. The British Deaf Association has an anomalous position in this analysis. It is the major deaf organisation representing the views of deaf people, but because it is identified with a particular view of deaf education, for convenience, it is thus described with the more specialist groups[1].

BATOD, NDCS

While good practice does not emerge as a topic within the policy statements of most organisations, conclusions can be drawn from their general statements with regard to education. Both BATOD and the NDCS describe the need for a range of provision, and have a broad view of the aims of deaf education with a focus on the whole person.

---

[1] See appendix 2 for further information on these organisations.

For example, BATOD states:

> Some deaf children and young people will grow up to be part of the deaf population: some will live fully in the hearing world and some will move between the two so they have the right to develop appropriate skills to enable them to participate in hearing and deaf communities to the extent which they themselves choose and to be valued in terms of both their deaf and hearing identities.

The NDCS states:

> Deaf children and their families should be able to participate positively in the shared experience of deafness. To assist this process they should have access to the widest range of deaf people; this includes Deaf people in the sign language-using community, deaf people who use spoken language as well as those who use both.

> Both organisations recommend a continuum of provision to meet individual needs, and that the wishes of parents should be recognised and considered.

BATOD asserts that:

> All children and young people have the right to a developed communication system which enables them to communicate effectively in a variety of settings and for a variety of purposes. The desire to communicate must be fostered in order for language to develop. The methods of communication used with a child must be based on his/her needs, as assessed by all concerned with the child's development.

The NDCS view is that:

> Deaf children should have the appropriate technology, resources and support so that they have full and equal access to the language and cultures of the wider hearing community.

Deaf children need to develop fluent language skills, to understand and influence the world around them, by whichever approach is the most appropriate for the individual.

BDA, LASER and DEX

The BDA, LASER and DEX advocate bilingual education with access to both English and British Sign Language (BSL) as appropriate for most deaf children. This depends on the acceptance of BSL as a language equal in status to English both in society and in education. These organisations have a particular perspective on what it means to be deaf. They have a pluralist view of society within which deaf people are a linguistic and cultural minority, signified by their use of the capital letter in 'Deaf'. Therefore, they would argue, a deaf child has a right to a sense of deaf identity and access to the Deaf community. This would include developing self-esteem as a deaf person and the promotion of positive role models and positive images of deafness. In addition, their acceptance of the social model of disability means that one of their aims is the removal of oppression and empowerment of deaf people. For example, DEX writes, 'Although the term "hearing impaired" is used widely throughout education, DEX will not use it, on the basis that if we are to learn to become positive about being Deaf then negative language can only serve to undermine that process'.

An important prerequisite therefore is the ability to communicate in a shared language, hence the need for sign bilingual education to be offered right from the start. There would also be involvement of deaf adults and the Deaf community and the opportunity to learn about deaf culture and history within an appropriate and relevant curriculum giving the same access to the knowledge, skills and experiences as hearing children and enabling them to move freely and comfortably between communities – deaf, majority society and family (BDA).

Due to the concern for links with the Deaf community, these organisations have reservations about placing deaf pupils in mainstream schools, where they may be isolated without the support of a reasonably sized deaf peer group. 'There is, and always will be, a role for Deaf schools... these must be centres of excellence... where BSL is used, Deaf professionals are employed and the curriculum is appropriate' (BDA). The BDA and DEX would both want the Deaf community to be involved in placement issues since, 'Hearing parents cannot make informed choices about their deaf children's education as they are not, themselves, deaf'(DEX). The members of DEX consider mainstream schooling was a 'negative and disturbing experience which has left them isolated and in limbo between the hearing society and the Deaf community'.

DELTA and the Ewing Foundation

DELTA and the Ewing Foundation would take a very different position because of the importance they place on audition and on spoken language. 'The right to spoken language is a human right of immense benefit. Deaf children who speak can be at ease in society where most communication is by spoken or written word. The only fair alternative would be for everybody to learn to sign fluently' (DELTA). For these organisations the important function of deaf education is that deaf children acquire their mother tongue and for the vast majority this will be a spoken language. Whilst lipreading, visual clues and gesture are not ruled out, they are not emphasised.

For DELTA the aim of achieving a place in society means in the hearing world, and the Ewing Foundation would stress the ability to choose to live and to function independently within hearing society, to achieve success and to progress in education and employment.

This gives a basis from which the deaf individual can choose the extent to which they wish to live in deaf and hearing worlds.

For DELTA and the Ewing Foundation the importance of the family in encouraging language acquisition is linked with the need for the child to share the family's means of communication. Parents' wishes should be respected with regard to choice of mode of communication and placement and parents have the right to take responsibility for and make decisions on behalf of their children. These organisations would prefer as many children as possible to be in their local mainstream school 'in an environment where spoken language is the routine medium of communication' (DELTA), but neither would rule out the use of sign language or specialist school provision where necessary. However, they do argue that learning sign language first inhibits the acquisition of spoken and written English.

Overview

Implicit in these documents are some shared principles concerning the education of deaf children. These relate to reaching potential, achieving a rightful place in society and developing good language and communication skills. Good practice can thus be related to the means of achieving these goals.

However, particularly for the smaller organisations, policy documents such as these tend to stress those aspects of policy on which they themselves have a unique or identified policy. Thus differences, rather than similarities, are emphasised. These differences relate to specific aspects of the overall aims of education and the particular means by which these should be achieved. It is clear that if these are taken as a basis, a consistent and coherent view of good practice in deaf education would be difficult to achieve.

Views of parents of deaf children, teachers of the deaf and deaf adults

Questions about good practice in deaf education form part of the questionnaire that was distributed at the start of the research project. As was described in chapter 2 this was widely distributed. We were delighted by the response – overall we received 628 replies. These fell into the categories as follows:

Parents of a deaf child	290
Teachers of the deaf	140
Deaf adults:	
General	35
FE students	46
Mixed categories:	
parents/deaf adults	18
teachers/deaf adults	7
parents/teachers	5
parents/teachers/deaf adults	1
Other:	
professionals working with deaf children	62
relations of deaf children/adults	10
other interested parties	6
Not specified	8
Total	628

Not only were we delighted by the overall number of responses, we were also pleased to note that the largest category of responses came from parents of deaf children, 314, including those 24 who also fell into other categories. The next largest response category was teachers, 153, including 13 who fell into other categories. We were also pleased to note an encouraging response from other professional groups, 62. There was a range of respondent, the main ones being speech and language therapists and communication support workers.

The questionnaire was designed both to identify examples of good practice for the case studies and to survey the views of respondents about the nature of good practice. The questionnaire gave people the option of only filling in the first part which related to specific examples of good practice, but nearly all respondents took the opportunity to complete both sections (see appendix 1). Part two of the questionnaire was introduced by a statement following which there were four questions with space (about 5 cm deep) in which to answer each one.

There are different views about aims and what constitutes good practice in deaf education. For example, different approaches to the education of deaf children place different emphasis on the importance of language and communication, literacy, access to the curriculum, and the development of self-esteem and identity. We would welcome your views on these matters.

1. What in your view are the most important aims of deaf education?
2. What do you think most helps deaf children and young people develop their full potential?
3. What in your view are the main obstacles to deaf children and young people achieving their full potential?
4. Please state here any further comments you would like to add concerning your views on what constitutes good practice in deaf education.

The responses to this part of the questionnaire were rich, complex and diverse. Many respondents did not simply fill in the questionnaire, but included additional lengthy and detailed responses. It has not been possible to do full justice to the unexpected richness and diversity of responses to part two of the questionnaire within the time frame agreed for the production of this report. To date, we have therefore only undertaken a preliminary survey of views, the results of which are presented below. The research team will report separately and in greater detail on data collected in part 2 later in the year, with support of additional funding from RNID.

To provide an initial review of the data, three members of the research team reviewed questionnaires from the main categories of respondents – parents of deaf children, teachers of the deaf and deaf adults (deaf adults who were parents were added to this group to increase the numbers) – to identify the emergent themes relating to factors that help or restrict deaf children in reaching their full potential. About one hundred questionnaires (or the total group if smaller) were reviewed for each group. It was necessary to treat the responses to this section of the questionnaire as a whole rather than considering them question by question because respondents differed in the way they distinguished between aims and objectives, factors that help deaf children and factors that are obstacles in deaf education.

Overall, where respondents suggested aims they tended to reflect the aspects of deaf education listed in the introductory paragraph to part two of the questionnaire – language and communication, literacy, access to the curriculum and the development of self-esteem and identity. In addition, many respondents mentioned features of adult life – deaf young people taking their place in society, being full members of their community, and assuming an adult role including a career or work. While, overall, the aims expressed tended to be similar, respondents differed in the emphasis they placed, or the priority they gave to different aims. This will be reviewed in detail in the further analysis of the data.

In looking at factors which help deaf children and those that were obstacles to deaf children, the three researchers inspected the questionnaire independently and then combined their findings. A main factor was defined as one that was identified by all three and occurred at least three times in all the samples taken. A minor factor was identified by all three and occurred more than once in all three samples. Consideration was also given to factors that were identified by two of the team and occurred more than once for both.

The factors that were identified for each group and give representative quotes from the questionnaires as illustrations are listed below.

Parents of deaf children

The results of this analysis suggested that for parents there were four main factors that contributed to deaf children developing their full potential.

The development of self confidence and self-esteem in pupils

The development of their self-esteem and identity enables greater potential to be achieved

Child's sense of identity, feeling of belonging should be addressed

Self-esteem and identity are paramount because without these, together with a feeling of security and happiness, the young children and older students are unable to apply themselves fully to their academic studies

A flexible approach to communication

An open mind by experts in advising parents in oral vs signing routes, less political correctness about the whole process

Give them the full communication needs, i.e. sign, gesture, visual aids, good hearing aids, speech therapy, not either/or.

Recognising the child's right to communicate in their chosen language

Good family support

Support from parents, encouragement from parents to assure the child they are no different from any other hearing or speaking children

A positive and supportive attitude from all family members and friends

The continuing support from their family and friends throughout their whole education, without which they will never develop to their full potential

Access to the curriculum
It is important that children are exposed to the full curriculum to allow a deaf child to have full access to the National Curriculum, wherever possible

Having full curriculum available to deaf child regardless of their disability

When we considered factors which are obstacles to deaf children reaching their full potential, the main factors parents focused on were as follows:

Low expectations of deaf pupils
Treating them like they are stupid or slow which holds them back

Some schools take the opinion that because kids are deaf they cannot achieve good marks so they might not give them the chance to meet their full potential

Trained staff often have low expectations – is this part of the training?

Attitudes of society to deaf people, discrimination against deaf people
The ignorance of other people is quite a hindrance to a deaf child

Ignorance, stereotyping, fixed attitudes and opinions, fear

The general attitudes, lack of knowledge and prejudice of some who have no experience with deaf children

Inadequate support and poor resources, particularly in mainstream schools
Wider availability of aids (classroom support) would help the children overcome obstacles which they come across on daily basis

Lack of support in the process of integration

I don't understand why a deaf child in a mainstream unit setting does not have support (signing or otherwise) as long as they need it. .. At college they automatically have access to full time communicators. Surely primary and secondary school are equally as important – without the foundations in place everything collapses. No wonder deaf children are so far behind

Lack of understanding of deafness by teachers
Lack of understanding in schools both by other teachers and hearing children

Lack of deaf awareness and poor expectations within mainstream schools
e.g. secondary school teachers with deaf children in their class

Teachers in school not wholly understanding the psychology of teaching
deaf children

Rigid views held by teachers of the deaf and other professionals
Extremist groups such as DELTA (pro-oralism) and deaf organisations (pro-sign,
anti-cochlear implants)

Attitudes of zealots who think their way is best and there is no alternative way

The education system – everywhere we have polarised choices, either signing or
oral and never the twain shall meet. The individual needs of the deaf child seem
rarely to be considered

The main focus for parents thus seemed to be the whole child, on the importance of self-confidence and self-esteem in order for the child to reach their full potential. Lack of understanding of deafness within school and negative attitudes to deaf people in the wider world were seen as limiting factors. Language and communication were mentioned, not in terms of advocating a particular approach but usually in terms of the need for choice and flexibility. The rigid attitudes of professionals was seen as an obstacle. Curriculum issues largely emphasised the access to a broad curriculum and saw a major barrier as the lack of adequate support in mainstream schools. Not surprisingly, parental support was recognised as a factor which helped deaf children reach their potential.

Teachers of the deaf

Teachers of the deaf identified three main factors that helped deaf children reach their potential.

Good linguistic skills through a systematic approach
An education that allows them to develop their English language and particularly
reading to an independent level

Regular and comprehensive linguistic assessment, formative in nature

High levels of spoken language and written language competence

Pupils reaching their potential through access to a wide curriculum

Integrating children at all ages and following the normal curriculum with support

Skills which enable the child to communicate effectively and access the curriculum

Access to a full curriculum which is differentiated for their individual needs

The development of confidence and self-esteem in pupils

To be encouraged from a very early age to believe that they can succeed and be confident

To develop their full potential they need to develop self-esteem and find their identity

A positive self image promoted at home and at school

In the analysis that we completed, due to the range of responses, only one factor emerged as a major factor for teachers which proved an obstacle to deaf children reaching their potential. We thus also mention the more minor factors that emerged.

Low expectations of deaf pupils

Teachers and others who believe that deaf children cannot ... and set restrictions on their experience as a result

Adults, including parents, who do not have the belief in their children's ability to reach their full potential

Attitudes which suggest that 'young deaf people can't' or that the young person is doing very well 'for a deaf person'

Minor factors:
Lack of support in the classroom

Insufficient learning support to assist meaningful integration

Insufficient and inappropriate support in schools

Lack of parental support

Poor parental involvement and low parental expectations

Parents making unnecessary concessions because they [the children] do not hear very well

Late diagnosis

(This was mentioned but not expanded upon as a topic.)

(There were a further twelve factors warranting consideration, including poor language, poor hearing aids, poor training, lack of resources, late diagnosis and confused teaching methods.)

Thus for teachers, while self-esteem was important, also important were good linguistic skills and access to the curriculum. Obstacles arose due to low expectations but also because of inadequate provision in a number of areas.

Deaf adults

For deaf adults there were three main factors that contributed in a positive way to the deaf child reaching their full potential.

Development of deaf identity and self-esteem

I believe that with good deaf identity and self-esteem and with good practice at school they can achieve and do well in education

Awareness of their deaf identity, that they are not disabled

Flexible communication and choice with respect to communication

The encouragement and full use of the best and most far reaching means of communication available

If they are given freedom to choose communication methods then I think it helps later on in life

Access to a wide curriculum

As with the education of hearing children, the education of deaf children should start from where they are, encouraging them to develop skills in all areas of the curriculum

A wide curriculum with diversity as well as conformity

The main inhibiting factors deaf adults mentioned were:

Low expectations of deaf pupils

Some teachers seem to think deaf people are not very clever
Expecting/accepting lower standards of achievement because they are deaf

> **Lack of awareness about deafness in schools**
> Not listening to deaf adults who have direct experience of living in a mainstream society with no peer group support
>
> Lack of understanding of how deafness affects learning and language acquisition
>
> **Education holding a medical deficiency model of deafness**
> Society, mostly in the professions, seeing deafness as a medical condition not an ethnic difference
>
> Pathological attitudes towards deafness
>
> **Discrimination against deaf people**
> Discrimination is a problem as it smashes a deaf person's confidence
>
> Attitudes of ignorant or narrow minded people restricting the deaf child's exploration of their identity and place in society

Overview of the responses to the questionnaire by category

While we would not suggest that this procedure provides a robust quantitative analysis and there are some difficulties relating from the definition of categories, we would suggest that this provides evidence of similarities and differences between the groups in terms of priorities in deaf education.

There was some a general consensus about the factors that 'helped deaf children and young people develop their full potential'. All groups agreed on the need for, firstly, self-esteem and self-confidence and, secondly, access to a broad based curriculum. All the groups emphasised aspects of language and communication but there was a difference – teachers stressed the need for good linguistic skills and a systematic approach, while parents and deaf adults focused on the need for flexibility in approach. It is maybe not surprising that parents also added the need for good family support as a priority.

In general there was less consensus when we considered 'the main obstacles to deaf children and young people achieving their full potential'. All groups agreed on one factor, that low expectations have a negative effect. Parents and teachers agreed that poor classroom support was a problem. The additional factors that were mentioned by deaf adults and parents were similar and tended to be social or relate to attitudes;

discrimination by society against deaf people, and lack of awareness of deafness in school and in society. Parents were also concerned about the rigid views that they perceived. Teachers added late diagnosis and poor parental support.

Thus in response to the questions there is some consistency, while differences in emphasis remain. While the dominant themes should be recognised – expectations, self-esteem and access to the curriculum – some differences need to be noted particularly in the context of the preceding discussion of the views of deaf organisations. Parents and deaf adults tend to look for a flexible approach to education and parents feel the commitment to particular language and communication approaches, that they perceive, is unhelpful. Teachers, however tend to endorse the need for a systematic approach to communication.

Challenges provided by the notion of good practice

The complexity in the notion of good practice created certain challenges in carrying out this research and more particularly in writing this report.

The main corner stone of the study was that good practice would not be decided by the research team – 'the academic view' – but by consumers and practitioners. This was successful in terms of identifying case studies. We received a large number of responses to our questionnaire and this gave us a range of potential studies from which we selected 15 based on the way they contributed to the whole picture. Finding case studies to provide a sample to tap the required range of aspects of good practice was unproblematic. However, in reporting aspects of good practice, there were a number of issues that we needed to take into account.

Firstly, there were instances which had been recommended as good practice where some things observed were not good practice, for example hearing aids not being used where they should have been. There were instances where we were confident there would be a general consensus that it was not good practice. Secondly, there were case studies where the account of practice was not borne out by what was actually observed. The description of policy on its own would be good but the practice did not match up to the description, for example a programme for teaching hearing children to sign, when the signing class itself seemed inadequate in major respects. In both these instances we were guided by our own response, so we took out observations where we felt that what was observed was not good practice or where theory/policy and practice did not match up.

More problematic were those situations where the views of the research team were at variance with the perceptions of consumers. A couple of examples can be given with respect to parents. In general, if parents were offered regular support in the early years they were most appreciative and perceived this as good practice. However, in these early years parents are not able to draw on a wide range of experience with which to compare. We, ourselves, were aware of significant and relevant differences in the nature of what was provided. We also know from research (Gregory, Bishop, and Sheldon, 1995)[2] that parents' views may change over time. Support that is valued and positively received at the time, on later reflection can be perceived as having been less adequate as parents develop an understanding of the implications of deafness and the possibilities for support.

A further related issue was that of the importance of the child's well being. As we have seen from the questionnaire responses, parents (and others) laid a great deal of stress on the need for self-confidence and good self-esteem. These were often seen as a prerequisite to learning. The research team would endorse these factors as important but would hold the view that they are not the only elements of good practice and must be part of the total provision. Good self-esteem is not a substitute for access to a broad and balanced curriculum. This presents a problem in settings where there was an emphasis on the child being happy, but relatively little attention to curriculum issues. We have tried in our reports to be selective and also to focus on those aspects that were good practice while recognising that on their own they cannot constitute a whole picture.

There were, inevitably, more controversial areas. There were case studies where we feel there could be difference in opinion as to whether they constituted good practice. The report of good practice from the deaf organisations and from the questionnaire response has clearly indicated that what is good practice for one group may not for another. For example, we were impressed by the fact that the case studies recommended to us were largely from situations where there was strong and positive leadership and a commitment to a particular approach, or particular approaches, to education. Inevitably the best practice with respect to a particular approach is where there is a commitment to this way of working. But there are issues. Firstly, a commitment to a particular ideology may lead to casualties, as the needs of not all children are met by such an approach. Good audiology and a commitment to speech intelligibility may mean that provision for those children who do not benefit from this approach is less well-developed or even very difficult to obtain. It has been suggested that a commitment to a sign bilingual approach may have consequences for the development of speech intelligibility as attention to good spoken language must be emphasised from very early on. We are aware these are controversial statements and it may be that it is possible for a number of approaches to exist side by side. However, we did not observe an instance where there was significant strength across the

[2] Gregory, S., Bishop, J., Sheldon, J. (1995) *Deaf young people and their families.* Cambridge: Cambridge University Press.

board. This raises the questions as to whether it can be good practice if it works for most, but what if the consequences for others are serious, sometimes extremely so? Our procedure in this report has been to focus on the good practice we observed and report it without necessarily examining wider implications.

This strong commitment to a particular approach has another consequence. Paradoxically, while it is effective, it seems to lead to an 'expert' model with respect to parents and families [3]. 'Conventional wisdom' would indicate that the expert model is undesirable. The collaborative approach that treats parents as partners may be more difficult to achieve where commitment is strong. Yet it is difficult to see how a more flexible approach could run alongside strong commitment. This dilemma would seem an important one for providers to consider.

A further observation linked to strong commitment, but also a feature of the case studies we observed, was the demands that effective practice makes on staff. A number of us observed that teachers and others were working long hours, often over and above what might normally be expected. This raises a number of issues. Firstly, is good practice only achieved by this degree of commitment? If so, is it good practice in terms of the implications it has for other aspects of life? Does this way of working exclude certain practitioners who for various reasons may not be able to make this level of commitment? Does this exclusion have implications for the 'roundness' of what is provided? We offer no resolution of this issue but feel it should be raised.

Conclusion

This chapter has demonstrated that that notion of good practice is complex and at times paradoxical. There is significant consensus on what should be the aims of deaf education although some variation in the priority which should be given to each one. It has not been difficult to arrive at a number of themes which need to be addressed in a consideration of good practice. There are differences, however, mostly between professionals, on how these aims should be realised. At the same time it is important to be mindful of a strong voice from parents that suggests that the debates in deaf education are not helpful and that disagreements are seen as destructive.

In putting together this report, the focus has been on good practice and the various ways this is achieved. The aim has not been to encourage evaluative comparisons, but to enable the best aspects of a number of processes to be examined. While the research team itself represents a range of views, and not every member would endorse every practice described, nevertheless there has been a consensus that focusing on commonalities and strengths rather than seeking to elaborate difference has been a powerful exercise. Thus the main body of the report presents a number of themes judged to be significant in deaf education and examines examples of good practice with respect to these with a view to informing practice in a constructive way.

---

[3] Cunningham, C., Davis, H. (1985) *Working with parents: frameworks for collaboration.* Milton Keynes: OUP.

Summary

Key findings in this section are summarised as follows:

- The notion of good practice is complex and at times paradoxical.

- There is significant consensus on what should be the aims of deaf education although parents, teachers and deaf adults vary in the priority which should be given to them.

- It has not been difficult to arrive at a number of themes which need to be addressed in a consideration of good practice.

- There are differences on how the aims of deaf education should be realised.

- Parents do not find the debates between professionals helpful, and disagreements between professionals are seen as destructive.

Chapter 4

Main themes

Main themes

4.1 Leadership and management

The topic of leadership and management did not emerge from the questionnaires but emerged from the case studies themselves. That is, no schools, services or colleges were nominated for this aspect of their work but in many of the case studies the topic was raised in a large number of discussions. Many people we spoke to saw this factor as central to the effectiveness of their work.

The discussion here almost entirely concerns services for deaf children – very little is said about special schools. This should not be taken to mean that we regard leadership and management in special schools as unimportant – clearly it is important – but it is simply a reflection of the case studies where this topic emerged.

The section is under two main headings, leadership and management.

Leadership

Although not selected originally as a theme for investigation, leadership emerged as an important factor during the case study visits. It is also a topical subject in the light of the government's training initiatives for serving and prospective headteachers. As one of the roles of a leader is to establish a particular culture for the organisation, parts of this section may overlap with the section on ethos.

Vision

Asked why the service was successful, a teacher of the deaf (ToD) replied '[name of HoS]! She's a real inspiration to all of us; the most inspiring person I've ever worked with. A great figurehead for us. She eats, breathes, sleeps deaf children!' (case study F [1]).

The headteachers and heads of service provided strong leadership based on their commitment to specific educational goals and often also on their allegiance to a particular philosophy of deaf education.

> The head of service (HoS) in A explained that previously in the service there had been a 'very narrow language-communication policy' when 'significant numbers of children were felt to be, by a number of staff... to be significantly disadvantaged by what was available'. Together with this understanding came a recognition of the low

---

[1] The reader is reminded that brief descriptions of the case studies appear at the end of chapter 2.

profile that deaf people had in the city. The twin aims of the initial policy therefore related to (i) the improvement in standards for deaf children and adults (ii) raising the profile of deaf people by improved attitudes in the city. Employing deaf people to become part of the educative process for deaf children made the 'biggest impact' on this agenda.

What emerged as a sign bilingual policy we did in order to say that not all children in X were being taught in two languages, sign language and English, but in order for those that needed it to have it we had to have a policy in place that meant that we could legitimately employ deaf people and CSWs and have a large sign language programme and so on... The policy emerged from a need to be absolutely clear about who was going to work for the service, where we were going to have children placed, how we were going to move on in terms of professional development, what the issues were around curriculum and assessment. So the policy issues emerged that way.

(HoS).

In order for the school or service to be consistent and effective in achieving its objective of high quality education for deaf pupils, the personal vision of the leader must be converted into a form that can be communicated to others. This is sometimes in the form of a vision or mission statement. However, despite their prominence in management training since the 1980s there is often scepticism about the use of these in education where they are sometimes considered yet another example of the infiltration of business thinking. They can be vague or even smack of insincerity. Provided the statements are a reflection of a shared sense of purpose and priorities they can serve as a means of focusing on a particular school's or service's core values in the continually changing context with which we are all familiar in education. We saw many examples of these statements in the various policy documents we were shown.

Shared philosophy

The embodiment of vision and values in policy documents is one of the indicators of the ethos of the school or service. By formalising ideas in writing and setting out their practical implications, the leader's vision can be more effectively diffused throughout the whole staff team. Our case study reports consistently remarked on the commitment of staff to the aims and philosophy of the school or service.

In case study E, the policy states that the specific method adopted by this service is a natural aural approach. This was also the clear understanding of the staff. At F, a ToD said that the success of the service depended on 'The grounding we have all received from [HoS]. It's enabled us to work as a team and we are all coming from the same position'.

At school P it was clear from a number of discussions that the school has a coherent set of aims for the pupils. The major priority is given to pupil happiness and well-being and there were many comments to the effect that children could not succeed if they were not happy. The second priority was establishing good communication, in whatever mode. The third priority was access to the curriculum and/or literacy. It was a feature of the school that these aims, in this order, were mentioned by almost everyone we spoke to.

Developing teamwork

A skilful leader will engender a team spirit where the commitment and loyalty of the team members can be balanced by a sense of belonging and ownership. We encountered many such examples of team identity.

In A while high expectations clearly make demands on staff, this does not seem to be an issue, though different people put in more or less at different times depending on their personal circumstances. The HoS also pointed out that the staff liked to be a part of this particular service with its particular approach, they like to feel they were developing new ideas and some of them had 'blossomed' as the service developed.

There's a momentum there, it's the only way. I work on the basis that people are also getting a lot from it. They've come such a long way, blossomed as people. It's a very demanding role...They love being at the cutting edge. They own it... That's what I have set out to achieve for both teachers and pupils, it's not just about the children. It's creating that environment where people are thriving, that atmosphere, that culture.

Valuing the contribution of individuals and recognising their professional autonomy, creating an atmosphere where innovation and experimentation were encouraged, and at the same time having high expectations of team members were important factors which we noted on our visits. It is also significant that they reflect the moral dimension of the educational enterprise which is the core purpose of school or service.

'The strength of the team is in the actual leadership and management of the team leaders in conjunction with the teams they manage so that there is a feeling of belonging, common policies and flexibility of placement. The quality of the team leaders is paramount'

(HoS, case study B).

At E, all staff are aware of the service policies and also understand their own roles and responsibilities. Yet within this structure there is room for individual teachers to use initiative and implement new ideas. The head of service expressed it as having; 'High quality people in the service and allowing them to make their vision the reality'. There were several examples of individual teachers putting forward ideas which they were then given encouragement to implement.

At H, the HoS emphasised the high quality of his staff. All teachers he has appointed have had the ToD qualification and have been high quality. There is a strong team ethos, with each member of the team feeling that their views are taken into consideration. '[HoS] is very clear about where he wants the service to go, he's very focused; also it's very demanding because he expects a lot of us. We put a lot in but then we get a lot out. If anyone sees a need for something [HoS] will listen'

(ToD).

In F, there is a strong sense of teamwork and good personal relationships. Everyone's role is valued, whether it involves teaching or administrative or technical support. The secretary is described as their 'relay station'. She co-ordinates the system: 'Everything comes through me from parents and audiology staff'. She also goes to DELTA days with the HoS.

The commitment and dedication of the team, the HoS and individual ToDs is recognised both within and outside. 'The teachers all have a love for the children and want to do the best for them. They even have people ringing them at home, they are totally committed... [HoS] cares so much and it comes right down the line' (secretary).

The HoS looks for quality in her team and has high expectations of them. The strength of the team was summarised by the Head Educational Psychologist (line manager) as being a result of:

> Strong positive management that actively promotes strong team links. The team manager has picked a strong and enthusiastic team, she recognises individual strengths and uses them... All the teachers in the service work well beyond the requirements of their job, it is recognised fact. The team has a mindset that coincides with the Board in seeking to promote inclusive practice. They make it work.

Delegating responsibility and using expertise

Clear and visionary leadership can become at best charismatic and at worst autocratic if too much of the decision and responsibility remains with the leader. We saw various examples of powersharing strategies.

At H, the senior teacher is a rotating post which carries extra responsibility (for example, assisting in appointing new staff) but no financial reward. Staff volunteer, and can in this way find out more about how the service works. Usually there is a discussion about who this person should be although the HoS will probably have an idea in mind. 'It depends on the route the service is taking at that time. You want someone that year to coordinate that aspect. Some might say that they don't want that role, which is fair enough' (HoS). The HoS delegates management of the resource bases (for which the service is responsible) to the teachers in charge to allow them to adapt to local needs and to feel responsibility for their work environment.

Service A has a number of ongoing projects which are the responsibility of individual staff members. They are allowed half a day each week to work on these, but the project must have measurable outcomes which are of benefit to the service. Recent and ongoing projects include; teaching maths, accrediting SNA training, assessment, development of a parent handbook for early years.

One advisory teacher in case study E has responsibility for continuing professional development for teaching staff which includes a training needs analysis for each teacher in relation to their current post, a possible future post and their personal interests.

In H, each of the teachers takes responsibility for keeping up-to-date on a designated area and in this way they can draw on each other's expertise. Individuals have different interests and strengths and are allowed to develop this with the support of the whole service. Everyone contributes.

This aspect is very important for future development and progression. If the success of an organisation rests too much on the individual personality of the leader or a long-established, but taken for granted philosophy, what happens when there is a change of staff or leader?

In C, we gained a clear sense of the whole staff sharing the same vision for the school, supporting its ethos and committed to the same oral and 'maternal reflective' approach. The school makes a real effort to make sure this method continues to be applied consistently. Many we spoke to remarked on the quality of the staff, their skills and commitment, being crucial to the school's success. The school is aware that an important issue for them is that some of its most experienced staff have now been there a long time and will not be around for ever. There appears to be a strong move to more sharing of expertise and knowledge, partly through written materials.

Professional leadership

However demanding the role of leader, he/she must not become too focused on the task at hand and risk losing the wider view. It is important for heads to demonstrate expertise in professional skills by keeping up to date in their specific field. They also need to be aware of what is happening in education generally and the implications of current legislation.

The head of service in case study A explained how important is was for a service to be aware of developments in deaf education and related areas, a responsibility she took upon herself.

If a head of service did not subscribe to the main journals and did not read the latest books or even the reviews and did not go to conferences it would be very difficult to sustain, because these people [the staff] can't. They need to be in the classroom with the children. I report back as much as I can. I don't know how important they feel this is.

The head of service E was appointed with the brief to identify trends in deaf education and to act as professional advisor to the units.

Management

Educational management can be conceptualised as the process of ensuring that the leadership vision and shared team philosophy is translated into the necessary activity to bring about the objective of quality education. The process comprises a network of activities such as devising or operating an organisational structure, establishing roles and responsibilities, compiling useful documentation and methods of record-keeping, facilitating the continuous development of staff, fostering good external relations, evaluating the quality of the service and planning strategies for change.

The head of service A had to tackle what could be a difficult and controversial area in sorting the finer details of the management team to support the bilingual framework. In the early days the roles of teachers and deaf people working in schools were defined on the skills they had at that time. Hence, teachers of the deaf had few signing skills but could teach, deaf people had 'native' signing skills but no experience of educating. However since then, the signing skills of teachers of the deaf have dramatically improved and a comprehensive training programme has allowed deaf people a development of pedagogic skills. The head of service description of the situation was:

> What you see now in the classroom is totally different from what we started off with partly because people's skills are light years away from where they were there and their knowledge is light years away but also because the education system is totally different at X now than it was in '86. Deaf instructors now bring their unique insights to bear on areas such as teaching children literacy skills and strategies for communication with hearing people.

Documentation and record keeping

Documentation and record keeping plays an important role. Schools and services we visited used development planning to guide their mid- and long-term progress. These were linked to the INSET provision for members of staff. For example, at A, individual professional and personal development plans are worked out with the Co-ordinators. There is some flexibility but they must link in a general way to the Service Strategic Plan, for example when the literacy hour was introduced, this development became part of the service plan and the professional development plans reflected this.

Although it is necessary to avoid unnecessary bureaucracy and additional paperwork, succinct documentation with a clear purpose can cement the ethos and philosophy, aid the induction of new staff and explain the intent of a service or school to those outside. Good policies and procedures can form the link between the vision statement and the educational outcomes. Good practice at the grass roots level can be sporadic and inconsistent without the guidance of a written framework and can lack direction without a clearly defined purpose. Conversely, clarity of vision and superb documentation is meaningless unless they are implemented in good pedagogical practice. Ideally, there should be a consistent thread running from the vision statement through the documentation and into observable practice. This may be even more important in a service where staff attend a central base infrequently unlike the daily face-to-face contact of a school.

> In case study H, a consistent approach is central to the work of the team. There is detailed documentation, kept up-to-date, on all aspects of the Service. The service development plan provides structure for the implementation and improvement of the service's provision and for the training of all its employees. All the teachers

have copies of the documents so they have a shared understanding of and commitment to the purposes and direction of the service. An interesting feature of the documentation was that for each topic – for example, Parent Support – there were three documents referring to the different levels of operational management; Policies, Procedures, and Practices. One ToD told us. 'As someone who's come to the service relatively lately, I've found the 'Policies, Procedures, Practices' file really useful. It gave a very good picture of the role and the approach'.

In addition, the IEP clearly plays a central role in the support work of ToDs both in resource bases and those working as visiting teachers of the deaf. One ToD told us:

> I think we can do a lot with an IEP. It's got to be a working document. If you've got quite a large case load of children it's got to be something that's not too intensive ... not too long to put together ... bearing in mind that planning sessions are very difficult to get hold of in any school ... you've got to make sure it's precise and specific.

Service B has written materials which clearly define a number of aspects of work including: the philosophy and role of the service, the model of service delivery, the role of the ToD and the LSA, criteria for monitoring the caseload, INSET materials, handouts, staff development, methods and resources for assessment, links with parents, links with other groups, call back sessions, links with schools, and services for babies and young children. These materials are held at each resource base in a file for reference with extra copies for staff use. There are detailed induction files for both new ToDs and new LSAs.

There also needs to be available standard forms of documentation for recording pupil progress, and in the case of a peripatetic service, where several visiting teachers of the deaf (VToDs) may be working in one school and with a range of mainstream teachers, efficient means of communication and liaison.

A feature of service D valued by mainstream teachers and parents is the effectiveness of the system of written records and opportunities for communication. Key features of this system are; the individual support plan, teachers' logs, liaison memos, the home liaison book, timetabled liaison time, and the provision of in-service training for the schools.

> The detailed records of all pupils kept on the database (for which one advisory teacher has responsibility) enable the head of service to respond quickly and accurately to any request for information from the county. It also means that trends and the performance of deaf pupils on some assessment tests which are carried out regularly can be identified and appropriate responses implemented.
>
> (case study E).

Self evaluation

> 'Although it's hard to do we have to evaluate the service work in relation to the impact it's having on pupils and schools. Therefore people have to make some sort of connection between their own professional development and the impact on schools and children'
>
> (HoS, case study A).

The following instances of reflective practice occurred in our case studies.

> The staff set themselves high standards and are self-questioning in their approach. The ToDs also see the achievement of targets from the Annual Reviews and IEPs as a measure of their own performance. 'We are always looking to improve the children's performance'
>
> (HoS, case study H).

> The service reviews its policies on a regular basis and modifies them as necessary. Staff are reflective about their practice and willing to make changes. 'Whilst the preschool programme will remain the same, we are rethinking how we support deaf children at primary level. We may have over-supported them and thought less about independent learning skills'
>
> (ToD, case study K).

> Part of the staff development budget has been allocated to finance a visit by the HoS and two teachers to investigate the use of support assistants in another service.
>
> (case study F).

Quality assurance

Two different approaches to monitoring quality in services were encountered. One of these reflected the concept of total quality management by the use of target setting or performance indicators and the other was a 'customer care' model using feedback from 'clients' or 'consumers' of the service.

The service handbook in case study K sets out operational criteria for each activity which clearly define the standard to be achieved and how this is to be monitored. For example, for hearing aid breakdown during the school holidays the standard is 100% response rate within two working days by duty ToD and/or technician; and this is monitored on the technician's computer and on the 'contact record' in the child's file.

There is a regular survey of schools by postal questionnaire covering: perceived quality of support provided, ongoing advice, support to technical equipment, how direct teaching support complements the school's curriculum and the value of contributions to assessment, IEPs and Reviews. 'How effectively they [the hearing impaired children] are included functionally would be good feedback. Whether you've given them the tools to enter the classroom to do the job, the confidence they do it with, the security they seem to have within the placement'

(HoS, case study H).

Organisational structure of services

'Variations in organisation can be a source of strength as they allow a flexible response to be made to challenges in very different geographical and demographic situations' (BATOD, 1994[2]).

The services we visited came under their LEA Special Needs Services. In some cases the head of service was responsible for other aspects of special needs, for example, a Head of Service for Hearing and Visually Impaired Children (case study D), a Coordinator of a Physical and Sensory Support Service and Head of Profession for Hearing Impaired Service (case study E). In one instance (case study F) the service was one of six responsible to the head of the educational psychology service.

Heads of service were keen that the special nature of their provision should be maintained and differentiated from other special needs work, for example where multidisciplinary teams operate. One HoS told us, 'It has taken me a long time to get them to realise that if a child has a statement with reference to deafness, they need a teacher of the deaf not just any teacher'.

The service for the hearing impaired became part of the county's learning support service, which brought several services under one umbrella in a federal structure, then a further change brought the learning support service into the Education Children's Service. The Service for the Hearing Impaired and Visually Impaired became the Sensory Support Service, with Physical Disability added to become

---

[2] The organisation and management of LEA educational services for hearing impaired pupils and young people in England and Wales. *BATOD Magazine*. November 1994.

Physical and Sensory Support from September 1999. The head of service becomes Coordinator for Physical and Sensory Support Service as well as Head of Profession for Hearing. Throughout these changes the Service for the Hearing Impaired has retained its status as a discrete service within a larger service. Thus the specialist nature of the service has not been lost. The Head of Profession has a devolved budget for running the service.

The decision to appoint phase coordinators for the county contributed to the stability and expansion of the service at a time when services in other areas of the country were being cut back as it led to a coherence across the area teams. There were meetings arranged for the preschool and primary teachers and others for secondary teachers. Encouragement was given to establish consistency of provision and practice across the county and they were able to retain the sense of being a county service rather than becoming part of area teams catering for pupils with different SEN.

(case study E).

Organisation of caseloads

Services, especially those that cover large geographical areas, need to give careful consideration to how ToD caseloads are organised. Two of the main factors involved are age of child and geography.

Service B, in a large county, is organised around three separate teams based around the county. The team leaders' main role is to support other team members. They have much smaller caseloads (around 1/3). They aim to have a weekly meeting with each team member, to organise team meetings, to perform much of the administration, to support INSET delivery and to arrange the Parent Support Group. Each of the team leaders has a high level of additional training, two being qualified Educational Audiologists. 'The team leaders must be proven experienced practitioners' (HoS). The caseloads of the ToDs in each team are largely based on the age of the child.

In E caseloads are organised by area and phase. The team of advisory teachers is organised into four areas with an area coordinator. ToDs within these areas largely work within one of three phases – preschool/primary; secondary and post 16. There are phase coordinators with responsibilities across all four areas. The phase coordinators are responsible for regulating caseloads to ensure they are similar.

In H the peripatetic ToDs deal with the whole age range of children working on a geographical basis to accommodate the demands of the large area covered although individual's preferences and strengths are recognised. The policy is to avoid a change in ToD at times of transitions because of the additional stress on parents and child.

In K the ToDs are organised in teams – preschool, primary, secondary, FE – and some have specialist knowledge and expertise in other areas, e.g. audiology and working with children with additional disabilities. So there may be a change of ToD supporting a particular child every few years. '... additional specialisms allow parents, schools and pupils to benefit from the specialist teachers through understanding of phase learning needs and curriculum'

(service handbook).

Units (resource bases)

Units may or may not be under the direct supervision of the LEA service. We encountered both situations.

In F the primary secondary units are under the control of their mainstream schools. Links with the service are maintained by annual meetings, and an open invitation to attend weekly staff meetings is extended to the unit teachers. Time constraints normally prevent the unit teachers being able to take up this opportunity. The lack of line management for the teachers in the units is an area of concern for the service.

The aim is to use resources flexibly so that they chase the children rather than vice versa – resource bases are 'always opening and closing' (HoS). This is made possible by ToDs being appointed to the service rather than to individual schools. There has been no pressure from the LEA or schools to change this arrangement.

(case study H).

Table 4.1.1 illustrates some of the different types of service management structure.

Table 4.1.1 Examples of different types of management structure in LEA services for deaf children and how case loads are organised

Case Study	Management structure	Roles and responsibilities	Units (resource bases)
B	ToDs work to three team leaders responsible for different parts of the county. HoS for Sensory Impaired Children is a QToD.	Team leaders have small caseloads. They meet with individual ToDs weekly. Caseloads organised largely according to age of child.	The 'resource base' for each team is also used for intensive work with pupils in a 'call back' service
E	ToDs work to four area coordinators. Also three phase coordinators. County Coordinator and Head of Profession (Hearing) is a QToD.	A large team allows caseloads to be organised by area and phase. Phase organisers regulate caseloads.	HoS acts in advisory capacity to resource bases.
F	ToDs work to Head of Educational Audiology Service who is a QToD.	Caseloads organised by area.	Units under control of mainstream schools. Unit ToDs not able to attend weekly meetings of service.
H	ToDs work to HoS for Hearing Impaired Children who is a QToD. There is also a deputy HoS.	Caseloads organised by area but recognition of individual strengths.	Resource bases under control of the service; they open and close according to need.
K	ToDs work to HoS for Hearing Impaired Children who is a QToD.	Caseloads organised by phase.	There are no resource bases in the country.

Income generation

Although there would be some difference of opinion about whether the topic of income generation was appropriate in an account of good practice, the issues of funding and fundraising arose in several of our discussions during the case study visits. It seems inevitable that schools and services should attempt to maximise the resources available to them. In some services we gained the impression that it was the strong leadership style of the HoS which kept the needs of deaf children on the agenda. In other cases the HoS became skilled in knowing what funding was available from government schemes and charitable organisations.

At Q, the service has been proactive in seeking financial support from a number of sources. Money has come from a fund for joint planning by the health and education authorities, from government initiatives and from the trustees of the hospital next door.

Two of the schools we visited were addressing the need to increase funds and to attract sufficient numbers of pupils. School C employs a promotions and marketing coordinator who, as a parent of one of the pupils, can speak with knowledge and enthusiasm about the provision.

As a non-maintained school, J is well attuned to fundraising in a way that most maintained state schools and services are not. The school can afford to pay for the services of a professional fundraiser. The fundraising habit has meant the attraction of resources which surpass those normally found within the maintained sector of education. For example, the provision of a spare hearing aid for each pupil is possible because of a specific fundraising activity. The proposed sports/performing arts facilities will undoubtedly be the envy of the average state secondary school. Hence, greater than average resources contribute greatly to the quality of education provided for the pupils.

Summary

Key findings in this section are summarised as follows:

- Effective leadership is a key component of good practice.
- Heads who have strong commitment and high expectations, who also value the contributions of individuals and allow professional autonomy are well regarded by their staff.
- Many of the schools and services we visited have a strong sense of team spirit.
- Clear and detailed documentation can ensure that a shared vision and philosophy is translated into a consistent approach.
- A joint approach to self-reflection and evaluation is a common feature of good practice.
- There is no one model of organisation to suit all services; factors such as size and geography play a role.

4.2 Ethos

The Concise Oxford Dictionary defines 'ethos' as 'the characteristic spirit of community, people or system'. It is a popular word in educational discourse as a shorthand for the kind of values we would want to see in place in an educational institution and also for the kind of intuitive sense we have about an organisation which is 'getting it right'. It is more often written about in management and organisational theory as 'culture'.

In most of our visits we were looking at two different types of organisation – special schools and services. Their different structure and functions means that the ethos they wish to promote has to be established and fostered in different ways. The special school, particularly when it residential, is a closed institution where prolonged and frequent contact between its members facilitates communication of goals and rules. There are regular and formalised rituals such as assemblies, concerts and parents' evenings which embody and perpetuate the prevailing ethos. All of the pupils share the characteristic of being deaf so that their needs within the specialist environment provide the focus for all activities. A service, on the other hand, is a more open and fluid organisation. Its members may meet face to face less frequently. They have many interfaces with other organisation who may or may not share their goals and methods such as health services and mainstream schools. For these reasons the ethos of a school is more observable and measurable.

Ethos may be thought of as a more abstract way of thinking about the same kind of issues involved in the day to day activities of leadership and management. Consequently, many topics are common to both. This section of the report should, therefore, be considered complementary to that on leadership and management, for example, the importance of the vision of the leader and the need for it to be thoroughly and specifically communicated as a shared philosophy or direction for an organisation. However, unlike leadership and management which we see as conscious activities, the abstract nature of the word might make us think of 'ethos' as something which 'just happens'. On the contrary, establishing or maintaining the 'right' ethos requires deliberate effort especially in times of change as the following two examples illustrate.

> An important feature of school N is the commitment of the headteacher to the success of the resource base. He came to the school twelve years ago already committed to inclusive education and with a clear idea of what he wanted.
> He worked to break down the barriers that he saw existed and to create a system where the deaf pupils and their teachers were seen as an asset to the school.
> He now feels the right ethos has been established but thinks it can't be taken for granted.

Originally a religious foundation school, C now has its first lay head and deputy. The head says that the ethos 'became ingrained in the mortar' over the decades when sisters worked as teachers and carers. The staff were all concerned not to lose this special quality when the sisters left but 'people have worked harder to maintain it and to take on responsibility. Staff have become more involved'.
For example, the school is looking at appropriate skilling of care staff with more advanced counselling skills than in the past, making it a priority for in-service training.

'The ethos of care, the legacy that the sisters left, it's crucial, we nurture it'.

(parent).

The ethos of the school needs constant monitoring. 'We have to work at it all the time, keeping the whole school moving forward ... promoting a strong ethos. ... A place where people will want to learn'

(headteacher).

Ethos is not unidimensional. The word is a collective way of speaking about a whole range of practices related to interpersonal relationships by which an organisation may be more or less successful in achieving the educational ideal and/or its individual vision or mission.

Clearly ethos is not something that is easy to measure. We therefore have to look at indicators such as documents, procedures and practices to find the evidence which supports our intuitive response, 'This school/service has a strong ethos'. The following discussion will describe some of the indicators we observed or heard about during our visits. Furthermore, ethos is essentially to do with how people treat each other. It is not only about how organisations see themselves and how they would like others to see them. It is very much to do with how they are perceived by others. It is, therefore, essential to ask those who are part of, or come into contact with the school or service, about their experiences at first hand. The Good Practice Review achieved this by the questionnaire survey and by talking to staff, pupils, students and parents during the case study visits.

Ceremonies and rituals

School life provides many opportunities for occasions to reflect and reinforce core values. In a special school for deaf pupils, these occasions also illustrate the school's particular approach to deaf education.

In C, there is a daily act of collective worship either on a whole school, departmental, class or group basis. All staff participate. 'There is a great deal of good will. It strengthens the sense of community, common identity fostered by the Christian ethos'

(head of religious education).

The head of primary in school G told us, 'We have a happy box in assembly and the children can write anything they want and put it in, and it will be read and valued, whatever the level of writing or drawing'. The children line up at the front with the head to talk about their work. The head makes comments and asks questions about each of their work and also invites other children's comments.

Policies and documents

The importance of meaningful documentation is noted in the section on management (section 4.1). It was also stressed that the values expressed in the documents must be consistent with the overall vision of the school or service and also ostensibly carried through into practice. The schools we visited used documents to explain and enshrine their value system. For example:

A Code of Conduct, 'Five Ways to make our School a Happy Place':

- We should all try to understand other people's point of view.
- In class you make it as easy as possible for everyone to learn and for the teacher to teach.
- We should all move quietly and in a sensible way around the school.
- We should always speak politely to everyone, and make [school] a welcoming place we can all be proud of.
- Out of school set a good example. Always remember that you belong to [school].

Positive Behaviour Partnership:

- This is a partnership between staff and pupils. Its aim is to encourage positive behaviour and mutual respect.
- As we take notice of unacceptable behaviour we must also take notice of and highlight what we consider to be positive behaviour. Respect, good manners and good behaviour are all important if [name of school] is to be a safe caring place for all those who live and work here.
- The aim is to support rather than punish.

The pastoral policy includes caring for staff and parents as well as pupils.

A *Beat Bullying* booklet has been compiled by students with staff help.

(case study C).

- 'Respect for All' – a policy created by staff and students working collaboratively – is prominently displayed at the school and expresses teachers' and students' commitment to equal opportunities for all, regardless of differences.
- The bullying policy incorporates the appointment of two student counsellors within each year who have a special responsibility for instances of bullying. One of these counsellors is deaf, the other hearing.

(secondary department in case study G).

Valuing individuals

Although ethos is a reflection of collective commitment, in educational contexts in particular it involves respect for individuals' needs, talents and abilities. This not only applies to pupils and students but to staff and parents and all those with whom the school or service comes into contact. Other sections of the report on professional development and leadership also deal with this topic with regard to members of staff. Discussion of schools' attitude to involving parents which is a related subject is to be found in section 4.11. Here we will explore the demonstration of school ethos through attitudes to pupils.

In C the spiritual, moral and cultural policy states, 'The uniqueness of each individual is celebrated and we actively promote the value of each person'. The theme [caring for the individual] permeates both work in the classroom and the pastoral aspects of school life. 'The school looks at each child's strengths, weaknesses, and needs and caters for them, teasing out of them whatever strengths they have. Whatever contribution they wish to make in the classroom is valued, so they feel valued'

(parent).

In the context of deaf education, valuing individuals may mean the need to maximise opportunities for communication so that the pupils both acquire information about what is happening in the school and have the ability and opportunity to express themselves and their ideas and opinions.

'Hearing impaired pupils don't pick up information incidentally. You have to be forthright in getting things to them' (headteacher). Each week begins with a staff briefing followed by a whole school assembly which includes a briefing session where pupils are informed of the week's events (for example, who was visiting, who had a birthday).

> The school council meets monthly with the headteacher or deputy headteacher. All secondary classes are represented. It proposes ideas for improvement of the school and themselves. Developments have included allowing the girls to wear trousers, a lighter summer uniform, and a cold drinks machine.
>
> (case study C).

> At an assembly we attended in G there was a lengthy discussion of the situation in Kosovo. Children were keen to participate, and expressed a range of opinions. The head explained, 'Children are given lots of opportunities to give their opinions; their thoughts and opinions are taken on board'. The head of primary told us, 'We value the children's contributions and bring them into our teaching. Assembly is one of the key times. The children can choose what they want to say in assembly, they can bring issues up. For example, some of the pupils were concerned about the rubbish being dropped in the school, they themselves brought that up. They explained that as we don't want that as we want our school to look nice .... and that came from the children themselves'.

Caring about others

We saw many examples of concern for the wider world being fostered in the schools. As our visits occurred at the time of the terrible happening in Kosovo, we found the children very preoccupied by these events. At school C the children were collecting clothing and toys to be taken to the refugees, and because of pressure from them to talk and learn about this situation the topic had become the focus for their work in spoken language and literacy for one of the primary classes.

> In G children are encouraged to think about others, not only themselves. This was both in terms of explicit consideration for the feelings of others, and in raising money for particular causes. Regular fundraising events are held. Often representatives of the charities are invited to the school to explain how the money will be spent. As the head said, 'Children like to feel that what they do is appreciated by people out there. It raises them from "poor little deaf children". It changes their attitude from "I'm deaf" to "I'm fine, I can do a lot to help other people"'.
>
> (case study G).

Staff-pupil relationships

Many would see 'caring' as an essential component for education, this is particularly so when parents entrust their children to a residential school.

'Pastoral provision is highly valued. The pastoral role is expected of all staff at some time – this may be a listening ear or a reassuring smile. Informally this means being a listener, encourager (to boost confidence), supporter (established pupils help new ones)' (school documents).

- Residential staff work on a personal level and use first names. The care office and duty room door is always open whatever the time. Weekend boarders have meetings to decide menus and activities. They try to make it like a home. Pupils who spend long periods away from home are given to opportunity for weekends away, e.g. a visit to London. 'The duty room is like a debating chamber. We never dictate the terms' (deputy head of care).
- Pupils choose a member of the care staff as a key worker to talk to if something is concerning them.
- The school is a registered site for the Rainbow programme for pupils suffering some form of loss (including divorce, separation in the family or bereavement).

(case study C).

This aspect of ethos will also be evident in the efforts made to promote the personal and social development of the children and to encourage their independence and sense of identity. More detail on these topics can be found in section 4.9.

There is a very strong ethos in the school of developing the confidence of the youngsters as a way of developing their own identity. With confidence, self-respect and realistic self-esteem there is the belief that the deaf young person is ready to face the world. According to one mother, 'My son doesn't feel he has a problem, only people who don't take the time to listen have the problem. This is because the school has built self-respect ....'.

The task of creating confidence, individuality, self-esteem, and self-respect is addressed throughout the pupils' waking hours, through the curriculum, particularly drama and PSE; through staff-pupil relations and through very carefully managed care and activities out of school time.

(case study J).

A sense of satisfaction

...from the cleaners through to the headteacher – everyone has the pupil's best interests at heart. My son has never been happier, he even wants to go to school on weekends. Sometimes professionals take over [but] I'd class [name of ToD] as a friend.

If you feel your child is special to her, she [the ToD] is obviously doing something right.

(parents in various case studies).

The impression we often gain of the current atmosphere in the world of teaching, for example from media reports, is one of dissatisfaction and disaffection – teachers stressed and disillusioned, parents complaining. It was therefore good to hear teachers who spoke of the rewards they found in their work and of the job satisfaction they gained. We also received questionnaires from and met very many parents who spoke with great warmth of the care and attention their children had received and praised highly the commitment and skill of the teachers of the deaf. The cliché of the caring, happy atmosphere is reality still in many places.

Summary

Key findings in this section are summarised as follows:

- The ethos of a school or service derives from and is inextricably linked with the features of its leadership and management and its underlying philosophy of deaf education.

- School life provides many opportunities for occasions to reflect on and reinforce core values which can help maintain a strong ethos.

- An important feature of ethos is valuing individuals, and staff-pupil relationships which reflect mutual respect.

4.3 Professional development

The issue of what constitutes appropriate training for those working with hearing impaired and deaf children is the focus of continuing debate. A consensus on the content of initial training courses for teachers intending to work within this field is provided in *Content of Courses* (Andrews et al., 1995[1]). This was written to suggest the knowledge, skills and experience a training course should provide for those already holding qualified teacher status. It is recognised that the demands of delivering such a course cannot be met in full within the present structure of course delivery, rather, a common core is covered with differing courses offering specific areas in more detail than others. All such training courses are recognised as initial training within the field of deaf education. There is an identified need to develop further training and expertise within this specialist area and to consider the place of formal accreditation of such learning by the profession (Garner,1997[2]). The current review of teacher training arrangements for specialist teachers working with pupils with special educational needs by the Teacher Training Agency (TTA)[3] makes this discussion of training issues for teachers working with deaf pupils and students particularly timely.

In addition to stressing the importance of being able to employ teachers with an appropriate qualification as a teacher of the deaf, all the schools and services nominated as examples of good practice in this study emphasised the importance of continuing professional development for teachers already holding the mandatory qualification as a teacher of the deaf. The need for a clear programme to support further professional development is summed up by two heads of service.

> Initial training is just that – it is essential for all staff to have on-going training to keep professional skills well honed and to continually upgrade. Without the development of staff skill you cannot provide a high quality service.
>
> (HoS, case study B).

---

[1] Andrews, E. et al (1995) *Training Teachers of the Deaf:* Content of Courses. University of Manchester.

[2] Garner, M. (1997) Training teachers of the deaf – time to move on? *Deafness and Education,* 21,2, 46-48.

[3] TTA (1998) (i) *Consultation paper on national standards for special educational needs (SEN) specialist teachers.* (ii) *Consultation paper on options for the delivery of training for specialist educational needs (SEN) specialist teachers.* October 1998

> I make sure people see personal development as part of the job. It isn't a bolt on. It isn't a perk. In order to do the job you have to continuously develop yourself. We talk about personal and professional development rather than training, so that people can see it as not just going on a course. There are lots of other ways you can improve your skills and understanding. It's something we give great priority to.
>
> (HoS, case study A).

Schools and services follow a range of approaches in achieving further professional training. Several noted the importance of auditing staff skills, undertaking training needs analysis for individual teachers or considering the training needs of all staff through a service development plan. The size of the service, school or college dictates how such training is organised. In some areas this is the direct responsibility of the head of service, whereas some schools and colleges employ a development officer. In other settings a member of staff is identified to complete this task.

The importance of regular, in many cases weekly, non-contact time for professional development is a common feature stressed as being important by services. In addition to completing administrative tasks, a staff development session allows an opportunity for sharing expertise and pooling resources. Continuing professional development was identified as having a number of main elements including attendance at external courses, whole staff INSET (usually five days per year) and regular meetings of the staff to discuss, amongst other things, training issues (case study D). Staff meetings are also used for the presentation of materials to the team in the form of mini INSET. This approach allows ToDs to develop their professional skills in providing INSET delivery and to investigate a specific area that benefits the whole team (case study B). In addition to the further professional training for ToDs, services and schools stressed the need to consider all staff and families in the training continuum.

> In one example the team decide between them areas that need developing by reflection on practice. For example this year it was literacy, next year it will be numeracy. A speaker from outside is invited to 'kick-start' the process. From this initial impetus, activities cascade down with meetings, in-service training and workshops, training for SENSAs and meetings for parents. This process is further enhanced by the involvement and the commitment of the whole team.
>
> The HoS will identify days for training/development, maybe a couple of days in a nice hotel. Then some will take it away to develop it further, working in evenings and weekends. The team can be quite critical of what is proposed, and it is worked on until everyone is happy with it. So really it is very much a whole service production. Everyone is involved. Individual

> teachers take responsibility for keeping up to date on a designated area and in this way the team can draw on each other's expertise. Individuals have different interests and strengths and are allowed to develop this with the support of the whole service. Everyone contributes
>
> (ToD, case study H).

In one service (case study A) individual members of staff are permitted one half-day per week for on-going projects. Such projects must have measurable outcomes that are of benefit to the service.

> Staff are encouraged to attend conferences which they had to write up and circulate or present to the service. However the head of service felt this was not totally effective.
>
> If they go to a conference they have to write it up, although we do not send everything round now. Cascading work does not work incredibly well. In the end it's the person who goes who is affected
>
> (HoS, case study A).

Staff skills as a resource

There is a recognised need to keep abreast of rapid developments within the profession and in education in general. All services and schools stressed the importance of employing fully qualified teachers of the deaf. The present situation, where a qualified teacher may work with deaf children for three years prior to undertaking the qualification to teach deaf children, was not recognised as good or effective practice. Rather the heads of schools, colleges and services stressed the specialist skills of their ToDs and the importance of upgrading these skills and the grafting on of new ones. In addition, service providers noted the importance of auditing skills outside the traditional ToD remit that may enhance the provision made for deaf children and young people, for example skills and knowledge in counselling, modern foreign languages, and literature studied at 'A' level. Such skills and knowledge, when audited, provide a pool of additional information which allow the HoS to make the most efficient use of resources (case studies D and L). Within the public sector such skills were widely used to upgrade other team members. The income generating potential of specialist staff was noted as an important aspect of a skills audit, specifically in the non-maintained sector.

> I was appointed to coordinate the training needs of college staff and also to take advantage of the skills and expertise available to provide outside external courses.
>
> (case study L).

The majority of nominated settings met the requirements of 'Investors in People' in that they have:

1. a professional development plan which is based on a strategic and operational plan

2. an appraisal-type process through which progress to achieving professional and thus service development objectives is monitored and evaluated

3. an induction programme in place

4. an effective system of communication in place, within the service and between the service and others

Areas for professional development

There were several topics repeatedly mentioned as important for continuing professional development for teachers already holding the mandatory qualification as a teacher of the deaf. The two main ones were:

*   Audiology
*   Sign language skills

Curriculum initiatives such as the Literacy hour and the Numeracy hour were cited as areas that teachers of the deaf require training to allow them be part of the process of developing strategies ensuring that deaf children gain maximum benefit.

A wide range of other areas were being studied by ToD to improve the quality of school/service provision for deaf children. These included:

*   Appraisal training
*   Early diagnosis (universal neo-natal screening)
*   Deaf awareness
*   Racial equality
*   ICT training
*   Further Education Funding Council pack on inclusive learning
*   NVQ training for residential care staff
*   Professional development award for communication support worker for deaf people
*   Profound and multiple learning disabilities and sensory impairment certificate

Funding issues

There is no clear pattern concerning the allocation of funding for further professional training for ToDs. The move to Local Management of Schools led to many resource bases being devolved to host schools. In many cases this separated resource base staff from further professional training within the field of deaf education. At the same time services for deaf children became part of the central funding mechanism of the LEA. The result of this is appears to be an uneven and unequal opportunity to allocate central funds for further professional development. Fair Funding appears to have made less money available for centrally funded LEA to support continuing professional development of qualified teachers of the deaf.

> Prior to LMS allocation from the LEA pot was approximately £180 per person per year. Staff apply to the HoS for INSET training – they are all entitled to one INSET day per annum. The freeze on county council money meant that there was no budget set aside for the sensory service last year. Staff had access to the LEA training programme, for example, a three day numeracy course. This was run by the LEA, it was useful and could be cascaded back to service staff. The service has managed to claw back some funds equivalent to £70 per person per annum. Recent useful INSET for service was on the literacy hour, which was used as a basis to develop a service literacy hour policy.
>
> (case study B).

For those ToDs working in a devolved unit, opportunities for professional development may be limited to the school's training days, with little or no opportunity to develop further specialist skills and expertise. This can be further exacerbated by lack of easy regular access to other teachers of the deaf.

> I do feel rather isolated being the only teacher of hearing impaired children in the school. I don't always have someone to bounce ideas off. Also your point of view is not always understood fully. There's always that ignorance about the education of hearing impaired children'
>
> (ToD, case study F).

The complexities of providing high quality service/school provision are well recognised within the profession. A common feature of schools/colleges and services for deaf children/young people is the high level of professional expertise displayed by ToDs.

> When we were tired and apathetic she [the ToD] was there full of enthusiasm. We rely on her judgement, she has lots of experience, and reference points we don't have.
>
> (parent of deaf child, case study F).

Teachers of the deaf at present have a range of options available to gain further professional expertise, including membership of the professional association, the British

Association of Teachers of the Deaf, which provides access to a journal and magazine in addition to the provision of update courses and regular meetings. Also, several universities offer opportunities for further professional studies although funding for ToDs is frequently reported to be problematic.

The overall commitment to professional development is evidenced in discussions and conversations with many staff members. Many talked about their current professional development initiatives, or what they hope to do in the future. Those engaged on particular projects described them in some detail and always talked in terms of how they saw them benefiting the service as a whole (case study A).

Conclusions

Continuing professional development is essential for teachers of the deaf in whatever setting they work. In addition to the training needs that are held in common with all teachers with regard to curriculum initiatives, teachers of the deaf have specialist skills that need on-going development. In a one year or equivalent initial specialist course it is only possible to provide the level of skills that teachers need as newly qualified teachers of the deaf. Research continually informs the profession. The introduction of new technology, sign language assessment tools and other innovations require opportunities for teachers of the deaf to extend their expertise and to ensure that benefits are accrued for deaf children/young people and their families. Good practice at any point in time is dependent not only on a perspective of the objectives of deaf education but also on access to training, both initial specialist training and on-going professional development. Many heads of service specifically noted that all the teachers employed held the specialist qualification and that it was policy not to employ untrained staff. The value of further professional development is well summed up by one head of service:

> The role of the ToD in supporting hearing impaired children in mainstream schools is rich and varied and the totality of skills required are unlikely to be fully met during initial training. Furthermore continuous changes in the field of education of the deaf itself, e.g. the introduction of a sign bilingual approach, new technology in hearing aids, together with the rapid changes occurring in education generally, demand continuous professional development, training and updating.
>
> (HoS case study D).

The same notion holds true for any setting. Training is a continuum rather than an end point. The importance placed on such continued development strongly supports the introduction of a system of continuing professional accreditation. Such a system would encourage all teachers of the deaf to keep abreast of developments, allow the profession to make more effective use of 'good' practice across regions and help to ensure that all deaf children and young people and their families benefit.

Summary

Key findings in this section are summarised as follows:

- Regular team meetings which specifically evaluate the service or school, consider areas for development and share expertise across the team are seen as vital.

- Heads of schools and services emphasise the importance of employing teachers who hold the mandatory qualification to teach deaf children.

- A comprehensive audit of all staff skills is helpful which includes all areas of expertise together with a clear plan for development of the individual to enhance service delivery.

- A proactive head of school or service can ensure funding opportunities are put to maximum use.

4.4 Inclusion

Introduction

Inclusion means many things to many people (Powers, 1996 [1]). In the past inclusion might simply have implied the *location* of a child with a disability or special need in a mainstream school. Later there has been emphasis on *integrating* the pupil with a disability into the mainstream school, offering various kinds of specialist support in order for the pupil to benefit from what is generally available (Lynas, 1986 [2]). For those who currently might term themselves 'inclusionists', for example Dyson, 1994 [3]; Booth, 1996 [4]; Ainscow, 1997 [5], inclusion means more than placement or integration; it means *welcoming all children* into the local school regardless of ability, disability, background, religion, ethnicity, as a matter of human rights; it means top-down, whole-school policies whereby the staff of the school take full responsibility for the education of all the children in the local catchment area; it means teachers planning their teaching and reflecting on their practice in order to accommodate diversity; it means collaboration between mainstream teachers and as many specialists and support staff as are necessary to ensure that all learners have a worthwhile learning experience and make systematic learning progress.

Inclusion can be perceived as an educational *process* and an educational *goal*. Inclusion as a process implies that all learners are educated together as a means of offering equal opportunities, celebrating diversity, of enabling each pupil to achieve her/his learning potential, of improving the quality of education not only to pupils who are traditionally excluded from mainstream schools but all children. The practice of catering for diversity is believed to lead to overall school improvement and more effective schools for all (Ainscow, 1995 [6]). Inclusion as a goal, however, need not imply the location of every learner in the mainstream classroom for all or even part of the time (Powers, 1996). The goal of inclusion might be thought to be achieved by a variety of routes, for example offering the pupil with special needs finely-tuned positive discrimination; offering specialist or intensive learning experiences in a separate location which will lead ultimately to the goal of inclusion in the wider society as an independent, confident individual.

---

[1] Powers, S. (1996) Inclusion is an attitude not a place: Part 1. *Journal of British Association of Teachers of the Deaf,* 20, 2, 35-41.

[2] Lynas, W. (1986) *Educating the Handicapped into Ordinary Schools: a Study of Hearing-Impaired Pupils.* London: Croom Helm.

[3] Dyson, A. (1994) Towards a collaborative learning model for responding to student diversity. *Support for Learning.* 9, 2, 53-60.

[4] Booth, T. (1996) A perspective on inclusion from England. *Cambridge Journal of Education,* 26, 1, 87-101.

[5] Ainscow, M. (1997). Towards inclusive schooling. *British Journal of Special Education,* 24, 1, 3-6.

[6] Ainscow, M. (1995) Education for all: making it happen. *Support for Learning.* 10, 4, 147-155.

Inclusion as a goal

The variety of practices observed during the Good Practice Review case study visits reflected the complexity of the concept of inclusion. All of the case study provisions, whether LEA service, resource-base, college or special school, share the goal of inclusion of the deaf individual into the adult world as a confident, participating, independent member of society. The good practice we observed means high aspirations, high expectations and a concern for equal opportunities. But there were different practices in relation to the means of achieving those goals: for some, a separate education of high quality is the means of achieving equal opportunities and later inclusion; for others inclusion means participation in the life of the mainstream school as a way of achieving equal opportunities and later inclusion in the adult world. However, with all the case study provisions that were offered within the mainstream school context, we observed a combination of discrete, separate tuition *and* participation in the mainstream class and the two forms of provision were not perceived as incompatible: intensive or specialist work was perceived to support academic and social inclusion. Furthermore, with the special schools, firm links have been established with nearby mainstream schools and/or the local community: a special school education does not, therefore, necessarily mean complete segregation.

The special school and the goal of inclusion

The special schools which feature in the Good Practice Review merit special mention. First, there is no doubt that they share the goal, with all other providers, of inclusion into the wider society. Second, each special school contributes to this goal by offering direct links with the 'wider society' during the school years. The two residential schools encourage and support links with the local community through a variety of extra-curricular activities in order to develop the pupils' social skills and confidence in using spoken language in hearing contexts.

The two day schools (primary) have active links with local primary schools, for example in lessons, lunchtimes, play-times and certain extra-curricular activities 'to prepare our children to integrate both academically and socially in mainstream schools and within the hearing community'. That many of the children use sign as their main means of communication is not believed to be a barrier to the links with hearing schools. The support of communicators and the ingenuity of the pupils themselves in developing communication strategies with hearing pupils facilitates social interaction. Furthermore, hearing children take signing classes to encourage mutual accommodation. Deaf pupils from both primary schools transfer to secondary provision in mainstream schools. There is an emphasis, where deaf and hearing groups come together, on 'respect for all' regardless of difference.

In general, the special schools visited as part of the Good Practice Review reflect the idea that special schooling does not have to mean isolation and segregation. It is doubtful, 20 or so years ago, whether this would have been the case.

Inclusion as a process: mainstream provision

Enthusiasm for inclusion as a practice was evident both from the specialist and mainstream sectors as the following statements indicate:

> 'We have always believed in inclusion, it underpins all the work we do... We like the inclusive approach – they're out in the mainstream sector but we're matching it with 100% support. We do not want segregated provision. We get young people ready for life and life is in the hearing community with links with the deaf community. Students will be living and working within the hearing community. That is the real world. We need to offer very good and very clear support in the real world'
>
> (principal, case study L).

> 'Integration/inclusion, whatever, all coming to the same school gives them the opportunity to mix socially. They have to operate in a hearing world so, if possible, it makes sense for them to come to a normal school' (headteacher, case study B).

> '[I am] ... very, very happy that these young folk seem to be well integrated into the life of the school and have become part and parcel of school life'
>
> (headteacher, case study F).

The idea of 'celebrating diversity' by educating deaf children in mainstream school was perceived as a special benefit to the children's normally hearing peers:

> 'The children were great with him [the deaf child]... they still are. They can sometimes understand better than the teacher. They'll translate for him. He's just part of the class'
>
> (mainstream primary teacher, case study F).

> 'It's good for the other children as well. They'd never dealt with a deaf child before but [now] just accept her as a normal child. They will speak clearer and slower. The others make sure she knows what to do'
>
> (mainstream primary teacher, case study F).

> The children are totally integrated... there are spin-offs for us too – the impact it has on the other children. For example, when G had her implant they could see the site of the operation and that she had had her head shaved. They showed real concern and empathy for her'
>
> (headteacher, case study F).

The role of the teacher of the deaf in promoting positive attitudes

For the practice of including deaf children in mainstream schools to be effective, top-down commitment and a whole-school ethos of acceptance is important. According to the findings of the Good Practice Review, commitment to inclusion and a welcoming ethos is sometimes a feature of a school before the arrival of a deaf pupil and schools are often selected by parents or by the educational service for this reason:

> The ethos of a school is very important. The school has been excellent, bent over backwards. The teachers would ask what they felt they should do. This school is totally supportive, it welcomes all the children'
>
> (parent of three deaf children, case study F).

> Inclusion is implicit within the articulation of the school, and within this framework the opening of the resource base was seen as a positive development by the school'
>
> (HoS case study B).

That management attitudes are important is illustrated by the following example of changes in ethos towards inclusive practice on the appointment of a headteacher committed to inclusive principles:

> When I came there were demarcation lines and it was a matter of breaking these down and creating an ethos where we would be working in a truly inclusive way. It had to be seen to be a positive thing by everyone in the school to have hearing impaired children here. About 12 years ago there was perhaps the idea that the deaf children and the unit were a bit of a nuisance and an extra burden on the school. We had to develop a system where class teachers would see it was a real benefit to them, to have hearing impaired children integrated as much as possible... team teaching developed and people planned together and the ethos changed... the Hearing Resource Base [formerly called the 'unit'] came to be seen as a positive asset for the school'
>
> (headteacher, case study N).

Teacher of the deaf support of inclusion

In the case of several schools attitudes of acceptance and welcoming of diversity have to be worked at by the service or by individual ToDs, and positive attitudes seem to a very important extent to depend on ToD support. The following examples and citations testify to the contribution of teachers of the deaf in developing welcoming attitudes towards deaf pupils in mainstream schools:

I felt terrified. I nearly died when M [deaf child's mother] said she was sending him here. We've learned so much since then'

(mainstream teacher, case study F).

'We honestly couldn't do without the support. It's back-up for ourselves'

(mainstream class teacher, case study F).

Last summer I thought "How will I cope? How am I going to understand what she's saying?" But I really enjoy having her'

(mainstream teacher, First School, case study K).

The interpersonal skills of the ToD helps enormously in encouraging staff to be as helpful as possible. We can accommodate with right support. The staff have made sure that X [the deaf pupil] has a fair crack of the whip. The two ToDs are key to the success: you can't underestimate their importance. They gently nudge staff along ... to be better whilst reassuring'

(headteacher, case study B).

[Inclusion] has worked mainly because of the LSA and the visiting teacher of the deaf... pointing out things we'd never thought about... the school have taken him [the deaf child] on lock, stock and barrel'

(headteacher, case study B).

...the quality of staff is crucial. ToDs have a high level of commitment. [The ToDs] really are very supportive. From the technical side, maintenance of equipment happens without problem'

(headteacher, case study F).

This last example reminds us of the important role that ToDs play in audiological management and support. Mainstream teachers typically cannot perform the tasks associated with hearing aid management unsupported. Yet it is doubtful if deaf children can be successfully included in the mainstream system if hearing aids are not effectively maintained and managed.

Collaboration as integral to inclusion

The Good Practice Review has more than confirmed that for effective inclusion there is a need for planning and collaboration on the part of ToDs, LSAs and mainstream teachers. Good practice means finding the time, whether a lunchtime, after school or during a timetabled session. That liaison time is coming to be seen as crucial is evidenced by one LEA service (case study E) endeavouring to timetable liaison so that it does not depend so much on the goodwill of staff, for example in giving up lunchtimes. The National Curriculum and its attendant record keeping, weekly plans, half-termly plans and detailed definition of learning targets undoubtedly provides the basis for successful ToD-mainstream staff collaboration. Where ToDs and LSAs 'know what's coming' facilitates planning work with class teachers, enables ToDs and LSAs to participate in class lessons, and helps the ToD in her/his pre-tutoring of the deaf pupil. Examples of careful liaison and joint planning can be found in the section on Support in the Mainstream.

A finding, though not a universal one, from the Good Practice Review, was that the recent introduction of the National Literacy Hour (and in the same vein, the forthcoming Numeracy Lesson) has positively supported the inclusion of deaf pupils in mainstream lessons. For example, a teacher of the deaf working in a primary school, comments that the Literacy Hour 'has absolutely supported' the deaf children because of its similarity each day. The following is an example of good practice reported by this teacher.

> The mainstream teacher and the ToD plan the lessons together. The teachers plan the questions they will specifically ask the deaf children (reflective, speculative and descriptive). The teacher of the deaf teaches two hours of the Literacy Hour a week. On the occasion of the case study visit the mainstream teacher was taking the Literacy Hour and repeated answers so that all children can hear them.

Teacher of the deaf input contributing to school improvement

Some writers (e.g. Ainscow, 1997 op cit) fear that effective inclusion cannot be achieved through the mechanism of introducing the child with a disability into a mainstream school with some kind of specialist support. Support from special educators, so it is claimed, will inevitably become 'velcroed' to the child and this will interfere with inclusive practice and will deflect attention away from the need to improve school policies and practices. The good practice we observed bears testimony to the fact the specialist educators can, from the 'bottom-up', be a positive force for developing whole-school policies, for collaboration, for helping create positive attitudes, for enabling and empowering mainstream teachers in catering for diversity, in offering appropriate differentiation, and in adapting their teaching for the benefit of all the children in the class. Of equal importance, is that, far from being 'velcroed' to the child, the good practice of ToDs and support staff is aimed towards creating independence in learning as a primary goal; efforts are made to prevent dependence and over-protection.

Specialist staff, primarily teachers of the deaf, support assistants and deaf workers, far from detracting from the process of inclusion by segregating pupils for special attention, made a very positive contribution not only to the overall ethos of inclusion but to the quality of teaching in the school and to school improvement. Several comments and examples from mainstream staff and schools affirm that adapting teaching for the deaf child improves the learning environment for all pupils:

> 'It does benefit everyone. It's good practice'
>
> (primary mainstream teacher, case study E).

> 'A good teacher of the deaf benefits all children and the school'
>
> (headteacher, case study B).

> The principal of the college for deaf young people (case study L) was a consultant to the production of the FEFC resource pack, Inclusive Learning Quality Initiative. She is introducing the pack, rated as an 'excellent resource which helps colleges to move forwards towards more inclusive practice', throughout the college as a valuable whole college approach to inclusive learning.
>
> (case study L).

> The classroom was carpeted to make it more acoustically friendly ... the teacher of the deaf takes the class while the class teacher works in one-to-one withdrawal with the deaf child... the teacher team teaches with the class teacher.
>
> (case study F).

What is significant about the indirect support practices referred to above and in the section on Support in the Mainstream is that they are perceived as successful in modifying teacher behaviour, not just for the benefit of the deaf pupil, but also for the well-being of the teacher her/himself as this comment from a secondary teacher indicates – 'I'd much rather they understood than that they muddled through'. Of greater significance perhaps were that some support practices we observed, direct and indirect, were judged by practitioners to contribute to the class teachers' teaching abilities, so they felt enabled to take responsibility for the deaf pupil in her/his class. That the school and the class teacher take responsibility for all the pupils in their class and do not think of children with disabilities as primarily the responsibility of specialist staff is, of course a key principle of current thinking on inclusion (Dyson, 1994 op cit).

The following examples and citations testify to the important role of the ToD in contributing to empowerment of class teachers and hence to the principle of inclusion:

> As a teacher I have benefited from her [the ToD's] expertise; I have used this to develop my own teaching ... All the children I teach benefit from [the ToD's] expertise'
>
> (mainstream primary teacher, case study F).

> One LEA's support practice document states that 'direct support teaching should enhance the child's ability to receive the curriculum and empower the mainstream staff to deliver the curriculum'. The activities of the ToD working alongside the class teacher, making use of strategies such as developing listening and communication skills, checking understanding etc., known here as parallel teaching, have the effect of transfer of skills to the class teacher in a non-didactic way. 'We always see integration as a two-way process, not as an aim but a process... which I think is nearer to inclusion than some other people's interpretation of integration'
>
> (HoS, case study H).

> I thought about what the teachers of the deaf had explained to us and tried to think how I could help make the library more user friendly. I saw a programme about subtitling and thought I could do that. I talked to the headteacher and wrote to the NDCS explaining what I wanted to do. They came up with half the money and the school matched it. For the deaf kids I can subtitle anything they want but I always subtitle Newsround and Brookside. It provides a really good example of standard and non-standard English. It benefits all the pupils in the school'
>
> (school librarian, secondary school, case study B).

Discrete provision as a means to the end of inclusion

In many of the case studies the importance of discrete, specialised provision is seen as entirely compatible with the goal and/or the practice of inclusion. The following citations reflect the idea that focused, intensive or specialised learning experience in a separate location can be a means to the end of educational inclusion or eventual inclusion within the wider society. The following examples and citation reflect the notion of special provision being a valid route towards later inclusion:

A school such as (X) acts as a safety net for pupils with particular needs, or pupils with restricted local options, enabling them to have access to a normal educational experience with relatively high levels of support allied to clear and consistent expectations. The ultimate objective for the school is to equip pupils and their families with the necessary skills and experience to re-integrate fully into college or the world of work at the earliest appropriate point.'

(staff handbook for teachers, case study J).

Inclusion can be seen as an authority wide response to the diversity and range of needs of pupils and students, whereby institutions are encouraged to ensure maximum entitlement for all. The aim is for all schools to be inclusive. Resourced mainstream schools are part of this aim even though children do not attend their local mainstream school. The contribution to be made to the wider community by the language and culture of Deaf people is a positive feature of inclusion. The Salamanca Declaration within the UN Standard Rules, recognises the unique position of deaf children owing to their language and culture. Whilst the goal of inclusion into society is a human rights issue, inclusive education can take many forms. In the case of deaf children, specialist provision such as a resourced school can be inclusive.'

(Policies and Procedures document, case study A).

We want our children to go to their local mainstream school – that's what we aim for. So independence is the thing; they have to be able to cope on their own at the big school and that's what we're about with the children and that's what we impress on the parents'

(ToD, head of nursery, case study M).

Most of our examples of discrete provision supporting inclusion come from the mainstream sector itself. For many of the services where deaf children and young people are placed in mainstream schools or colleges, full inclusion into the mainstream class is perceived as a goal to be worked towards rather than a practice to be slavishly adhered to. Discrete, specialist, intensive work with one or a small group of children or young people are commonly perceived in our Good Practice Review to be an essential way of enabling ultimate independence in learning. Discrete provision allows for the development of, for example, sign language, listening skills, spoken language, literacy, and social interaction in a way that is not so easily achievable in the everyday life of the noisy mainstream classroom. Furthermore, skilful pre-tutoring allows for more genuine participation in lessons; post-tutoring reinforcement and consolidation of learning permits genuine access to the curriculum. The following citations and examples illustrate these points:

The tutorial system run by the college promotes inclusion by ensuring that the cognitive and linguistic underpinning necessary for course access are developed. Support in college may be a small group but will always include some one to one work as well

(interview with college principal, case study L).

'We would always be talking as the ultimate goal functional inclusion, functional integration as it might have been termed, not locational or social, is what we're after... [but] if at the end of the day a child hasn't got the language appropriate to cope in a mainstream class, withdrawal for tuition is offered'

(HoS, case study H).

'We really treat it [withdrawal tuition] as an investment in time... we're building up skills that will let them back later'

(ToD, case study H).

One LEA makes minimal use of LSAs and in-class support. Much of the support is indirect, e.g. INSET, regular liaison, and part of the policy of 'working through the class teacher'. Support offered to the deaf pupil is generally direct and individual in a withdrawal situation away from the (often) poor acoustic conditions of the mainstream classroom. The aim is to develop language and literacy, to pre-tutor for lessons to come in conditions of high levels of on-task engagement. The support ToD's close understanding of the child's learning abilities and extent of her/his knowledge enables skilful 'scaffolding'. The service believes that this form of support contributes more to inclusion than in-class support because of the demands it makes of the deaf pupil to access information for her/himself when in the mainstream class; in short, it facilitates independent learning which is a central goal of inclusion.

(case study D).

Parents and inclusion

Parents, of course, do have views about educational placement and about educational inclusion. Unfortunately, the case study notes based on our visits do not include comments from parents on this issue. We do have a wealth of such comments but they feature as written comments in part two of the questionnaire that we used to select our case studies (see discussion in chapter 3).

Inclusion as a way of achieving natural auralism

There was evidence from the Good Practice Review that some educators believed that the process of inclusion was itself a means to goals in the education of deaf children other than academic and social inclusion, in particular, the goal of developing spoken language. According to one HoS:

> [the natural aural approach is underpinned by] natural experience rather than direct teaching. Both parents and teachers must aim to create a consistent atmosphere in which children wish and need to communicate naturally. Children will construct language from the natural environment'
>
> (HoS, case study B).

Inclusion and deaf adults

Inclusion implies equal opportunities. For children with disabilities to genuinely believe in themselves as future contributing members of society then they need to see that adults who share their disability are indeed socially and economically active. To this end the employment of deaf adults in the educational service for deaf children can be seen as a positive step. The proportion of deaf adults employed in schools and services cannot be ascertained from the Good Practice Review because we did not ask this question. However, examples of good practice in this respect can be found in some of our case study notes; in case study A, 11 deaf instructors are employed working in a team which included 20 ToDs; in case study D, one of the seven teachers of the deaf was profoundly deaf and there is another deaf adult employed as a communicator for the sign-bilingual children; in case study P, a deaf signing instructor is employed. In case study G, the headteacher is deaf; in case study N, a head of unit is profoundly deaf; in case study M, there is a deaf support assistant employed part-time; in case study J, one of the ex-pupils is a care manager; in case study N, there is currently discussion about the need to employ a deaf person.

There could be further examples of employment of deaf adults but these are not revealed in the case study notes. Furthermore, in the case of 'oral' deaf adults who perhaps do not see their identity as primarily anchored to their deafness, their employment may not have been seen by some of the case study providers as anything of particular note.

There could be scope for a higher degree of employment of deaf individuals in the education of deaf children and young people as a way of truly embodying the spirit of inclusion. However, there are almost certainly greater numbers of deaf people in deaf education than there used to be and this is to be welcomed.

Summary

Key findings in this section are summarised as follows:

- There is a universal support for the goals of inclusion among providers whether mainstream or special school.

- The goal of inclusion is supported not undermined by a component of separate, discrete specialist provision for deaf pupils.

- Welcoming attitudes and a commitment to inclusion on the part of the receiving school contribute greatly to the perceived success of the practice of inclusion.

- Teachers of the deaf are seen to play a significant role in overall school improvement and in promoting whole-school policies.

- The practice of inclusion is perceived by some providers as underpinning the natural aural approach.

- Deaf adults are increasingly playing a role in the education of deaf children and young people and this is seen as a positive step towards inclusion and equal opportunities.

4.5 Support in mainstream schools

Support in mainstream is a major theme in this report. It was a selected theme in six case studies but also emerged as a theme in another two.

This section concerns the support, both direct and indirect, offered to deaf pupils in mainstream schools by teachers of the deaf (ToDs), learning support assistants (LSAs), mainstream teachers, interpreters, deaf assistants and others. It includes but does not entirely concern support in mainstream classes. The discussion relates to practice in either resource base ('unit') provision or the support offered to deaf pupils individually placed in their local schools. It is presented under the headings; two contrasting approaches, arrangements for support, joint planning, roles, delivering INSET and monitoring progress.

Background

It is easy to forget that although the idea of educating deaf children in ordinary schools has a long history in the UK, it was not until the second half of the 1970s onwards that there was a significant shift of deaf pupils away from special school provision and into ordinary schools. The most recent figures show that currently about 85% of all deaf children are being educated in mainstream schools (the figure for severely and profoundly deaf pupils is 65%)[1] (Eatough, 1995)[2].

The trend away from special school placement for deaf pupils over recent decades is illustrated in Tables 4.5.1 and 4.5.2. Table 4.5.1 shows that the number of special schools in both the UK as a whole and England and Wales has fallen by approximately 50% over a twenty year period from the late 1970s to the present day. Recent figures provided by Eatough (1995) compared with figures in Table 4.5.2 show the change has been even more dramatic when we look at pupil numbers; the number of pupils placed in special schools in England and Wales fell from over six and a half thousand in the mid 1970s (Table 4.5.2) to only two and a half thousand in 1994 (Table 4.5.3).

---

[1] In the UK deaf children are educated in special schools for deaf children, in schools that have been specially resourced for deaf children (these specialist provisions are sometimes called 'units') or on an individual basis in mainstream schools. Also, there are some deaf children educated in other types of special school. Ignoring this last group, the most recent figures show that over 85% of deaf pupils (with all degrees of hearing loss) are now in mainstream programmes.

[2] Eatough, M. (1995). BATOD Survey 1994: England. *Journal of the British Association of Teachers of the Deaf* (19) 5, 142-160.

Table 4.5.1
Number of special schools for deaf children [3]

Year	Source of information	Number of schools England and Wales	Number of schools UK
1968	Lewis Report	54	
1971	NCTD Report	52	65
1975/76	NDCS Directory	61	78
1978/79	NDCS Directory	59	74
1982	Jordan		75
1988	Child		40
1998	BATOD data base	30	42

Table 4.5.2 [4]
The number of deaf pupils attending special schools in England and Wales

Year	Number of pupils
1968	5,141
1972	5,781
1976	6,633
1977	5,938
1979	5,566
1980	4,849
1983	3,808

Source: Lynas, 1986 p13 [5]

[3] It was difficult to get this information. The DfEE do not keep records on the number of special schools for deaf pupils and have not kept data on numbers of deaf pupils since the 1981 Education Act. Also, the main deaf organisations, the National Deaf Children's Society, the British Association of Teachers of the Deaf and the Royal National Institute for Deaf People, were not able to provide it. Eventually it was possible to locate a 1971 report from the National College of Teachers of the Deaf and some old copies of the NDCS directory which between them provided the information in this table.

[4] From the comments on p14 of Lynas (1986) it is clear that these figures refer to the special schools for deaf children and do not include deaf pupils in other types of special school.

[5] Lynas, W. (1986) *Integrating the Handicapped into Ordinary Schools.* London: Croom Helm.

Table 4.5.3
Deaf pupils in England and Wales in 1994 by educational placement

Placement	Number of pupils (nearest 100)
Special school for deaf pupils	2,400
Mainstream school	16,100

Source: Figures derived from Eatough (1995, 1996[6])

The move towards mainstream school placement has been matched by a move towards the teaching of deaf children in mainstream *classes*. It would appear from previous reports (e.g. Powers, 1990[7]) and our observations during this study that almost all deaf children in ordinary schools are taught for the majority of their time alongside their hearing peers, although, as we shall describe later, in many cases arrangements are also made for tutorial support outside the ordinary classroom.

Two contrasting approaches

In this study we came across two contrasting approaches to supporting deaf pupils in mainstream schools. From our observations it appears most other approaches fall somewhere between these two.

In the first approach D the emphasis is on ToDs offering tutorial support to deaf pupils with very little use made of LSAs. In the second approach E, ToDs offer almost no direct support to pupils but instead concentrate on providing indirect support to mainstream teachers and directing the work of LSAs.

The first approach

The model of support in service D is for ToDs to provide direct support to pupils in tutorial sessions. There is very little use of non-teaching support assistants except in the case of sign bilingual children or occasionally for notetaking purposes for pupils at KS3 or examination level. Predominantly, the support involves the withdrawal of pupils for tutorial time on a one-to-one basis with the aim of developing core language and literacy skills and spoken communication skills and to prepare the pupils for full access to the curriculum. Withdrawing the

---

[6] Eatough, M. (1996) BATOD Survey 1994: Wales. *Journal of the British Association of Teachers of the Deaf* (20) 2, 50-61.

[7] Powers, S. (1990). A survey of secondary units for hearing impaired children. *Journal of British Association of Teachers of the Deaf* (14) 3, 69-79.

pupil from the mainstream class for support, we were told, ensures good listening conditions, a lack of distraction and a high level of on-task engagement. A knowledge of the pupil combined with a knowledge of the work to be covered in class enables very effective pretutoring; the pupil is familiarised with what is to come and this has the added beneficial effect of boosting the pupil's confidence.

The service believes that in-class support would not facilitate more access to the curriculum since pupils need intensive language teaching which can only be achieved in a withdrawal situation. However, the approach is not a rigid one so that where there is a particular need for in-class support, for example some form of practical work, the teacher would arrange to be alongside the pupil in the classroom. The time pupils spend unsupported in the class situation is considered valuable for developing independence. This model of support together with the indirect support provided through INSET to schools is considered empowering for the mainstream teachers and maintains the important link between pupil and class teacher without the mediation of a third party.

The second approach

Case study E provides a contrasting model of support. In this service ToDs have an almost purely advisory role (and are known as advisory teachers) and the only direct support is given by LSAs and mainstream teachers. Inservice training for mainstream staff is given special emphasis.

One key function of the advisory teacher is to observe pupils in class noting on a checklist aspects pertinent to a pupil's ability to follow oral communication. The checklist focuses on the pupil's ability to access both the teacher and other classmates, in pairs or groups. Use of audiological equipment is also monitored. The advisory teacher uses the checklist as a basis for discussion with the mainstream teacher after the lesson. In some instances, a tick list of 'recommendations' is left in the school for the relevant teacher. A complete list of communication strategies is also available as an information document.

Information relating to the pupil's progress is collected on a 'Round Robin' report form which is filled in by all the staff concerned. This information provides the basis for the advisory teacher's yearly report and from which suggestions and recommendations can be made.

The two models of support in D and E differ essentially in the relative emphasis given to direct as opposed to indirect support from ToDs. It is probably true that in recent years there has been a general shift towards ToDs taking on a more advisory role, although from our visits it would appear that the approach taken by E is unusual and that most ToDs provide at least some direct support to pupils.

Arrangements for direct support to pupils

The two main factors discussed under this heading are the amount of support and the type of the support.

Amount of support

Where there is a resource base in a school it is often possible for a pupil to have some direct support every day. This is more difficult for visiting teachers of the deaf (VToDs), but most of the services we visited offer several visits a week to some pupils.

> In service K maximum levels of support from VToDs are decided according to levels of hearing loss; five times a week for profoundly deaf pupils, three times a week for severely and once a week for moderately deaf pupils. For example T, a severely deaf six year-old in year one in a mainstream Infant School, is visited three times a week by the ToD. Two sessions are 1:1, in the other the ToD takes a group of four to six children including T (reverse integration).

> In service H many pupils are visited by the ToD several times a week. The HoS is responsive to the advice of ToDs if they feel increased support is required. Conversely, there is a policy of reducing the level of support when this is appropriate. In this way, the HoS feels, the credibility of the service is maintained with the authority so that requests for increased or high levels of support are listened to sympathetically.

In several of the case studies final decisions on levels of support are made after consultation with parents and mainstream teachers.

Type of direct support

In most cases ToDs appeared to exercise considerable autonomy over the nature of the direct support offered to pupils. Also, in almost every case (the main exception being service E) most pupils were for some of the time taught separately from the mainstream class, either by ToDs or LSAs. That is, we came across very few cases of pupils being fully included in mainstream classes.

> In H it is largely left to individual ToDs to decide what form the direct support should take. According to one document 'Teachers of hearing impaired children

should determine the balance necessary in consultation with mainstream colleagues'.

You have to really look at how they're performing in class with or without you. And if they haven't really got the toolkit, as it were, you need to arrange some withdrawal, perhaps in a group or even one-to-one.

(ToD).

Tutorial support is offered on an individual or small group basis. The service aims for a 'high level of inclusion' where it's feasible but will arrange withdrawal sessions '... if at the end of the day a child hasn't got the language appropriate to cope in a mainstream classroom' (ToD). Withdrawal for tuition is provided to develop deaf pupils' skills in language, speech, listening, literacy and social interaction; also as an opportunity for reinforcement and consolidation of learning, and for pretutoring to enable pupils to take part in future classroom activities. Emphasis is given to the need for careful planning of how withdrawal time will be used and the need to develop study skills rather than concentrating solely on the content of the particular lesson.

[It is important to be] ... very specific about the reasons for withdrawing them from a lesson, having a good justification for that... We really treat it as an investment in time... So that later we're building up some skills that will let them back in later.

(ToD).

This approach is in line with that required under the Code of Practice (DfE, 1994)[8] which requires clearly stated reasons for withdrawal to take place.

In the primary resource base N, ToDs decide levels of integration. The stated aim is to integrate in mainstream for 70% although at the moment this is not met because of the demands of the literacy hour. Opportunities for tutorial work are seen as crucial because of the opportunities for concentrated language work. Arrangements are flexible and there is the possibility for a pupil or group to be withdrawn to continue in the resource base if they are not understanding. The need for flexibility was mentioned by several people. In the secondary unit in E they operate a 'reserve timetable' so that should pupils not be requiring the timetabled support, the supporting teacher can consult the timetable and discover with which pupil she can more usefully spend her time.

---

[8] DfE (1994) *Code of Practice on the Identification and Assessment of Special Educational Needs.* London: HMSO.

During our visits we saw several examples of reverse integration, that is a group of hearing children withdrawn from their mainstream class to work with one or more deaf children, normally in the resource base and normally taught by the ToD or sometimes the LSA. If managed well there would appear to be clear potential benefits for many pupils in such arrangements compared with supporting in the mainstream class, including:

- the acoustic conditions should be better

- speech reading should be easier, due to smaller numbers and better seating

- teaching is by a person trained to teach deaf children and familiar with the deaf child

- with smaller numbers it is easier to pace the lesson appropriately for all pupils

- all the pupils have more opportunity to contribute to discussion

- there is possibly better opportunity for pupils to 'shine', with benefits to self-esteem and therefore motivation

Also, the hearing pupils in reverse integration groups should receive more individual attention than they would in the mainstream class.

It is likely that many ToDs would say they find reverse integration work more satisfactory than supporting one child in a mainstream lesson. Also, there is the opportunity for the ToD and the class teacher to swop roles where the ToD teaches the main group and the class teacher takes the reverse integration group. This provides an opportunity for the class teacher to become more familiar with the particular needs of the deaf child.

It is clear to us that reverse integration is often used effectively, however it is only one among several approaches to supporting deaf pupils in mainstream schools and clearly has its limitations. In some subjects the ToD or LSA will not have the subject specialist knowledge required, in others the necessary equipment will not be available. Undoubtedly there are also many cases where deaf children are achieving well in the mainstream class and enjoy the challenge of the large group. Also, many ToDs will want opportunities for intensive one-to-one or small group sessions with deaf pupils.

Where reverse integration is used it is important that there is a clear understanding of roles between the adults involved, as demonstrated in the following two quotes:

> One of the issues that has sometimes come up is when a teacher throws a whole lot of children with a whole medley of needs in with this hearing impaired pupil who might be quite different and their needs are not being met. You have to stand up. On the other hand if we can be of help when it's relevant to bring others into the group that's an added bonus and it's part of our goodwill that we do that but we have to keep in mind the needs of the hearing impaired.
>
> (LSA).

Sometimes we have to support the support assistants in that because they haven't got enough status to say to the teacher 'Look this is not working. I'm getting too many difficult children here'.

(ToD).

We came across the following two cases where the level and type of support had been negotiated with individual pupils. It does seem right to allow older pupils, and perhaps younger ones, the opportunity to become involved in decisions made about their support arrangements.

R is a profoundly deaf pupil in a mainstream sixth form. She began to lose her hearing at two and a half then suddenly went totally deaf at nine years.

In secondary school she started with 15 hours of support but this reduced in years 9 and 10. She had found the support '... got a bit much at times. Sometimes when I needed the help it was good, sometimes not. In Maths and Science it was helpful. I couldn't do algebra so we concentrated on that.' She prefers to have the lesson with the class and then go over it with the ToD so she has 'two different ways of explaining it'.

At GCSE level she negotiated where she wanted help. In the sixth form she has one hour a week available from the ToD, but will ring her if she needs her more. She is studying Biology, History and Environmental Science.

(case study K).

In D particularly at the secondary stage, pupils have a say in their own support programme. They can negotiate the amount of support they receive and up to a point the subject(s) they omit from the curriculum in order to receive support – they can elect to have 'support' as one of their curricular options. Support teachers and the class teachers rely heavily on the comments and feedback offered by the pupil, pupils are encouraged to take responsibility for their own learning needs from as early an age as possible.

Joint planning

Joint planning emerged as a major theme in our discussions with ToDs, mainstream teachers and others. For example, one ToD in K said:

As a service we're coming more and more to realise that you can't carry out our work without liaison time.

In service H 'joint planning and preparation' are given special mention in service documents. Reference is made to 'regular, positive meetings' between the ToD and the classteacher 'with close co-operation between both parties' and where decisions will be made concerning the 'role the ToD will play', 'planning the optimum use of the assistant support' and 'preparation and planning for non-curricular and social events in school'.

In several cases reference was made to the importance of having sessions written into the timetable for regular liaison between ToDs and mainstream teachers, although this is undoubtedly easier to arrange in primary schools where fewer mainstream teachers are involved with each child, and in resourced schools where ToDs are permanently on site.

In the primary resource base N, weekly planning between the ToD and classteacher is central to the work of the ToDs – according to one ToD 'a vital part of the whole week'. This meeting between the ToD and the relevant classteacher is written into the timetable for lunchtime or after school each Thursday or Friday. Up to one hour is set aside to look at the classteacher's plan for the week for all subjects including games and PE. The meeting is used to look particularly at language, so that any language that needs to be introduced beforehand will be.

In service D, a weekly session of formal liaison between the VToD and the primary school classteacher is timetabled, even if this has to take place at break, lunchtime or before school. As a result of this liaison schemes of work and lesson plans are converted to specific language and concept development plans for the deaf pupil. Weekly plans of work are devised and worksheets and resources prepared beforehand. Each day's programme is well planned, with all the necessary materials to hand and with clear ideas about the work that is to be carried out and the targets to be achieved. We were told by the ToDs that the National Curriculum has greater facilitated planning and liaison with mainstream teachers.

In K, joint planning sessions most frequently occur before school, at lunch time or after school, usually once a week, but for some children they are much more frequent, three times per week for one pupil who was observed. The ToD looks at the plan for the next two weeks for the mainstream class and discusses with the classteacher those areas with which the deaf pupil would need support and the nature of the support. This is then written as a plan and a copy given to the classteacher so that she knows what the ToD will be doing in support sessions. The ToD differentiates the curriculum and frequently provides worksheets or supporting material that will be useful for other pupils as well. Most frequently the hearing impaired pupil is withdrawn to a quiet room, along with a group of hearing pupils (reverse integration).

Having planned with the classteacher, the ToD visits the parents to go through the work to be covered in the next two weeks so that support can be given at home.

In service B, weekly collaborative planning is seen as vital and normally includes the ToD, classteacher and LSA. In one primary school each Monday lunchtime the classteacher shares her detailed planning with the LSA and the ToD. From this the ToD is able to establish her involvement and prepare materials. An example in practice of this was observed. From her close liaison the ToD had prepared carefully designed flipchart sheets on which she wrote as the teacher delivered the lesson. She then used these sheets as a basis for withdrawal reinforcement and group work.

In B, the ToD and the LSA produced materials for the deaf pupil that were often seen as useful to other children in the class as well. There were also other visits where ToDs mentioned the importance of being able to offer some 'payback' like this to mainstream teachers for the additional time they were giving the deaf pupil.

Joint planning in secondary schools is often more difficult because of the number of mainstream staff involved. In B, before the end of the summer term the ToD in the resource base asks the Heads of Department for the names of the teachers who will be teaching the deaf pupils the following year and for schemes of work. Also, two weeks prior to each lesson she sends out sheets to each teacher asking for more information about lessons, and worksheets and any tests which will require modification. From this she holds a weekly liaison meeting with the LSAs in which she shares a summary of what she has gleaned and its implications.

In H, liaison between the ToD and the mainstream teacher can be directly timetabled or take place informally, according to the needs of the particular situation. It is often in break and lunchtimes but we were told any of the ToDs would make themselves available to see classteachers at any time.

Some concern was expressed on our visits about the amount of time liaison was taking. One headteacher in a first school in K said her only reservation about the support arrangements in place was about the amount of time the class teachers had to spend on planning for the deaf children. One classteacher in the same school said, 'There is a lot of time involved. Lunch times I would usually be mounting pictures and so on, but each Monday and Friday lunchtime is my planning time with [ToD]. The other ToD phones the other classteacher on Sunday night to prepare. I have several other special needs children to prepare for as well, and half-termly meetings with the SENCO'.

However, one classteacher we spoke to did not resent the extra time involved.

> I think [my planning] is more detailed now than it used to be .. because I am having to plan not just for myself but also a another member of staff. It's been very beneficial for my teaching because it has probably meant that I've been more organised. ... Some teachers might not want to take on the extra work. [But] I feel that my planning's valued.... It really does show when [the deaf pupil] comes into the lesson. [The ToD, LSA and parents] have all the information [about the work coming up] It would be wonderful to do that for the whole class.
>
> (classteacher case study H).

A positive note was also struck during our visit to the primary resource base at N. According to the head of resource base when the weekly meeting between ToD and classteachers was introduced the classteachers thought it was going to mean lots of extra work but have since realised that they are doing the same amount of work but are just having to do it earlier rather than over the weekend. The head of resource base also thinks that classteachers appreciate the benefit of sharing ideas with the ToD in this meeting (this might be especially true in a one class entry school).

> In service H, the individual education plan (IEP) is central to the planning process and clearly plays a pivotal role in the support work of ToDs both in resource bases and those working as VToDs. Comments from two ToDs were:

> > In all the changes over the last however many years in education and special needs, I think the IEP is the best thing that's come out. I think we can do a lot with an IEP. It's got to be a working document. ... you've got to make sure it's precise and specific.
> >
> > (ToD).

> > It's a very, very powerful document.
> >
> > (ToD).

> > Its hard work on preparation side. A lot of the effort is in the discussions, the liaison, actually writing it up is quite a slog but then it makes planning and recording so much easier.
> >
> > (ToD).

An IEP is produced for each pupil each term and is completed by the ToD after discussion with the classteacher. The LSA and parents also have an opportunity to contribute.

> The IEP form now in use in H is the result of several attempts by the service to produce the most useful working document and is one of the products of the staff development programme. Areas which can be included as appropriate to the

individual pupil include: Audition/Use of hearing, Communication/Interaction, Receptive/ Expressive language, Literacy, Speech, Learning Behaviour and the Wider Curriculum. The plan has three sections; 'Review' of last term's targets, 'Objectives' for the current term, and 'Arrangements' which states what's to be done to meet the objectives and who is responsible. Two ToDs said they found the 'Arrangements' column of the IEP particularly helpful in that it helped to focus right at the beginning of the planning process on how particular objectives could be achieved. They also found this section useful to establish the need for regular liaison time with classteachers and to highlight and monitor necessary action required of them. It was also a tactful way of encouraging appropriate actions by parents; for example, where a television was often on in the background in the home, the ToD explained to parents that this might provide difficulties for the pupil and wrote into the Arrangements section of the IEP 'Ensure quiet situation when 'working' with [pupil]'.

We came across many occasions during our visit to H where the IEP was being used. It was referred to in a weekly planning meeting between a classteacher and the ToD, it was mentioned by parents and we saw it used to record progress made by one pupil. One LSA described the IEP as 'the programme I work to', a lot on the IEP refers to what is taught in the class, the teacher's plan, 'it is all sort of mixed together'. The IEP helps her to see what the pupil has not yet grasped.

In the secondary resource base in service B, IEPs were also specially mentioned. When a new IEP is to be produced all mainstream staff are sent a form asking for details of a pupil's strengths and weaknesses and targets they would like to see on the IEP and these are summarised and represented on the form. The new IEP is then fed back to each member of staff.

Roles

The roles of learning support assistants and teachers of the deaf are discussed briefly below. The role of deaf instructors and communication support workers is discussed in section 5.3.

Learning support assistants

We have already seen the role LSAs play in joint planning. Other than this we found they work in a variety of ways, both supporting in mainstream classes and giving tutorial support out of the main class, apparently sometimes fulfilling similar teaching roles to ToDs, but under their direction. LSAs sit alongside pupils and ensure they understand the lessons, sometimes by differentiating the language of instructions or the language of texts;

they prepare pupils for lessons and offer follow up; they withdraw to work specifically on aspects of language including reading, sometimes using the auditory training unit; they observe pupils; they note take; they sort out problems with hearing aids and cochlear implants; they liaise between classteachers and ToDs; and most importantly they often provide the regular point of contact with parents.

Teachers of the deaf

ToDs are involved in a variety of roles which have already been discussed, including joint planning, directing the work of LSAs, and directly supporting deaf pupils in class, in tutorial sessions or reverse integration groups. We came across the following two cases where they also sometimes reverse roles with mainstream teachers:

In N, two of the ToDs have a school-wide responsibility for particular areas of the curriculum, music and RE, and there are times when this allows the ToD and the classteacher to change roles, with the classteacher teaching the reverse integration group and the ToD teaching the main group. We were told there were plans to try to extend this arrangement. According to the Policy Document the reversing or roles is 'useful to establish both teachers with their "opposite group" '.

In service F, in order to promote acceptance of the service teachers as part of the schools they work in, some of the ToDs reverse the teaching situation allowing the class teacher to work in a one-to-one withdrawal session whilst the ToD takes the class.

Recognition of the importance of being clear and happy about roles was apparent in the secondary unit in E. To assist in gauging teachers' likes and dislikes unit staff had designed and distributed a questionnaire to their colleagues. Questions related to the role which mainstream teachers would like the unit staff to take whilst in their class, for example was it acceptable to help other children, discipline other children, speak to the deaf pupil while the teacher was delivering information to the whole class. Data from these questionnaires were found to be useful in determining comfortable styles of support. Unit staff also take into account teachers' strengths when deciding on level of support.

The danger of oversupport

The danger of oversupporting pupils was a recurring theme in several cases studies. In one service we were told:

> ... we are re-thinking how we support deaf children at primary level. We may have over-supported them and thought less about independent learning skills.
>
> (ToD, case study K).

In B, there is a general concern that deaf children are over dependent on LSA support. The VToDs are trying to address this at both primary and secondary levels.

In H, the need to avoid over-supporting pupils has been given recent prominence and was a training day issue for LSAs. A 'Learning Behaviour' section has been introduced into the IEP and has emphasised to support assistants the need not to do the work for the children and to encourage them to take responsibility for their own learning. For example, one LSA told us she may sit at the back of the class to know what the task is, or even go in after instructions have been given, check the pupil has understood but then leave and return in 20 minutes to monitor progress.

> [Our job is] supporting a pupil in being as independent and active as they can. For example, it's their job to look after the FM system as soon as possible, it's their responsibility to sit themselves in a sensible place.
>
> (LSA).

> [We try to] see that they are working independently of us which is quite a hard thing. It's hitting the happy medium. We're not there joined at the hip with them but we're there if they need us but still try to get them to go to the teacher as well because they're responsible for seeing that they're following the work properly.
>
> (LSA).

This LSA sees her role as helping pupil X access the curriculum and giving the right sort of support, not 'over-supporting', to keep an eye open and to help when she is really needed, 'not to be a parrot on her shoulder'. The LSA feels she can decide when to leave X on her own. 'You have to just work it out on the spot'. She often works with X in a group with three hearing children which means that it isn't only X getting the extra help. 'This is important because she doesn't see me as another mother figure chasing after her ... she has to get on like everybody else ... It's giving her more independence.'

Delivering INSET

Case study B was chosen partly for its recommended INSET work with mainstream teachers and others. In this service, all the teachers are expected to deliver INSET, indeed it is part of their job description. In order to encourage all staff to improve their skills in INSET delivery, each member of staff is encourage to present a case study at one of the fortnightly team meetings.

> A wide range of materials is readily available for use indexed according to age group, intended audience and computer reference number. In order to encourage staff to make more use of video material and to provide a richer resource,

individual ToDs are asked to review at least one video. This review is shared then filed for future reference. The service also uses longitudinal studies of children in video form (parental permission is needed to use these). These videos are used in several ways, for example, with new staff who are unfamiliar with a pupil. Also, prior to the establishment of a new resource base, the ToD concerned gave a presentation to the governors and staff using video footage of the pupils who would be coming in the first year.

(case study B).

In B, when a new pupil with a significant hearing impairment is about to enter the school, substantial INSET for staff takes place. In two cases that we were made aware of INSET for the staff occurred over two days. On one day a basic training was given to all staff, including playground supervisors. On the next, the teachers who would actually be teaching that pupil were given more advanced training.

In a school with a resource base, all staff are given INSET at the beginning of a new school year and individual preparation is given to teachers taking on a new pupil in their class.

INSET has been delivered to a range of audiences including mainstream staff, Health Visitors, early years teams, parents and school governors.

In other case studies where INSET was discussed, it was difficult to see any common approach emerging. Different amounts of time are available and in some cases INSET is not compulsory. In more than one case the importance of including all ancillary staff was emphasised.

In service H, when a hearing impaired pupil enters a school there is an initial INSET session. A two-hour session is given to the whole staff which covered a range of topics including deafness, language, literacy and social skills. Then each year there is a session with the individual class teacher. They also provide leaflets, information packs or insert information into school handbooks.

In F, all teachers who are going to have a deaf pupil in their class are now invited to a half-day INSET.

The service D offers INSET at the beginning of the year when a pupil enters a mainstream school. In addition to the normal topics, this may also include visiting each room where the pupil will be working and advising on improvements to the physical environment where possible (for example venetian blinds, curtains) or how to minimise problems (for example the best place for the pupil to sit). The in-service training is considered to be a whole school issue so that everyone from headteacher to dinner ladies are expected to attend.

K provides a two-day INSET course annually.

In E, secondary resource base staff have experimented with different ways of delivering deaf awareness training. Last year they tried an induction lunch where new mainstream staff were invited to attend lunch in the resource base, to meet the staff and to have the opportunity to listen to hearing aids through stetoclips and receive basic training. At the same time, INSET continues to be delivered to established staff. A recent innovation was an activity in 'quiz' format aimed to help staff to reflect upon and improve their communication strategies.

Deaf awareness

'Deaf awareness' is a term in everyday use in deaf education meaning, broadly, 'creating an awareness in hearing people of what it means to be deaf'. Within the work of services, 'deaf awareness training' is often part of the menu for in-service training with mainstream colleagues or for sessions or assemblies with hearing children. Commonly the starting point is to present sound as it might be to a deaf person so that hearing people can consider the implications for communication, learning and social and emotional development. For some this will be a negative interpretation of the term with a wish instead to emphasise the positive aspects of deafness in relation to its language, heritage and culture.

Monitoring progress

Service H was one case study where strong emphasis is given to carefully assessing pupils' progress. We were told that progress is monitored all the time. 'If she was in class and getting nothing from it she would be straight out and doing something else' (ToD). A wide range of assessments are used including formal and informal measures, and the decisions about the assessments to use have been made by the whole team of ToDs. A battery of assessment results for each individual pupil gives a 'view of where their language development is', but moderated and tempered by watching them in the classroom, being with them and getting feedback (ToD). 'Assessment [is] informing our teaching' (HoS) and 'shows up weaknesses' (ToD). 'We've tended a bit towards standardised assessments but we've had to keep a kind of healthy scepticism as to what we do with the scores' (ToD). 'Much of our assessment is descriptive and that constitutes much of our reviews' (HoS). The details of how progress is monitored in case study H are given below.

All children are videoed regularly (younger children every three months, older ones every six months or a year) and all ToDs are trained to use assessments.

There is a ongoing staff development programme which reviews the assessments used and several of the procedures currently in place have been devised by team members. Four examples illustrate this:

(i) The *profiles for hearing impaired pupils* were devised by the team based on already published material. They cover a wide range of aspects of the pupil's development. The ToDs value them because they progress in small steps.

(ii) The *ECI (Expression of Communicative Intentions)* was developed from an article by Beattie and Kysela (1993), in the Journal of the British Association of Teachers of the Deaf, volume 17.

> A few of us had read it. [One of the ToDs] took it and put together a format that was serviceable. It's brilliant. It gives a clear picture of progression which is very useful to share with parents. Parents can see very readily... it also makes them think about their interactions a bit like the Pragmatics Profile, such as what elicits a spoken response and what doesn't.
>
> (ToD).

(iii) The *Schedule for Early Language Development* was put together by one of the team years ago and assesses the deaf pupil's early interactive pre-verbal and verbal development against normal patterns. It's used to show parents the sometimes small steps in development taking place.

> It's very disheartening if parents see other children talking but not their deaf child; but you can use this to show parents that there is a lot going on, and he's only been hearing for this length of time.
>
> That's a huge part of our job, giving parents encouragement .. and being positive .. and building upon what they know .. and giving them the confidence to carry on doing what they were doing.
>
> (ToD).

(iv) An *auditory development programme* has also been devised by the service which charts the pupil's progress in auditory skills. The objectives are worked towards through play activities, including recognising sounds and anticipating key words.

Summary

Key findings in this section are summarised as follows:

- In most cases a mixed approach is taken where support is offered in class, in tutorial sessions and in reverse integration groups.

- Teachers of the deaf adopt an approach where they seek to work collaboratively with mainstream teachers and learning support assistants, sharing the responsibility for the deaf pupils. The teacher of the deaf often takes on the coordinating role.

- Increasing emphasis is being placed on the need for joint planning between teachers of the deaf and mainstream teachers even where there are constraints.

- Some services involve parents and pupils in decisions about the amount and type of support provided.

- There is widespread awareness of the need to constantly monitor and evaluate levels of support.

- There is a strong emphasis on INSET for mainstream teachers which makes significant and specific requirements of teacher of the deaf.

4.6 Audiological management

All children with a degree of permanent childhood deafness have one thing in common. Early identification and good appropriate management will help lessen the impact of hearing impairment on the child, family and on society, (NDCS 1996[1]).

Identification of hearing loss lies within the remit of health service providers whilst on-going audiological management is shared by health and education providers and families. The degree to which a particular service is involved in identification of hearing loss in older infants and young children is heavily dependent on geographical location. Whilst some health authorities are fully involved others may not have sufficient resources. The structures within health to ensure that all children have access to a sensitive and efficient services are discussed in some detail in Quality Standards in Audiology Volume 2 (NDCS, op cit). The perceived lack of such structures or resources together with the importance placed on identification of hearing loss is illustrated by the role some education providers take in this process. The responsibility for part of these services have historically been shared by Health and Education. The role of one service is described in detail and includes:

> To test and assess hearing of school age and preschool children in conjunction with the Senior Clinical Medical Officer for the area. Additionally, the service sees its role as including the training of health visitors and school nurses in screening tests of hearing when requested.
>
> (case study F).

The recommendation for the adoption of universal neo-natal screening for hearing impairment is likely to move the identification process being firmly within the health sector with the exception of those children who have acquired hearing loss.

Initial contact with families

Families are central to effective service provision. The initial contact between families and educational support services is crucial. Fast, efficient and sensitive support can help families to regain control and begin to understand the new situation in which they have been placed.

---

[1] NDCS (1996) *Quality standards in paediatric audiology: the management of the child with permanent hearing loss* Vol 2. London: NDCS.

In case study K, emphasis is given to the need to 'support the family through the initial stages of crisis/shock so that they come to accept hearing aids in a positive way' (policy document). There is a Quality Standard which states that a ToD will visit or contact the family by telephone within 48 hours of diagnosis. The educational audiologist or a senior member of staff attends all diagnostic clinics. From the point of diagnosis the Service for the Hearing Impaired takes over management of the child. This is a policy which has been agreed with Health. The audiologist prescribes the hearing aids which are then purchased by Health. 'Liaison with Health is a real strength'

(ToD).

The head of service is always present at diagnosis of hearing loss and it is she who 'breaks the news'. So from the very start a teacher of the deaf is available for the parent/s when the 'news is broken' and plenty of time to talk is offered. There is a perceived need when supporting parents to 'break through' the medical model of disability – no matter how good the quality of support nor how efficient the hearing aids, nothing will 'cure' deafness.

(case study D).

Audiological resources for assessment

In one case, the Education provider has moved further in providing a resource offering visual reinforcement audiometry, a service more normally found within the health sector. This in itself raises some issues of the role of educational services for deaf children and serves to underline the interconnectedness of health and education in providing high quality services. Case study E exemplifies methods for ensuring good communication exists between sectors and that families receive sensitive and efficient services.

It used to be the custom for educational audiologists to have responsibility for health visitor training in the county and to staff second tier audiology clinics, working with a doctor. However, the service has relinquished responsibility for health visitor training and reduced the number of clinics which it staffs as these were taking up a lot of staff time. However, the teachers of the deaf work closely with the health service and frequently attend clinics when pupils have review appointments.

If there is no member of the service at a clinic at which a hearing loss is diagnosed, then the parents' permission will be sought for their child's name and details to be passed to the service and these details will be sent immediately, or a telephone message will be made to the service. All details of hearing impaired children are entered on the service database, including the age at diagnosis. The situation is monitored by the service to check that the reduction in teacher of the deaf time spent in clinics is not having an adverse effect on age at diagnosis.

(case study E).

For parents and families the issues surrounding who does what are less important than the quality of the service provided. The importance of providing an appropriate setting at the time of confirmation of hearing loss to families is well recognised. The ideal setting and type of personnel involved together with the timing and level of information are less clear. Where early contact with educational services are in place parents express considerable levels of satisfaction. When the system is not in place or breaks down the repercussions for families are considerable.

A parent who has a four year old daughter who is profoundly deaf had been promised contact with the education service at the point of formal diagnosis but the referral letter was not sent. The family received two hearing aids through the post from the hospital and recall the feelings of desolation. One mother told us, 'I had no idea what to do ... the hospital had given me a cup of tea and piece of cake and told me it would be OK ... here I was with my little daughter two hearing aids in boxes and no idea ... I cried for days.' This mother stated how she felt when she first met the ToD, 'She threw me a life jacket... quite simply she said this is what to do'.

(case study F).

For families where English is not the first language, the problem of isolation may be even more severe. The challenge of providing services in a sensitive way to minority ethnic families presents some challenges that are above those otherwise experienced – for example, the use of parental questionnaires with those who may not have written skills in English, and the social mores which see support as a family matter. An example of this was observed by one of the researchers.

Many of the hearing impaired children are diagnosed at a very late stage, quite often not before two or three years old. The health authority discontinued the distraction test because they considered it did not work and in any case only picked up 40% of cases. They substituted a questionnaire. So only those whose parents answered 'yes' when asked 'Are you worried about your child's hearing?' would be sent to the audiology clinic for testing. All 'at risk' children go from the London Hospital to the audiology clinic. Some cases of moderate to severe deafness are not identified until as late as five, six or seven years when the children are already at school. The HoS says that schools find it difficult, they say, 'When do we get concerned about their language not developing [because of a hearing problem] when they come in to school not speaking any English?'

(case study Q).

The head of service is trying to ensure that all families in the LEA have access to health and educational services in respect of hearing loss by taking into account the special needs of this group.

> B, the parent of a 10 year old deaf girl spoke through the interpreter. Her daughter was premature and drip-fed in hospital for four weeks. She was referred for a hearing test.
>
> I was really helpless. I thought I was the only one with this problem. There was no one to talk to and no one to ask advice. After [the HoS] visited, things started to get better. People started to visit me and I met people.
>
> (case study Q).

The simple availability of audiological services in itself is insufficient to meet the needs of specific groups. Access which recognises the cultural and social differences and seeks to meet these goes a long way to ensuring equal access for all families.

> The Head of Statement Support says that there is a move towards earlier diagnosis. Previously if there was a problem with a child under about three years the Bangladeshi family's attitude was 'we'll cope with it ourselves'. The home visits showed them that they could have information and support, and when the women began coming out to the centre they began to see that they could support each other. The service has very close links with the audiology clinic. They established the first nursery group there. 'It was a way of getting them happy about going to clinic' (HoS). Now all the groups are held at the SEN Centre but the link worker from the audiology clinic is at the service's base every Monday morning working with the children in the crèche and meeting their mothers in the crèche and in the signing class.
>
> (case study Q).

Provision and management of personal amplification

Following identification of permanent childhood hearing loss appropriate amplification should be made available. The NDCS Quality Standards document recommends that children should be fitted with appropriate aids bianually as a matter of routine and that replacement instruments should be available within 48 hours. In some situations the health service providers are able to meet the recommendation. In some cases the good working relationships allow educational services to administer spare/replacement aids. In these cases systems operate which are fast, efficient and family friendly.

Spare parts for hearing aids are readily available on request from the hospital clinic and the Resource Centre has a plentiful supply of spare hearing aids, batteries, leads, tubing etc.

(case study D).

The educational audiologist or a senior member of staff is present at diagnosis. The educational audiologist decides on the hearing aid prescription and aids are purchased immediately. Each child is automatically prescribed three hearing aids so that there is always a spare aid available.

(case study K).

Those schools for the deaf following an oral approach have audiological facilities on site and either a technician or audiologist who is responsible for ensuring consistency of amplification.

All hearing aids in need of repair have to be sent back to the issuing NHS authority and there are around 40 of these for all the pupils in the school. This could lead to problems of delay, but these problems are overcome by the centre having a spare aid, identical to the child's personal hearing aid, so that no pupil is ever without aids that are working. The clerical assistant plays an important role in liaising with the many different health authorities.

(case study J).

In a number of services we visited, educational services view consistency of amplification as a priority and in order to ensure this is achieved have undertaken to provide a resource bank of suitable aids.

Since the local hospitals are unable to guarantee that a replacement aid of the type prescribed will be available at any time for each child, seven years ago the decision was taken to set up a bank of loan hearing aids which could be borrowed whilst children's own aids were being repaired. Money was raised through fundraising activities and a supply of the most popular commercial hearing aids was purchased. The loan aids are held centrally, each one is labelled and a record kept of all aids and their whereabouts. Whenever a child's aid needs to be repaired and an identical replacement is not available at the hospital then the parent or teacher of the deaf rings and leaves a message for the teacher with responsibility for administering the loan aids. Since all records are kept on the service database, a replacement aid can be found and set appropriately using the information on the database. The aid is then despatched to the child by the quickest possible route to ensure that the child spends the minimum amount of time without the appropriate aids.

(case study K).

Such a system provides a fast and efficient service, but the reliance is on educational services to fill in for what is essentially the responsibility of health service providers. A formal agreement between health and education sectors that such a system is an efficient use of resources would ensure all children had the potential to receive replacement aids with the minimum delay. Piecemeal arrangements that put the onus on education services demand the commitment of staff who are convinced of the importance of consistency in amplification.

> Because my son uses a bone conductor which is unusual, the hospital wouldn't let me have a spare aid. The service bought one for him as a spare. It was fantastic, I didn't ask them for one they simply provided one.
>
> (case study F).

In some cases there is also heavy reliance on the education services to provide audiological information that is primarily the responsibility of the health sector. This is dependent on ToDs having a high level of audiological expertise or having an educational audiologist on staff.

> 'Early on there was friction with the hospital. I wasn't at all happy with the aids. It was obvious to me they weren't providing what she needed. The ToDs kept pushing, asking for more powerful aids. The clinic totally refused to listen. They kept saying the aids were OK and said the ToD had no business to talk about hearing aids ... In the end they had to admit they were wrong and we got stronger aids, the difference was obvious almost straight away'.
>
> (parent, case study F).

> 'The hospital weren't sure what they were dealing with. At first we were told he was severely deaf and given aids. D was very difficult. The ToD wasn't happy with the aids at all. Then the hospital said he was profoundly deaf and changed the aids. It was a ToD who suggested that a cochlear implant might be the best option ... he showed an immediate response ... it was fantastic. I'm learning sign language at night school. We want D to have the best chance we can give him'.
>
> (parent, case study F).

Services provided a variety of types of support in the management of amplification including the provision of stetoclips with attenuators, forced air blowers, retubing kits, batteries, training on the need to check aids daily and written information to support this aspect. Stress was also put on the importance of developing individual children's independence in taking an active part in managing their own aids.

> From the earliest age children are encouraged to be actively involved in management of their own amplification. A two year old with a profound hearing loss was observed removing her ear moulds and trying to attach one to a stetoclip before babbling to provide a check signal. At a secondary base all children use the testbox and are familiar with basic response curves and harmonic distortion.
>
> (case study B).

> Pupils are required to take responsibility for their hearing aids; when the aid goes wrong it is the pupil who has to decide what to do about it; self-sufficiency is strongly emphasised. In years 10 and 11, students have to do more than just drop into the school audiology centre – they have to think what they should do to keep their aids in working order and what to do if they go wrong, as though they were in the 'outside world'. All pupils can visit the audiology centre to have aids examined and if necessary, replacement parts/aid. They can only leave lessons with the permission of the teacher and then only if something is seriously wrong with the aid. Otherwise pupils must go to the centre during 'open clinic' hours, before school, lunch-times, after school. When visiting the centre, pupils must sign in and record what the problem is and the action taken. If pupils are issued with a loan aid they must sign for it and take responsibility for it. All aids are electronically tested and their amplification needs judged by objective measures. However, the pupil's view of their amplification needs are taken very seriously and are used in making decisions on hearing aid selection and use. All the pupils interviewed were clearly good hearing aid users and well motivated to have their aids working, 'I cannot hear without my aids, I am really dependant on them'
>
> (year 9 pupil, case study J).

Earmoulds have long been the weak link in the amplification chain schools and services took a variety of approaches in overcoming this problem including:

- taking impressions by education personnel (case study D)
- ensuring a specific technician takes impressions whenever possible and these are sent to a commercial manufacturer to ensure high quality moulds. In such cases, costs are met by the education service running a variety of fund raising activities with the help of parents (case study F)
- the school audiologist is carrying out research into ensuring children /young people with profound hearing loss at the school have the perfect ear moulds they need (case study J)

Audiological management is complex and demands not only that personal aids are well fitted and working efficiently, but that these are checked electro-acoustically on a regular basis. The Quality Standards in Audiology document suggests that this should be at least every six weeks (NDCS, 1996 p8).This standard was met in all services that were considered under this theme. In some cases weekly, fortnightly or monthly checks were made. In all these cases detailed records of hearing aid performance on user settings are kept for reference. Wherever possible children were actively involved in this process. The amount of audiological equipment available in services varies, but includes as basic equipment a number of test boxes and sound level meters available for use by ToDs as part of the weekly management programme. In special schools or small urban areas such resources can be kept in resource bases or specialist audiological facilities. The high quality facilities within the non-maintained sector provide an example of the resources that should be readily available in all services.

> There is an audiological centre in its own building, but close to the rest of the school. The centre has spare parts, spare aids, a computerised data-base, equipment for testing hearing and hearing aids, facilities for making ear mould impressions and specialised equipment for supporting research and developing new techniques.
>
> (case study K).

Services have also developed considerable specialist resources in order to ensure that audiological management is rigorous on behalf of the children and families being served. Such services have frequently to be more versatile than special schools as they work with a more diverse population, infant to adolescent, mild to profound hearing and temporary as well as permanent and functional hearing loss. The needs of children who have mild to moderate degrees of hearing loss are the responsibility of services. This large group have their needs which are different from those children with profound hearing loss, but they are no less real. One example of the level of resource given is provided by case study K.

> Advisory teachers can draw from a large bank of test boxes, sound level meters, spare radio aids and accessories, output level setters, conference microphones and audiometers. In addition, educational audiologists have available test boxes with probe tube facilities, warble tone generators, tympanometers and otoscopes. A further test box and hearing aid programmers are kept at the central base with the stock of loan hearing aids. All teachers of the deaf are expected to be competent in the appropriate use of audiological equipment and how to use it to encourage the maximal use of residual hearing. It is expected that they will carry out regular assessments of pupils' use of equipment and their listening skills – for example, listening in noise – and discuss any findings which appear unsatisfactory with one of the educational audiologists.
>
> (case study K).

In large rural areas that are sparsely populated there are different variables to be considered. The large distances and public transport and lack of nearby resource bases make rigorous management more challenging. One approach to meeting this challenge has been developed by case study F. This is an example of an education service taking a consumer friendly approach in aiming to achieve high quality amplification for hearing impaired children within the service.

> A fully equipped audiology van and technician/driver are based within the service. The van is a roving resource. It provides an acoustically friendly space for audiological assessments. Equipment available includes a Fonix test box, Kamplex audiometer with provision for soundfield testing, hand held impedance tester, auroscope, tests of speech perception, sound level meter, and a full range of spares for personal and FM systems. For many parents living in isolated areas a hospital appointment would mean a day trip. Instead, the audiology van can take the test to the family. The child can be tested at a time which best suits the family, without a long tiring journey. The van is used by all the ToDs on a rolling basis, as a flying service for problems, and additionally it is used to support the local health service providers in providing a quality environment in which 'difficult to assess' children can be tested. The technician and van are available during the holidays.
>
> (case study F).

Such a service seeks to ensure accessibility and underlines the services commitment to a high standard of audiology. Parents valued this service and the perceived expertise it provides.

Room acoustics

Poor room acoustics are recognised as presenting a major challenge to any listener with a permanent degree of hearing loss (Berg,1993[2]). Learning environments are frequently hostile to hearing aid users and as a consequence it may be assumed that special schools with acoustically treated rooms may have significant benefits. It was evident that parents in oral authorities were well aware of these difficulties of mainstream settings. Such benefits can also be accrued within mainstream settings usually as a result of the intervention of ToDs and educational audiologists.

> The service will look at the acoustics of the nursery and if they are not good they can ask the Deaf Children's Society to contribute to curtains and carpets on behalf of the school. The authority is also very supportive of the needs of hearing impaired pupils.
>
> (case study K).

---

[2] Berg, F (1993) *Acoustics and sound systems in schools.* San Diego: Singualar Publishing.

> At the beginning of the year the ToDs provided input to in-service training, explaining the audiological equipment R would use and giving general guidance about appropriate teaching strategies and pitfalls such as walking around whilst talking. His form teacher sits R centrally to maximise lipreading. Venetian blinds were purchased to prevent glare, but she feels the room is not good acoustically as it has a central arch which causes reverberation. At the beginning of the year one of the ToDs went round all the classrooms R would use to point out any problems and advise on the best places for R to sit. A booklet of information is provided for each department.
>
> (case study D).

One service is actively involved in the trial of soundfield equipment as a way of providing an improved signal to noise ratio for hearing impaired children and their peers (case study E).

FM radio aid systems are widely used to overcome the problems of distance and to provide direct access to a range of other technology. Regular checks to ensure electro-acoustic transparency of these systems together with efficient use of the transmitter microphones, easy access to such systems and to spares were reported in all the oral settings. A sensitive handling of both mainstream teachers and deaf students is reported to be essential for success.

> I didn't like the old system because it really looked so awful and was in the way. I could hear but I didn't want to admit it. This new one is much better.
>
> (secondary pupil using microlink).

The importance of auditory training systems in providing a high quality signal, covering a broad frequency range at high levels of amplification is stressed by all the oral services. Such systems are available for use with preschool cases at home and in a range of settings including secondary schools. The benefits of such quality amplification is noted not only by teachers and parents, but also by students themselves.

> I have to work harder – but I can hear so much clearer.
>
> (secondary pupil in resource base, case study B).

Listening programmes

There was no consensus regarding the importance of a detailed listening programme. In oral settings, management goes beyond ensuring the aids are working efficiently and the acoustics are acceptable. The quality of the signal going into the amplification system is recognised as being of fundamental importance in encouraging use of amplification. All oral schools and services monitor the development of listening skills longitudinally. All have high expectations of their hearing aid users. A structured approach is a key feature of case study D.

> The service operates a structured programme of Auditory Rhythmic Training to 'enhance listening skills and to promote rhythmic awareness and, in turn, to positively effect speech and language development'. Using games, music, songs and activities, physical movement to sound and music encourage awareness of rhythm and stress patterns, and assist the development of language skills. 'ART is not something which occurs in isolation from the rest of the service's work. It develops to become a tool to be implemented by child and teacher together in peripatetic language support sessions'. For example, the rhythm curve drawn for each child's name and later for familiar words or phrases may be used a means of teaching new vocabulary in the support session. "ART [in this service] has developed to be in keeping with the peripatetic nature of the work of the service.' Children come into the Centre once a week for session in small groups of children of similar age. The programme starts as soon as the child is diagnosed and can include a group of babies from 10 months old. For the preschool group, parents also attend and this begins their close contact with the service. 'Children continue to attend the groups for varying lengths of time, for as long as they continue to extend their skills usefully and the session continues to enhance their language development'.
>
> (case study D).

Interesting approaches to promoting hearing aid acceptance and positive management are illustrated by two services, case studies A and K.

> L was happily wearing his aids at first, but has since had continual ear infections when they were left out. Since then he has tolerated them less well. Now over the past three or four weeks he is only pulling them out three or four times a day. His mother found this worrying at first but was reassured when the ToD showed her the service's profile document, the first item of which was 'tolerates aids for ten seconds'. The profiles are not prescriptive and they do not teach to them. They are cross-referenced to the National Curriculum targets. One ToD found them especially useful for the very young children where more formal assessment is inappropriate. They are also helpful in writing IEPs, and are used as working documents. The job description of the ToDs specifies that they have to keep the profiles up-to-date.
>
> (case study K).

Children have IAPs (Individual Audiology Programmes) which are worked out with the audiologist. Each child has set targets, for example, year three targets might be to know whether a hearing aid is working and to change a battery.

(case study A).

Audiological competence

Services stress the need for ToDs to be audiologically proficient. The importance of this point is stressed by all oral and the sign bilingual services. For deaf children and their parents importance is clearly placed on the process rather than who is responsible for the process. For any child or young person using amplification those in daily contact or readily accessible must be audiologically competent. This requires not only quality in basic training programmes, but also the availability of on-going training. Where an educational audiologist is in post this responsibility is within their remit. Teachers of the deaf in initial training cannot afford to see audiology within a medical model. Rather audiological management sits firmly within education. For the majority of deaf children, audiological management is a key feature of inclusion.

The identified need for rigour in managing this aspect for the majority of deaf children identified in this study, together with the rate of change in technology, suggests audiology should be a core feature of any initial training programme. The importance of positive management has led to one authority seeking to ensure skills through second tier training.

There is a team of seven qualified educational audiologists, one of whom has a post of responsibility for audiology within the county, for which one day per week is allocated in her time. For a period of several years there was a rolling programme of secondment onto a one-year course to qualify in educational audiology. The educational audiologists offer support to the units, although unit staff are expected to carry out regular checks of hearing aids and radio aids and to test them on test boxes and balance radio aids. The postholder for audiology is a member of the service's senior management team and produces an annual business plan for audiology with targets for the year. A high priority is given to audiology within the service budget. All the educational audiologists are committed to keeping up-to-date through attendance at conferences and involvement in local, regional and national groups, for example the postholder is a member of the BATOD regional committee for educational audiology.

All advisory (visiting) teachers are expected to develop a high level of expertise in audiology, which is achieved by INSET and informal support from the educational audiologists. As one commented, 'I thought I knew a lot of audiology until I came here'.

The postholder for audiology said, '[I] decided that I had to train to be an educational audiologist to be a good peri, really' and added, 'I came from a good audiology background, but when I came here I found that expectations were really high'.

Unit staff (teachers of the deaf and learning support assistants) are expected to check hearing aids daily (more than once per day for young children). They are required to be skilled at using a test box and one member of staff (a teacher of the deaf or learning support assistant) will have time allocated on their timetable for regular electro-acoustic testing.

(case study E).

Conclusion

Whilst case study E was unusual in having seven trained educational audiologists, the knowledge and skills expected were found in all schools and services nominated for good practice in audiological management. Hearing aids are not designed for a paediatric population and the majority of schools are not acoustically friendly for any learners. For services and schools offering high quality audiological management it is seen as the right of any child using amplification. This is a demanding on-going task that is accomplished by skilled professionals on behalf of deaf children and their families. The centrality of audiological management for the majority of deaf children suggests that anything less than a rigorous approach is unacceptable.

Summary

Key findings in this section are summarised as follows:

- A positive working relationship with health service providers, early identification and early access to services for deaf children are key features of good practice.

- Access to appropriately fitted amplification and high quality earmoulds is essential.

- Teachers of the deaf should be audiologically competent and enable other adults and the child to become proficient audiological managers.

- Teachers of the deaf need to be fully conversant with the potential effects of room acoustics and the importance of daily access to an acoustically friendly area.

- There should be regular assessment of changing audiological needs in conjunction with an educational audiologist.

- A clear developmental programme to monitor and encourage optimum use of amplification is needed.

4.7 Spoken language development

The development of spoken language was seen as an important feature in many of the case studies, although the priority which was given to it varied from one to another. In some instances, although when questioned the staff said that they were concerned with the promotion of communication, this was taken to mean communication by the medium of spoken language. Thus the development of spoken language was in practice the primary aim. In other settings, the emphasis was on communication, with spoken language as one of a range of options. In these settings the promotion of spoken language skills did not attract the same emphasis, although its importance was still recognised. These different degrees of emphasis are reflected in the approach to the promotion of spoken language which each setting adopted.

Even in those cases in which the primary aim was communication via the medium of spoken language, there was variation in the way in which its promotion was approached, although each of the examples where it was given priority shared a belief that this was based on the foundation of the promotion of auditory awareness and listening skills.

Natural Aural approaches

In those settings in which the approach to the development of spoken language was described as natural aural, a fundamental principle was given as being the establishment of sound audiological foundations. There was concern to ensure early, accurate diagnosis of hearing loss followed as soon as possible by the provision of appropriate hearing aids, with support given to the parents in encouraging babies and young children to wear the hearing aids constantly. Teachers of the deaf in these settings welcomed the prospect of neo-natal hearing screening with the promise of even earlier diagnosis. Emphasis was placed on on-going, detailed assessment of the child's hearing levels and amplification needs, and ensuring that each child had the benefit of consistent listening patterns by the availability of spare hearing aids of the same type. Other amplification equipment was used and provided for use at home where appropriate, for example radio aids and auditory training units. The acoustic environment was also monitored carefully to provide sympathetic listening conditions. Parents were equipped with the necessary skills and expertise to play their role in securing these conditions, both in terms of hearing aids and the environment. 'It is believed that the development of speech and language is dependent on the use of residual hearing and auditory discrimination.' (Service policy document)

Building on the foundation of accurate diagnosis and appropriate hearing aid fitting is the development of listening skills, as the belief is that spoken language development is based on following premise:

that a hearing impaired child has the ability to speak and understand natural language…if these children learn to use their residual hearing effectively and are offered normal interaction they can acquire their mother tongue naturally.

In all case studies in which this approach was adopted, the children's listening skills were monitored closely. There was an emphasis on providing interesting and varied sounds for the child to listen to and encouraging them to listen and respond to them, showing the child the source of the sound to aid identification. In some settings no specific programme of listening was deemed necessary in addition to the approach just outlined, rather it was seen as a 24-hour programme in which the aim was to get children 'hooked on listening' so that they used their hearing all the time without thinking about it. This was the favoured approach in case study E, for example, and the ability of the majority of the pupils to exploit their residual hearing to the full was evident. All those involved with the deaf pupils treated them as if they expected them to be able to respond to sound and to access information auditorily.

An observation of a lesson with a profoundly deaf pupil and three hearing peers was made. All children made appropriate use of the radio transmitter in giving their answers. All the children were actively encouraged to repeat comments, share with others, turn take. There was clear language extension for all the children, new words were explained clearly to all children, then discussed by the group, examples used and drawn on the flipchart. The deaf pupil was able and expected to listen and respond appropriately without visual contact. This was observed to be quite natural behaviour for this deaf child.

(case study B).

However, other case studies stressed the need to institute a structured listening programme, for example in case study D the exploitation of residual hearing is supported by a structured programme, Auditory Rhythmic Training (ART) and all the teachers of the deaf in that service have been trained in the use of this programme. This programme is described in more detail under section 4.6 Audiological Management.

The question of whether to use some form of structured listening programme or not was the focus of some discussion and disagreement, particularly between some teachers of the deaf and members of some cochlear implant teams. It is possible that in some children, particularly those who are implanted early, listening skills will develop without a structured programme, as happens with hearing aid wearers in these settings, but that other children, especially those who are implanted later will benefit from a listening programme. There is room for further discussion between local teachers of the deaf in these settings and members of cochlear implant teams.

Having given attention to the children's audiological needs, the second tenet of natural auralism depends on the provision of an environment which will encourage conversational skills through interaction. The approach is described in one service policy document as resulting from:

> natural experience rather than by direct teaching. Both parents and teachers must aim to create a consistent atmosphere in which children wish and indicate the need to communicate naturally. Children will construct language from this natural environment.

This approach starts with work with the parents. Frequently this takes the form of regular home visits, but these may be supplemented by advice/counselling given to the parents as part of a group.

An example of this was a parent and toddler group which was observed. This gave the opportunity for parents to gain information and observe aspects of the approach demonstrated in an informal way. There were talks organised for the parents, with speakers who could discuss a wide range of subjects relating to deafness. While the parents attended the talk, the children were occupied in a nursery setting which was equipped for the purpose and staffed by a teacher of the deaf and nursery nurse. The audiology technician also attended and was on hand to test hearing aids. Parents were able to observe professionals working with their children. They could observe how the professionals interacted with their children and ask questions in a relaxed atmosphere. Occasional outings were arranged which extended these opportunities.

(case study K).

Teachers of the deaf working with parents of preschool children in all these case studies concentrated on conversation skills, encouraging the parents to stimulate language development through play. One teacher stressed she was 'not there to teach the child but to empower the parent and to play with the child in such a way that language develops'.

The natural aural approach is informed by on-going assessment and monitoring of children's progress. It is based on the premise that, given a facilitating environment the spoken language development will follow a similar path to that of hearing children. Therefore it is vital that teachers of the deaf supporting families of preschool children are thoroughly conversant with the stages of development of spoken language in hearing children so that they can monitor progress and advise parents. One mother said she had found it very useful to have someone present to notice progress and to explain 'what steps to look for next'. In most settings these informal assessments were supplemented by more formal assessments. Teachers of the deaf all stressed the need for assessments which were able to demonstrate 'small steps of progress'. One mother said, 'M could pick out things I didn't see at all ... then later I could see it. There were changes, progress, but I needed M to point that out to me'. Some settings had devised their own assessments based on published materials, with supplementary steps. In several case studies the importance of regular video monitoring was highlighted. The videos were then used as a basis for discussion with other professionals and with parents. In case study B, there was a pattern of making a video of the child two months prior to the annual review, which all those involved with the review were able to view.

Once the child enters school, the approach continues in a similar vein. The emphasis on conversational skills and the promotion of receptive and expressive language skills is to be found at all times. This starts with interaction between staff and children as soon as they arrive at school.

> A group of children at Key Stage 1 arrived at the Unit for the start of the day. Each child was allocated to a member of staff who saw them every morning to check their aids. While hearing aids were being tested, conversation with the children ranged over events at home, items the children had brought in to show and events of the forthcoming day.
>
> (case study E).

An in-class observation showed a teacher of the deaf using the following strategies:

- focus directed to listening rather than to lipreading
- expansion of children's contributions in the teacher's own speech
- clear models of sentence structures
- expressive face
- some use of gesture
- clear lip patterns
- expansion of vocabulary, eg. alternative words for 'take away'
- encouragement of turn-taking skills in children

Mainstream teachers are encouraged to adopt these same strategies, while also aiming to keep background noise to a minimum. In some settings the continued promotion of spoken language skills takes place in withdrawal sessions, with teachers of the deaf where the emphasis is on supporting language in order to assist the pupil in accessing the curriculum. This was the clearly stated policy in case studies D and H. In other settings, support is centred around the curriculum and tied very closely to it. It may be offered by teachers of the deaf or by learning support assistants who receive in-service training from the service for the hearing impaired.

However support is offered, there remains a concern to promote pupils' conversational skills.

> The teacher of the deaf in charge of a secondary unit introduced a weekly news slot in which deaf pupils took it in turns to present items of current news to the other pupils. This was seen as serving several functions:
>
> - students developing an interest in national and international news
> - practice in writing a coherent and interesting script for presentation
> - practice in delivering information accessibly by oral means
> - an increase in students' confidence in their own intelligibility
> - an active listening opportunity for other students
> - an opportunity for answering questions based on auditory information
>
> (case study E).

Many pupils in the natural aural settings observed had developed spoken language that was both fluent and intelligible by the secondary stage. However, there were some pupils who required assistance either with aspects of spoken language or with developing intelligible speech and there were systems in place for such pupils. Concentration on the conversational aspects was centred on the development of pragmatic skills. One example was a group of secondary pupils who were engaged in the RSA National Lifeskills Profile, part of which included taking part in group discussions; providing information and obtaining information from others. These pupils all had difficulties additional to hearing loss and benefited from having some of the aspects of communication skills made explicit to them. There were also examples of secondary aged pupils receiving some focused teaching on specific aspects of grammar where these had been identified as a weakness.

With regard to speech intelligibility, there were slightly different stances adopted towards intervention, although there was general agreement that there should not be any intervention beyond encouraging the child to listen until after spoken language was established. In some case studies there was no evidence of direct intervention work aimed at improving speech intelligibility, while in others the position with regard to developing speech skills was currently under review.

> In one case example they were reviewing their approach to speech intelligibility and contemplating the introduction of an auditory verbal programme, but with the determination not to introduce anything without evidence of its effectiveness and the insistence that any more structured work would be done 'with a very light hand on the tiller'.
>
> (case study H).

Where some work was undertaken with the aim of improving speech intelligibility, the approach which was favoured was not the analytical approach which used to be employed with deaf pupils but a phonological/contrastive approach. The emphasis was on ensuring that there was a distinction between different sounds articulated by the pupil which would aid the listener in understanding.

It was anticipated that pupils would have developed intelligible speech by the secondary stage and teachers of the deaf saw this as an essential goal. As one HoS put it, 'If we have not achieved good articulation by the secondary stage *we* have failed'.

Speech and language therapy

There was a similar degree of variation in the inclusion of speech and language therapy in the support offered to deaf pupils in natural aural programmes. In some case studies the involvement of speech and language therapists was limited to producing reports for statements and, where requested, in working with pupils who had difficulty with speech resulting from a condition other than deafness, for example cleft palate. Case study K had an agreement with the speech and language therapists under which the teachers of the deaf took full responsibility for the speech and language development of all children with hearing aids, referring them to a speech and language therapist if they deemed it necessary.

Close working relationships established between teachers of the deaf and speech and language therapists were seen as beneficial provided that there was a shared understanding between the two groups of professionals which enabled them to utilise each other's strengths. In these areas the speech and language therapists had undergone specialist training to work with the deaf and their main role was frequently in assessment.

There appeared to be a difference between those pupils with cochlear implants and those fitted with conventional hearing aids, with the former receiving regular speech and language therapy while hearing aid wearers in the same setting did not. Teachers of the deaf in natural aural settings mainly felt confident in their understanding and skill in promoting the speech and language development of deaf pupils.

Assessment of linguistic progress

Where teachers of the deaf were using a natural aural approach with its emphasis on developing conversational skills through interaction, often in an unstructured way, the importance of regular monitoring of linguistic progress was acknowledged. This served the purpose both of monitoring progress and also of combating any perception that the approach was *laissez faire*. Skilled practitioners who were observed implementing the approach were constantly monitoring children's progress as they worked with them and could give an accurate description of the stage of language development which the child had reached.

All case studies had a battery of assessments available for use with deaf children to monitor their linguistic progress. These were carried out on a regular basis and the results collated so that progress could be seen at a glance.

One service had a wide range of assessments available to teachers. These included:

The Renfrew Action Picture Test
The Bus Story
Webster profiles
CELF and preschool CELF
Sentence Comprehension Test
Pragmatics Profile
BPVS

There is no 'cut and dried' rule about use of these assessments. It is more usual to 'look at the child and see what's appropriate'. At primary level the annual report includes a speech discrimination test, in noise and quiet conditions.

(case study E).

Maternal Reflective Method (MRM)

One case study, C, used the maternal reflective method (MRM) which is described as an 'oral policy'. It shares some features with natural auralism, but is distinct from it. The emphasis is on the promotion of spoken language skills, and the importance of audiological support and the use of residual hearing are stressed. The approach is described as a conversational approach to learning language. A key feature of the approach is the use of the written form from a very early stage.

There are two elements to the maternal reflective approach, the maternal element and the reflective element, both of which are seen as fundamental. The maternal element is based on the notion that parents 'naturally use a different register' when speaking to babies and young children. This aspect of the approach has the same starting point of promoting interaction as natural auralism. The reflective element is, however, distinct. This describes the way that pupils are encouraged to reflect on language, considering such features as aspects of grammar, style, register and identifying forms of language such as colloquialisms. In order to achieve this reflection, the conversation is written down and prepared into a text by the teacher. The pupils are then required to analyse the text. The written form serves the dual function of preserving some of the features of spoken language which can easily be lost and of providing a text for analysis.

Staff are trained in the use of this approach. Many have worked at the school for many years, particularly in the primary department, and this is seen as a real strength. Since it is a special school setting, it is possible to maintain a consistent approach throughout the school.

Speech and language therapy

The provision of individual speech and language therapy is seen as very important in this setting. There was a decision to move away from the non-interventionist approach to speech to give more attention to individual speech therapy. Each pupil receives an average of three sessions of individual speech therapy per week. In addition, speech and language therapists and teachers of the deaf work together in setting language targets for individual pupils and classes. Teachers of the deaf are trained in teaching stress and syllable patterns and also in using the school's own phonetic system.

Assessment of linguistic progress

Stress is placed on the assessment of linguistic progress. The school has a programme of regular video recording of pupils and a battery of tests related both to listening skills and phonological skills as well as language tests.

> The school uses different kinds of assessment tests.
>
> *Listening skills:*
> MERKLEIN (a speech feature discrimination test)
> GRASP (this is similar to MERKLEIN but more detailed)
>
> *Phonological skills:*
> PETAL
> A phoneme test (the school has devised its own test)
>
> *Language development:*
> Reynell
> TROG
> Renfrew Action Picture Test
> CELF
> STASS
>
> (case study C).

A distinctive test is one related to imitating and repeating rhythms and demonstrating auditory memory for digits. This test is designed to reveal pupils who have sequencing problems and a weak memory for rhythm. The school refers to these as dyspraxic pupils and has special programmes for them.

Discussion points

The maternal reflective method (MRM) clearly offers a consistent approach to language development. In the setting of a residential special school where all teaching staff and care staff are trained in the approach and there is a low turnover of staff, it is possible to provide this level of consistency. The question arises how easy it is to implement such an approach in other settings. It would appear to be difficult to implement the approach wholesale. Aspects of the approach, for example the use of written language to support the development of spoken language, have been adopted by other teachers of the deaf although this was not evident in any other case studies. The reflective element has similarities with the metalinguistic awareness of language which is emphasised in other case studies, where it is seen as useful in comparing and contrasting languages for the purposes of developing literacy skills, for example in case study A.

Live English

In some settings, notably those in which some pupils use BSL as their first language, there is an emphasis on promoting what has been termed 'live English'. This does not relate exclusively to spoken language, rather it describes strategies for face-to-face communication with hearing people. It may include writing as a strategy alongside speaking and gesture, but the expression 'live English' is used to differentiate it from written forms of communication. In these settings it is recognised that children will need these skills and will require training in them. There is a recognition of an increasing place for spoken language in these sessions and it is emphasised that deaf pupils will be the ones expected to make the major adjustment to the audience.

> There are situations in your life and in your future life where the person you are interacting with won't have any Sign or any Deaf Awareness. You need to have a number of tools, a number of things up your sleeve which will mean that communication will be effective for you.
>
> (HoS, case study A).

Originally members of staff worked with speech and language therapists on a programme of training in strategies. It was built partly on an English as a Foreign Language model in the sense that these were recognised as skills for life and with a purpose and not for learning purposes. More lately it has been seen that such training might fit appropriately in a Literacy Hour context.

Again, originally teachers of the deaf and speech and language therapists were perceived as being the main deliverers of the programme, but as deaf instructors have become more involved with different areas of the curriculum they have brought their own insights about communication with hearing people. As the HoS observed, 'They are speaking from strength'. Interestingly, one of these insights is the place of 'pidgin' sign in communication with hearing people.

(case study A).

'Live English' is not timetabled in the conventional sense.

Summary

Considerable importance is placed on spoken language. In some settings it is seen as the main channel for communication and education, whereas in others it is seen not as the primary means of communication but as having importance as one of a range of strategies for communication with hearing people.

Key findings in this section are summarised as follows:

- A great deal of importance is placed on the development of spoken language. This is true regardless of setting or communication approach.

- It may be regarded as the main channel of communication or as one of a range of options.

- In oral settings spoken language development is seen as building on audition, with speech intelligibility receiving emphasis.

- Where it is one of a range of communication options the emphasis is on 'live' English to facilitate communication with hearing people.

- In all settings on-going detailed assessment and monitoring of progress are essential.

4.8 Literacy

The development of literacy in deaf pupils was considered extremely important in all case studies, with some settings, for example case study H, stating unequivocally that it was central to the support offered by the service. Literacy may assume a role of great importance in the lives of deaf pupils as they may wish to use subtitles or need to read for information. They may also wish to communicate by electronic means, for example via textphones or e-mail or to send faxes. If these extra needs for literacy are added to the current demands for high levels of literacy skills made by the National Curriculum and the push for literacy for all pupils represented by the National Literacy Strategy, then the pressure to achieve high levels of literacy for deaf pupils becomes acute.

There are different routes currently being pursued towards literacy for deaf pupils. These variations in approach largely mirror the different approaches to communication which are being pursued and are documented elsewhere in this report. For some deaf pupils the approach to literacy is not significantly different from that being used with hearing children but with extra support being given, whilst for others the route to literacy is seen as being a distinctive one which is closer to that used with pupils who are native speakers of another language.

Literacy via spoken language

For pupils whose primary means of communication is through the medium of spoken language, this is seen as being the route to literacy. Case study D expressed it thus:

> The route to literacy for the oral pupils is through spoken language. Hence developing spoken language is seen as a necessary condition for literacy development. The aim is to create an analogue of spoken language in the deaf child's mind so that the sounds and structures of verbal language are internalised; the goal is 'inner speech'. Inner speech forms the basis for literacy.
>
> Achieving literacy is the key to independent learning and deaf children need all the support they can get to read and write fluently.

There was general agreement that literacy development follows in the wake of spoken language development, although some aspects were seen as starting very early.

> The coordinator of the preschool and primary team talked of literacy starting at preschool and stressed the need to encourage parents to share books and stories with their deaf children.

All the teachers of the deaf encountered in this service appeared to be have a broad concept of literacy. There were comments such as 'teachers are conscious of the interactive nature of reading, not just listening to the child read, but word attack, phonics and comprehension'. The understanding of writing led these teachers of the deaf to be concerned to ensure that deaf pupils were not being expected to write structures which were linguistically more advanced than their development of spoken language and to get this message across to mainstream teachers.

In the early stages of reading, teachers of the deaf relied quite heavily on teacher-made materials. In line with the strategy of not expecting pupils to read text that was beyond their grasp, teachers made their own books using language within the child's own repertory. Frequently the text comprised the written form of what the child had said in response to a picture, or their own version of a story, or perhaps the child's news.

(case study E).

The importance of the early stages of reading was also stressed in a total communication setting. Interview and observation of the head of primary in school G yielded the following information:

The teachers of the deaf feel that pre-reading is very important. There are certain skills which must be established before children are expected to read text or even individual words, which are to:

- handle books; talk about books; talk about pictures; gain a notion of story
- identify their own written name
- identify individual letters
- be able to tell a story and understand a story

On introducing reading the child is not asked to speak or sign words in the first instance, but to respond to the text. For example the child might be faced with a written instruction 'blue car' and understand that this meant to colour the car blue.

The importance of delaying the matching of text to signs or words as long as possible was stressed:

If they start that too early you damage development later, because if they start that before they have a good understanding of print conveying meaning and looking for the meaning of words, what you've taught them to do is to 'bark at print'... to produce a sign for every word. And we get children who are very proficient at producing sign for every word but because they have never been through the stage of print conveying meaning, they think that is what reading is... reading is when you sit down with a teacher and just produce a sign for every word and that keeps the teacher very happy, but they are not reading for pleasure.

(case study G).

Once their language had reached the level to access the language of reading schemes, then these were used widely, often with supplementary material. Schemes such as the Oxford Reading Tree which contained stories to which the children could relate were the most popular.

Pupils of secondary age were observed in a school for the deaf:

They typically arrived at the school reading below their chronological age. There is a strong emphasis in the school on the development of reading skills, with the stated aim: 'our pupils are encouraged initially to gain confidence and pleasure in reading and ultimately to become successful and enthusiastic independent readers'. In pursuit of this aim the pupils are organised into Reading Groups, which are held for three half-hour sessions per week. The activities undertaken in these groups is based on a 'pleasure model' and is unconnected with the rest of the English curriculum. Pupils are encouraged not simply to read the text but to interrogate it and respond to it. However, even within a pleasure model it is recognised that there is a need to monitor progress.

(case study J).

National Literacy Strategy

The National Literacy Strategy, including the Literacy Hour, was initially seen as presenting a real challenge for teachers of the deaf. However, a positive response to it was evident in the case studies. It was apparent that teachers of the deaf had risen to the challenge and been able to take useful points from it, using some strategies as designed and adapting others to suit the needs of their pupils.

There was a belief that teachers of the deaf needed to be as well informed and familiar with the National Literacy Strategy as mainstream teachers. Some case studies had been able to arrange for their teachers of the deaf to attend the training offered to mainstream teachers and then to organise their own additional inservice training. The attention to details at text level, sentence level and word level was seen to have merit for deaf pupils. Case study J mentioned above had seen the relevance of this approach to their reading groups.

Teachers of the deaf had different responses towards the teaching of phonics to deaf children. Traditionally many teachers of the deaf were of the opinion that the teaching of phonics was inappropriate with deaf pupils, although there were always some teachers of the deaf who disagreed with this stance and concentrated on promoting phonic skills alongside other strategies. The Literacy Strategy has encouraged teachers of the deaf to reconsider their position to the teaching of phonics and it has been found that many pupils are able to develop phonic skills.

In some case studies, for example D, teachers of the deaf take prime responsibility for literacy development, whereas in others, for example E, this is seen as the responsibility of mainstream schools, supported and empowered by teachers of the deaf from the service. In this setting, explicit guidelines have been produced in relation to meeting the needs of hearing impaired pupils during Literacy Hour. The emphasis is placed on ensuring that hearing impaired pupils are making the maximum use of their residual hearing and that listening conditions are favourable. Attention is then given to seating position to enable hearing impaired pupils to see the teacher's face, particularly when Big Books are being used.

Explanation is offered to mainstream teachers on the way that writing of hearing impaired children frequently develops, reflecting the structure of their spoken language. Thus they may write sentences which appear to contain only the key words, but this will accurately reflect the level of their spoken language and should not be corrected for fear of introducing deviance into the writing. The necessity for differentiation is stressed and other aspects which the pupils may find difficult, for example they may have difficulty with high frequency words as they are not yet in their spontaneous language and phonic work may require a great deal of reinforcement, although it should not be omitted.

Work related to the Literacy Hour was observed in the same case study in a unit setting:

> In the example we saw, the unit teachers and classteachers had planned the Literacy Hour together to the extent that specific questions for the hearing impaired pupils were earmarked at the planning stage – reflective, descriptive and speculative questions. The two year 2 classes are together for the Literacy Hour, with the group session being taken two mornings per week by the teacher of the deaf and three mornings by the mainstream teacher. The hearing impaired pupils are fully included in the hour and the teacher (on the occasion we were there, the mainstream teacher) repeats answers so that all children can hear them. The mainstream teacher is aware of targets for individual hearing impaired pupils, for example behavioural targets, and can see that children are encouraged to follow them. The children were clearly fully involved in the hour and enjoying it. The unit staff reported that the hearing impaired pupils had responded positively to the structure and routine of the hour.

The Big Books are chosen to fit in with the topic being followed in other areas of the curriculum, which proves beneficial in reinforcing relevant vocabulary. A learning support assistant from the unit sits in on the group session and record the new vocabulary and notes any examples of hearing impaired pupils experiencing difficulty.

The hearing impaired pupils are taught separately from the mainstream class for the rest of the hour and they receive additional work on literacy. One day per week they are withdrawn for the Literacy Hour to go over any problems. They also have a spelling test during this session, and a writing session. Whilst the main emphasis in literacy is on comprehension and expression, the older children at Key Stage 1 are encouraged to use phonics and spell correctly. An emergent approach to writing is encouraged, with children attempting to write from a very early stage. Once writing is established, they are encouraged to move towards using conventional spelling. The pace of all the literacy work was brisk, with children kept on task all the time and frequent change of activity. The questions asked were probing and demanded that children think and speculate. They were expected to show an understanding of story grammar and to recall without recourse to visual prompts, although these were readily available if any child started to struggle.

(case study E).

Services working within a natural aural approach had developed guidelines for the Literacy Hour and deaf pupils. The role of the teacher of the deaf varies with individual pupils and with the nature of the lesson. It also has to fit within the structure of the service. Teachers of the deaf were seen as being involved in both the planning and delivery of the Literacy Hour. There was seen to be a great advantage in the structure of the hour and the necessity for clear planning on the part of the mainstream teacher. The structure was seen to have benefits for deaf and hearing impaired pupils, who enjoyed both the security of the routine and the opportunities which the hour afforded for repetition and reinforcement. Teachers of the deaf were able to pre-tutor pupils as the short and medium term plans for the hour were made available to them.

There was a considerable amount of liaison where teachers of the deaf and mainstream teachers were working well together. A prime example of the quality and amount of planning and preparation for the hour came from case study K. The example refers to the total package of support given to the pupil, but a large amount of the time was devoted to the Literacy Hour since this was seen as central to the child's needs.

Joint planning sessions are seen as essential to the ToDs work. There may be time allocated in the mainstream teacher's timetable, but most frequently they occur before school, at lunch time or after school. Planning sessions may occur once a week, but for some children they are much more frequent, three times per week for one child who was observed. These occurred at lunch times. Whilst the classteacher appreciated the opportunities for instant feedback on the child's progress and the chance to discuss any problems with the ToD immediately, it did involve her in devoting three lunch times to planning for the hearing impaired child's needs.

The ToD would look at the plan for the next two weeks for the mainstream class and discuss with the classteacher those areas with which the hearing impaired pupil would need support and the nature of the support. This would then be written as a plan and a copy given to the classteacher so that she knew what the ToD would be doing in support sessions. The ToD would differentiate the curriculum and frequently provide worksheets or supporting material that would be useful for other pupils as well. Most frequently the hearing impaired pupil would be withdrawn to a quiet room, along with a group of hearing pupils.

Having planned with the classteacher, the ToD would visit the parents to go through the work to be covered in the next two weeks so that support could be given at home.

(case study K).

Literacy within the maternal reflective method (MRM)

Case study C has its own distinctive approach to literacy in keeping with the maternal reflective method (MRM).

The policy document on reading states:

> One of the major causes of educational difficulties in deaf pupils is their very low reading standards .. In our view the conversational approach of the MRM is best fitted to developing the reading skills of deaf pupils.

The same document describes the school's approach to reading as including:

*   a conversational approach
*   additional reading lessons for pupils
*   annual assessment
*   broad reading experience
*   use of the library

Primary department

In the primary department, texts are initially based on pupils' conversations and when some independence is achieved, books from reading schemes and pupils' fiction are introduced.

Secondary department: the reading groups

Reading groups are used in the secondary department. The reading groups developed in the early 1970s and predated the introduction of MRM in the school, although in many ways the approach taken in these sessions is very MRM in nature. This approach to reading was developed by the previous head of English because of concerns about low reading ages of pupils. She based it on a remedial approach she took with hearing pupils.

> There are four English and four reading group sessions each week for all pupils in years seven to 11. Sometimes there have been debates in the school about whether one reading group session should be dropped, especially for those in year 10 and 11 doing GCSE. But the school believes it is mainly because of the reading groups that the reading of pupils continues to develop. Dropping the modern foreign language from the curriculum has provided some of the space needed.
>
> Pupils are grouped by ability, and sometimes personality, in years seven to nine. In years 10 and 11 they are grouped according to GCSE and other courses, unless there are large enough numbers to group by ability.
>
> Not all teachers are involved in reading groups; some subject specialists never get involved and part-time teachers cannot be involved because the reading groups occur on most days. The head of English previously thought that the reading groups should only be done by English teachers but now thinks that everyone should participate, for a certain period of time, because of the insights it gives to pupils' understanding and misunderstanding of what they read – 'the incredibly complicated way in which some deaf pupils can misunderstand'. She thinks for subject specialists who are concentrating on getting the content across it is useful for them to see this.
>
> (case study C).

The aims of the reading groups according to the policy document include:

- to develop greater understanding of language
- to develop formal knowledge of language (through reflection)
- to develop conversational skills

Each reading group teacher identifies specific objectives for the group from reading tests and IEPs (reading targets are set at annual reviews). There are guidelines for the reading groups which describe the typical session comprising:

- shared context – preparation/revision/anticipation
- reading silently
- reading aloud
- discussion – global meaning followed by specifics
- reflection – unknown vocabulary, technical difficulties, working out rules
- revision/follow up

Reading groups are used for extending reading skills and through continuing language development. According to the head of English the reading group offers a group approach to reading which encourages the sharing of ideas. 'The discussion about the reading is the crucial element ... this is where the reading group approach is very close to the MRM' (head of English). The main difference is that in the first the discussion arises from the text, in MRM the text arises from the discussion. The reflection/discussion in the reading group is first of all about the meaning of the text; from the ideas the pupils bring forward there is then a focus on specific sentences on any vocabulary or other features of language that are problematic.

The English department has a library of resources for the texts used including videos and written materials. They find the videos very helpful especially for less able pupils. For example, with a less able group at Key Stage 4 who have not reached 'the magic reading age of nine on the Edinburgh Reading Test', the teacher used the video *Kes* and managed to read four abridged extracts from the novel, 300 words each. She told us, 'There was no way this could have been done without having that video ... watching first, talking about it, then coming to look at the text'. It is difficult to find videos with the captions so the school is recording its own with captions. Teachers also need to produce particular resources for each group.

Phonics has an important role especially in the early stages, but it is 'more a spontaneous collecting approach rather than teaching in a specific order' using the opportunity when new words arise.

Literacy within a sign bilingual approach

For those pupils who are sign-dominant, there is a distinctive approach to literacy. The pupils are seen as 'bridging the gap' to literacy via BSL. The emphasis placed on the development of literacy skills is very strong. This is exemplified by a quotation from the HoS in case study A:

> If the child can't read there is so much independent learning, independent access that they will never grasp and if they don't become fluent or proficient in the written form, there are whole areas of communication and reporting and recording which are denied to them.

Children in an English-dominant programme may be accessing English through 'oracy' whereas the sign-dominant children are being taught through BSL 'without necessarily needing to go through the spoken route'.

The HoS described literacy as an area where her views and others' had changed and were continuing to change. The initial view was that 'it was going to be the target form of the second language'. The children's ability to 'crack the code of written English' was going to be dependent on their sign language competence and proficiency. At this time a lot of thought and effort was put into teaching through a 'top-down approach' to literacy.

Another early idea was that 'oracy would probably spring from literacy'. She outlined ways in which it does, especially in relation to using a spoken form of the written English in 'live English' environments. At the same time deaf colleagues were impressing upon teachers the importance of literacy in deaf people's lives and 'the things it has to do for deaf people that it doesn't have to do for hearing people'.

> That made us realise that we couldn't just look at the traditional aspects of literacy ... that you had to look at literature within the lives of deaf people and the place of literacy in face-to-face communication and increasingly, electronic communication.

New insights came in another way when the deaf instructors became involved in children's literacy. They seemed adept at demonstrating new ways of explaining points.

The early experiences for children of literature in the form of storybooks have always been held as important and the concept of 'reading readiness' has not been adopted. Although there were arguments for a sequential bilingual model, that is establishing BSL first and adding in literacy at five years of age, this has been rejected. A 'simultaneous' model has therefore been embraced although it is accepted that the two languages may be 'out of sync' in developmental terms. Two languages are presented throughout children's school careers.

Observation of work in progress showed how teachers' understanding continues to develop through reflection on practice.

One of the major developments in the team's understanding has been in relation to the 'top-down approach' to literacy. The perception is that they over-estimated what a concentration on it could achieve. As a result, 'we had to start looking at independent reading and giving children a range of strategies to access text, to crack the code'. One aspect of this seems to be the growing awareness that children need to have a 'mental representation of English ... that wasn't purely sign' to progress. This 'mental representation' was further described as a 'linguistic sense and metalinguistic sense'. Those children with a better mental representation were perceived to be progressing faster in literacy skills but this did not necessarily relate to whether a child was 'more oral'.

The institution of the Literacy Hour has been seen to be helpful in this regard, bringing with it a greater concentration on 'bottom-up strategies' and 'metalanguage' which is seen to relate to this. Consequently the team are now concentrating on this area. They have moved away from concerns over the text and grammar levels of teaching since they feel that these can be fairly easily demonstrated to children as two representations with the same meaning. Rather, 'it's the word level that's more of a challenge. That's where the two languages are so, so different. It's so hard to make parallels'. The team know that this is, 'where we're really struggling' but are aware that they must 'crack it' so that children can progress.

On the even smaller unit level of phonology, the HoS explained that in examining ways of visually representing spoken language they had looked at 'things that are potentially quite sensitive like Cued Speech'. She also said that they had 'underestimated the role of fingerspelling'.

The team are now at a stage where there is greater concentration on the link between the spoken and written form because there are now so many 'English-preferred' children. There is now a recognition that learning to read and write is a different experience for English-dominant and sign-dominant children and that teaching needs to reflect that. Their approach is becoming 'more sophisticated'.

One of the main insights in this development is coming from children themselves, 'We understand better but really it's the children are telling us, how the children are progressing is telling us about what's working and what isn't'. They recognise that 'for each deaf person it's a unique experience' and that what is needed is a number of ways in which 'we can offer access'.

(case study A).

The Literacy Hour

The Literacy Hour which was observed involved a group of Key Stage 2 children, a deaf instructor and the teacher. The children were reported to be 'close enough' in ability to be taught together. This situation was particularly aided by the presence of the deaf instructor with BSL.

The teacher of the deaf plans the work with her mainstream colleague, deciding which texts she will use, adaptations that need to be made and gaps that need to be 'plugged'.

On the day in question the children were being asked to interrogate a text from 'Yellow Pages'. This was presented in large form so that the children could read it together. The teacher explained how much initial work had been necessary to give the children a sense of what the Yellow Pages are before any work could be done. Clearly, hearing peers had been much more 'au fait'. The consequence was that, 'We don't get through everything that the mainstream class does in the week'.

Follow-up was mentioned to be a problem especially for children working at a lower level than their hearing peers.

The teacher mentioned the area of phonics, or linking word families to spellings and lip patterns. The point here was that although work in this area is usually associated with Key Stage 1, the teacher of the deaf was still doing 'a big blast once a week' with Key Stage 2 children, which had to be fitted into the available time frame. Nevertheless the teacher felt this to be a very important area since 'at their own level, the whole idea of English words and how English words are put together is beginning to make far more sense'. The effect of the Literacy Hour is that the teacher feels that she has become more consistent in this than she used to be.

Summary

Key findings in this section are summarised as follows:

- Great emphasis is placed on the promotion of literacy skills in all settings.
- Teachers working with deaf children in oral settings draw heavily on work with hearing children, based on spoken language development.
- Sign bilingual and Total Communication settings have developed their own distinct ways of developing literacy skills.
- An important feature of good practice is a continuing focus on pupils' reading development at the secondary stage.
- In all settings, creative use is being made of the Literacy Hour to enhance learning for deaf pupils.

4.9 Personal and social development

This section is concerned with the aspects of good practice which relate to the deaf child's personal and social development. The discussion will cover issues of self-esteem, independence, identity, and social skills and behaviour. There are sometimes strong links between the issues raised here and those discussed in section 4.2 on ethos and where this is the case, what follows should be read in conjunction with that section.

Concern with the education of the 'whole child' was much in evidence in the questionnaire returns with many respondents placing great emphasis on the need for educational services to help deaf children and young persons to become independent, to have high self-esteem and a strong sense of identity. A concern with non-academic educational outcomes such as these are shared more generally in education and have been given increasing recognition in recent years, for example in the Coopers and Lybrand Report to Government on the Local Management of Schools[1]. It appears there are two reasons for this development; first, the acceptance of non-academic outcomes as important outcomes in their own right, and second, an assumption that such factors as a pupils' self-esteem and independence have an important influence on academic achievement. However, it should be recognised that although a well established link exists between school achievement and self-esteem there is no evidence of a *causal* relationship either one way or the other; it is likely that other factors are also involved.

Hence, although many people in deaf education see the growth of positive personal and social characteristics as inextricably interlinked with learning, including the development of communication skills, opinions are divided as to which leads to which. Do effective communication skills and high academic achievement lead to high self-esteem or is it the other way round? Does a sense of identity promote learning or the reverse? Or is the relationship reciprocal or even synergistic? Intuitively we would probably assume a reciprocal relationship.

We set ourselves the task of investigating personal and social education (PSE) in different provisions. We take PSE to mean both a set curriculum designed to impart information to children in relation to social and personal issues, for example drugs and sex, as well as the fostering of positive attributes in children. The discussion is structured under a number of headings although we recognise in reality some of these elements are not discrete – for example self-esteem and independence. In addition, as we have already mentioned, in practice it has been difficult to separate out entirely personal and social education from ethos. Here PSE is regarded as the strategies used to foster attributes and knowledge in children rather than a pervading atmosphere in an organisation or school.

---

[1] Coopers and Lybrand (1988) *The Local Management of Schools*. London: HMSO.

The main source for strategies and approaches used to encourage the development of personal and social skills and attributes came from schools for the deaf, although many seem transferable to mainstream situations. The discussion that follows is presented under a number of headings but the reader will realise there is considerable overlap.

The development of self-esteem

The development of self-esteem and self-confidence in a child are often linked to a sense that his or her actions are valued and praised. We were not surprised to find the use of praise is a strong element in schools. For example, the headteacher at P said, 'We celebrate all children here, regardless of what they can do', and the head of primary in G told us, 'For a lot of things we go the praise route rather than the sanctions route if we can. Where children are having problems we try to catch them being good'.

Staff in a number of schools outlined their strategies to increase a sense of pupils' self-worth. The head in G during assembly invites children to share their news as recorded in their diaries. Teachers can nominate children's work for the effort involved. The head comments on the work, showing the other children and inviting their comments. Whatever the standard of work the children are praised for their effort. Similarly in case study C, 'Whatever contribution they make in the classroom is valued, so they feel valued'.

A major boost to children's self-esteem in school P is believed to be participation in the summer concert. All take part, and according to the deputy head, 'We encourage the children to project themselves in this way ... so they build up a lot of confidence'.

Clearly an underlying question is how to give children opportunities to express themselves confidently. We were given one example when we observed the head in G engaging the children in a discussion about the situation in Kosova. This assumed that the children had an understanding of international news, but many of the children of primary age contributed confidently with perceptions of what it would be like to leave one's home and the 'rights' and 'wrongs' of bombing Serbia. The head acknowledged each contribution as valid. The children were notably keen to participate and such discussions were clearly regular events.

Other ways in which pupils' contributions are valued include the 'Respect for All' policy in G and the School Council in C, both discussed in section 4.2. We also came across situations where individual pupils were involved in decisions made about the amount and type of support they received in mainstream schools (see section 4.5).

These approaches to developing pupils' self-esteem are probably obvious to many readers but it is nevertheless important to note the strong emphasis people gave to the need to value pupils' effort and contributions. As children advance up the school, it appears to be important to demonstrate that not only are opinions valued, but that they can make a difference in a very 'real' way.

Independence

Teachers pointed out they need to be careful that they do not 'oversupport' or encourage 'learned helplessness' in deaf children. A child needs an appropriate level and style of support to become independent. Too much support and a child will find it difficult to develop those skills. It was interesting that staff in several services we visited expressed such concerns (see section 4.5).

In the past the issue of deaf pupils' lack of independence was perhaps particularly a problem in some residential special schools. It is now widely recognised that all schools and services share the responsibility to prepare youngsters for the transition from school to independent living.

The encouragement towards independence begins for the very youngest children in education. For example, in nursery M with regard to the insertion of a hearing aid mould the teacher was heard to say, 'You're going to the big school. You try and put it back in.' The head of nursery communicates the same message of the development of independence and self-management skills to the parents.

In college L, providing students with the skills to become more independent is one of the key aims and is accredited through the Award Scheme Development and Accreditation Network, (ASDAN). The care officer who is assigned to the student on entry takes responsibility for the ASDAN plan.

In one service the approach taken to providing support in mainstream schools incorporates elements of training for independence.

> Service D believes that in-class support is not the most effective way to facilitate more access to the curriculum since the pupils needs intensive language teaching which can only be achieved in a withdrawal situation. The remaining time, spent without support in the class situation is considered to be valuable for developing independence. This model of support is considered empowering for mainstream teachers and maintains the important link between child and class teacher without the mediation of a third party. By being in the class unaided the pupils develop coping strategies, become 'their own person and advocate' and are encouraged to

'get on with being a normal child' rather than relying on someone to help them. Members of the service talk to parents about this issue of independence from the beginning. A satisfied parent commented:

> ... deaf children need extra support, not someone who will do the work for them. This not only restricts them of ability but encourages them to remain 'different' and this crushes their confidence and independence at a very early stage ... [this] will have repercussions as they get older as they find it difficult to function on their own initiative as they've always had someone to tell them what to do.

We had the opportunity to investigate the approach of one school in some detail and this described below.

The approach of one school to developing pupil independence

In J it is recognised that youngsters enter the school with a wide range of skills for self-sufficiency, whether they enter in year seven or for their FE years. The years pupils spend at the school are seen as the major opportunity for youngsters to develop skills for independence and the development of independence is clearly an aim of all staff, school and out-of-school. The interviews we made on this subject were with care staff and pupils and it from this perspective that we report.

> In J pupils are divided into groups based on age and live in different houses based on gender. There are out-of-school activities which are carefully chosen to promote personal and social development. Also each pupil has a care plan which is described as a document , 'which outlines activities and skills which pupils want to develop as well as personal goals'. Targets within the care plan are arranged under a number of categories: audiology, health and care, homework, activities, personal organisation and behaviour. For the youngest children care plans may address the most basic physical needs, eg. brushing teeth, whilst for older pupils complex social and emotional needs are addressed. Pupils themselves have been involved in identifying the areas to cover. Many of targets within each category relate to independence.
>
> Skills mentioned include cooking, planning menus, using the washing machine, ironing, using kitchen equipment, washing up, shopping, waking themselves up with alarm, reading timetables, buying a ticket, booking the minibus, using transport, awareness of environmental aids, use of minicom and Typetalk, awareness of reduced rates for telephones, awareness of Disability Living Allowance and other benefits, audiological management, money management and banking, study and study plans.

> The weekly progress of each student is monitored and recorded including an assessment of the degree to which support is still required for each target. Care plans are used with pupils until year 10. The progress of year 11 pupils and FE students is monitored in a meeting which care staff and the young person attend where the young person is encouraged to reflect upon his/her progress in different areas of personal and social development and to identify new targets.

The aim in J is that by the end of year 11 the young person will be entirely responsible for their own care.

Although the aim is for a relaxed and informal atmosphere within the living groups, there is also a clearly defined structure. This 'ensures that the young people know what is expected of them'. These structures relate to after-school activities which include homework and recreational and leisure pursuits. As the summary of the out-of-school policy states, 'As the young people progress through the school the aim is to relax some of these structures while at the same time promoting the development of independence skills', for example how time after school can be used and opportunities for free walks. Pupils of younger years engage in a structured programme of after-school activities while older pupils have a less structured regime allowing them to make choices as to whether this time will be used for relaxation, homework or socialising. Once young people reach the age of 14, as long as they have parental permission, they may go 'off-site' in a group of three without a member of staff. Once they reach year 11 they may go in pairs, and once in FE they may go individually.

One student in J, remembering a time before he took up FE provision with the school said that he used to be 'stuck indoors' but now was 'out and about'. Several of them spoke to us of the independence skills they were learning.

The new hostel for FE students is due to open in town shortly. Clearly, although it will be 'overseen' by members of the care staff, this will provide even more opportunities for independent living.

Identity

The concept of identity and deafness has different connotations for different people depending on their views of the aims of deaf education. Where deaf children are orally educated, using speech as their primary means of communication, identity issues often relate to their ability to communicate with people who have normal hearing and their sense of themselves as deaf individuals within the hearing world. There are undeniably difficulties in many situations, even for the orally very competent deaf person, so that a central role for educators is to acknowledge these difficulties and develop strategies for coping. For those working in sign bilingual programmes, identity issues often concern the deaf child embracing his or her identity as a deaf person with an associated heritage, language and culture. In these settings the deaf child is the recipient of a bilingual curriculum which includes instruction in BSL as well as education about the deaf world and its culture. This curriculum is usually taught by deaf instructors who act as role models to the child and a deaf identity is presented as one in which the child can feel secure and proud.

There is a tendency perhaps to present these as the two approaches that exist to helping deaf children in their search for identity. However, this is an oversimplification – it is a mistake to think it terms of a straightforward dichotomy. Witness, for example, the thoughts of the head of service in a sign bilingual setting.

We invited the head of service in A to talk about deaf identity.

> I would say *identities* ... a number of, because it's very easy to see this idea of a hearing identity and a deaf identity... I'm really interested in the multiple identities which children have. They have an identity that's around being deaf but they have an identity about being black or maybe Asian or being a girl ... or from being from a particular part of [name of city]. I think the deaf bit of the identity is far more complicated. It's not a case of I'm proud to be deaf or I don't like being deaf ... I think there are lots of ways of having an identity relating to one's deafness which may not have anything to do with deafness ... and I think we have to accept that it changes. So the children's deaf-related image when they're little, it'll change and that's right and it's alright to change and with some of the older students it's alright to be angry about being deaf. There's a danger with a service like this because we are so positive about deafness that you intimidate parents. They can't feel equally positive about it, so having all these people coming in saying, 'It's not a problem' – well it *is* a blooming problem, and for the children it's a problem and for deaf people it's a problem. You know, deaf people here, they don't sit here saying 'I'm proud to be deaf'. They say 'It's a b***** hard life ... there are a lot of positives from it and we've emerged from the system as having a sense of being deaf but actually it doesn't suddenly make everything alright'.
>
> It's not for me to say and a lot of it comes from role models. The people who work here are so varied ... They all have a sense of Deaf self but they also

have other senses of self as well and they need to be flexible. We've all got multiple identities. It's multiple identities and not having them too much in conflict ... for many people they are in conflict or they perceive them as being in conflict and I don't think they have to be, but we often make it like that and the Deaf community often makes it like that ... It makes it quite hard. If we're about enriching society then we've got to break down some of these exclusivity things and deaf people need to let go a bit.

The concept of 'identity' is clearly complex. The greatest worry perhaps is for those children and young people who find themselves caught in the complexity of the situation without any real feeling of belonging to any group.

Three strategies for the development of identity are now discussed, providing a deaf peer group, deaf role models and curriculum.

A deaf peer group

As children begin to develop and mature, inevitably they address questions such as, 'Who am I ?' 'Where do I belong?' and 'Where am I going ?' The beginning of answers to these questions emerge through a child's ability to identify similarities and differences between self and others. In ensuring that deaf children meet and perhaps learn with other deaf peers they are assured that they are not 'alone' and have the possibility of forming a secure concept of self within an empathetic group. Clearly, schools for the deaf – and units to a lesser extent – fulfil this need. Where a child is the only deaf person in a school many services make special efforts to create social links whereby deaf children can meet.

Within the authority of service D there is a youth club and a signing choir. Some children attend NDCS meetings while older students attend the training programmes offered by Friends of the Young Deaf. Students join in the activities of disabled sports groups and the British Deaf Sports Association. It is hoped that a group will attend an arts festival next year. The service organises adventure weekends and trips to events such as a performance by Evelyn Glennie, the deaf musician.

The service base has an atmosphere of a social centre and meeting place. Students and parents attending sessions appear very much at home there and older students and ex-pupils drop in for a chat over lunchtime.

In this service hearing impaired children are perceived as needing the opportunity to meet together with deaf peers to develop a positive deaf identity. The service aims for a more 'deaf-centred' and 'person-centred' programme so that students will leave with a good sense of who they are but the approach also accommodates the views of older students wanting an identity as an oral deaf person as well as, or instead of a deaf identity. The initial emphasis is on the promotion of confidence in a peer group situation as well as developing self-esteem.

The nursery M forms an interesting example of the formation of a positive deaf identity at a very young age. The strength of this model is perceived to be a nursery designed primarily for deaf children where deaf children outnumber hearing children, yet set in a mainstream school. By this arrangement the children are helped to realise that they are deaf but that being deaf is not odd. In this way they can develop a positive identity prior to formal schooling.

Deaf role models

By introducing deaf adults to children the question 'Where am I going?' can be addressed. It is important that deaf children realise they will continue to be deaf when they grow up and that deaf people live normal lives like everyone else – they marry, have jobs, drive cars etc.

In school G, deaf visitors are invited in particularly to talk about careers. According to the school this provides youngsters with the opportunity to ask detailed questions about the obstacles they have faced and how they have overcome them. Further up the school deaf adults are invited to speak to students in more depth about college and employment. There is also a plan to invite ex-pupils to return to the school for the Parent Teacher Association annual general meeting so that parents can meet them.

We saw examples of deaf adults employed in a variety of roles in deaf education. In school G, half the senior management team is deaf as are a number of the learning assistants.

At case study G, the headteacher and the head of Primary are both deaf, providing powerful inspiration to the children of possible levels of achievement. The head is able to use her experiences to good effect to tell the children about the challenges they may face as they get older and strategies for overcoming them. She told us that her approach is to say to pupils:

You can't do some things. It is not because you are stupid, it's because you are deaf. You have to work harder to achieve the same.

When you go into the world there will be people who've got no patience with you, they may not understand you. You don't apologise, you just bear with them. If they don't understand try to improve your speech or write it down. But you don't apologise for being what you are.

> The head sees the role of the school as giving the children a 'defence mechanism' which will help them to cope with life when they leave school.

Service A provides the most extensive example we came across of the employment of deaf adults, with eleven deaf instructors employed. Here there is an active policy to recruit deaf adults, first to raise the status of deaf people within the authority by making them stakeholders in deaf education and second due to the valuable insights which they are perceived to bring to deaf education. For deaf instructors for whom sign is their 'native' language, their role in teaching sign and delivering the curriculum in sign is also seen as crucial.

Identity and the curriculum

In some cases identity is dealt with directly through the curriculum. For example, the residential school J incorporates deaf issues into its PSE curriculum in an informal manner. Discussion begins 'when the kids are ready for it ... we tend to follow their lead, with a bit of prompting. The level we take it depends on their maturity' (teacher). The school encourages acceptance and tolerance of diversity generally and specifically towards non-oral deaf young people. The same teacher told us, 'What I want for them is to be able to function in the hearing world and have respect for the deaf world'. The school also sees its extensive programme of out-of-school activities as important in the pupils' development of sense of identity. By engaging in a number of these, a pupil establishes multiple definitions of self as well as having a deaf self.

In case study A, a very different approach is taken. 'Deaf identity' is given high priority and discussion around the issue is incorporated into the curriculum. For primary aged children a half day a week is devoted to the 'bilingual programme' where issues of identity, deaf culture, regional signing and social skills form major elements. The sessions are planned and delivered by deaf instructors in BSL with no hearing teachers present.

Behaviour and social skills

From a consideration of personal attributes we turn towards the development of social skills, although for many people these are strongly linked – a positive sense of identity and high self-esteem are the basis for appropriate behaviour. As one secondary deputy headteacher (G) put it, 'There is an expectation that these young people will behave in the same way as any other, from the basis of self-esteem and confidence'. Another (P) said, 'We give them the confidence to act socially'. In other words, appropriate behaviour towards others is built on the bedrock of having a positive view of oneself.

Here are three examples of approaches to developing social skills, beginning with the very young.

> In the nursery M, at snacktime the children practise turn-taking skills in handing round milk and biscuits, expressing their thanks as they do. Parents send crisps and sweets to nursery for the children to share in a controlled setting. Good manners and socially acceptable behaviour are emphasised throughout.

> At the primary level, one deputy headteacher (P) was keen to stress that teachers led by example, for example saying 'Excuse me, please' to a child and in time expecting pupils to say the same back. In this way politeness is fostered.

> In P, a primary setting, an interesting example was given of settling a dispute. It is recorded here not only as a strategy, but also as an example of handling relations between deaf and hearing children in an integrated context. The deputy headteacher drew the example from an incident which involved an argument between deaf children who were integrating at the mainstream school next door and their hearing peers. She called for all the children involved in the argument to meet her and to sit down in a circle together. Then she encouraged each child to 'have their say'. All were encouraged to listen. She said that she adopted this approach for two reasons (i) so that the children could hear each others' views and know 'how each other felt' and (ii) to foster a recognition that it is possible to sit down 'and talk it through' – in other words that discussion is a useful way of solving disputes. From this all the children were encouraged to reinterpret the incident that had caused the upset. The hearing children were encouraged to understand that the deaf children didn't like being called 'deafies' and that when the deaf child had picked up a hat and had thrown it on the floor they were trying to initiate a game, however inappropriately. The deputy head also drew attention to the fact that these were useful instances of incidental deaf awareness to occur.
>
> (case study P).

An extension of this need for deaf children to learn to understand the point of view and needs of others is where they are encouraged to become involved in charity appeals. There were two examples of this.

In two schools (G and P), we were told that regular fundraising events for charities are held. In the first school, representatives of charities are invited in to explain how the money is spent. In the second school, projects are carefully chosen to provide a balance between local, national and international concerns 'and then think of ourselves at the end, as a little treat'. This year they have collected for Romanian orphanages, Children in Need and the local hospice. In this way 'the children know that there are so many children that are more disadvantaged'. The teachers explain the issues in class and then collections and other action is taken in the context of the assemblies. The head in G told us:

> Children like to feel that what they do is appreciated by people out there. It raises them from 'poor little deaf children'. It changes their attitude from 'I'm deaf' to 'I'm fine, I can do a lot to help other people'.

Communication: a social skill

Clearly there are many skills involved in being competent in conversation. This topic is addressed in more detail in section 4.7, but a few points are relevant here.

> In the daily group conversation sessions with the teacher in nursery M, the children are encouraged to share their news by turn and listen to other children's contributions. The teacher fosters an understanding within the children that conversation is a reciprocal event by asking the children: 'Is anyone going to ask me my news ?'

> From the primary day school P we learned that once the children had developed the confidence to include visitors in conversation and ask questions the next stage was to impress upon the children the appropriateness of a question:
>
>> We build up their confidence but then what we have to say is, 'Yes that's good but in this situation you do this and that's not appropriate in this situation'.

At secondary level such guidance becomes incorporated into work on socio-pragmatic skills, sometimes under the auspices of speech and language therapists. In service A, these skills form part of 'live English' sessions:

The use of drama

> Drama is seen as a vital element to education at school J. So high is its status in the life of the school and in the development of the pupils that its place on the timetable is safeguarded despite the fact that it is extra to the statutory curriculum. Staff believe drama to bring many benefits to deaf children including a potential for developing personal and social skills. The policy document states:
>
>> For the hearing impaired child at [name of school] drama plays an essential part in assisting the development of personal and social skills. All lessons are planned with the aim of building self confidence, self-assertion and self-esteem within the pupils, as well as helping them to work co-operatively within a group and consequently relating successfully with their peers.

Among the many skills mentioned, drama is seen as a means of developing skills of negotiation, cooperation and being able to express ideas. The benefits include receiving a wider outlook and perspective on life, enabling the ability to make choices, the development of empathy, the development of an awareness of the complexities of human emotions and appropriate associated vocabulary and meaningful interaction. The eventual aims are long term:

> ... we are aiming towards helping pupils develop personal and social skills which will enable them to live their lives in a way which is most satisfying for them and the people they come into contact with. They are developing the ability to take on a certain direction or course, or perform a certain action, knowing that for them personally it is the right one at that moment in time. They are learning to interact with people in a meaningful way...
>
> (school policy document).

Health and sex education

Although undoubtedly issues of health and sex education are major elements of all PSE programmes there was only one authority where these topics were specifically mentioned.

In service D, the general PSE policy was developed in response to the appreciation that deaf children in mainstream schools, though following the same PSE curriculum as their hearing peers, often receive an imperfect understanding of the subject. This may be partly due to the mode of delivery, which is often discussion, and due to the use of materials at an inappropriate level. The deaf signing teacher, after consultation with other professionals such as health education advisors, has worked in conjunction with a hearing teacher to research and develop a PSE programme which particularly aims to give deaf students the same access and understanding of personal safety and mental health as the hearing children. Also the views of parents have sometimes been actively sought for example to decide how to approach more 'difficult' issues, such as sexual development.

Pastoral care

Pastoral care is used here to describe care for students by staff in school and on the residential side. Clearly for all pupils it is important they feel they have someone who will listen and care. However, for those living away from home this is even more crucial. The discussion that follows comes from information collected in a number of residential settings about their approaches to pastoral care out of school and college.

In school C, residential staff work on a personal level and are called by their first names by pupils. The care office and duty room door is always open whatever the time. 'The duty room is like a debating chamber. We never dictate terms' (head of care staff). Pupils choose a member of care staff as a key worker to talk to if they are concerned about anything and a regular weekly slot is available for pupils to use if they wish. Conversations are treated as confidential unless there are legal implications. The school is a registered site for the *Rainbow Programme* for pupils suffering some form of loss and there are several qualified facilitators for this.

In school J, pastoral care is organised around a number of group leaders who stay with the same group of about eight youngsters for two to three years. The emphasis is on well-trained care staff who have many opportunities for continuing professional development. One group leader described the role as providing support and care without in any way replacing a parent figure. The relationship is perceived as being 'honest and open', instilling a confidence to talk, even about very personal issues.

In college L, although students are expected to take full responsibility for themselves, support and guidance is still offered where necessary. We were told that many students arrive in emotional turmoil with a need for intensive support both with communication and life skills. A care officer is assigned to each student on entry to college and an independent deaf counselling consultant is available for students who need this service.

Trips and activities

As well as a chance for firsthand experience and language development, trips and activities frequently provide opportunities for developing social skills in interaction with peers and members of the public as well as the development of organisational skills. Other aspects of PSE can also be addressed. Here is the approach taken by one residential school.

In school J, a wide range of activities and facilities is available. Some of these are on-campus: orchestra, drama club, swimming, table-tennis, pool, football etc. and more besides. By the time the youngsters are in Year eight, they are very much encouraged to go off-campus to join in clubs and activities in the local town, for example, youth clubs, sea cadets, scouts, swimming club, dance club, trampoline club, line-dancing, golf, weight training and football training. The staff have detailed knowledge about the social and recreational facilities within the local area. For the future, there are plans to develop the school's facilities – particularly the sports hall, outdoor sports facilities and performing arts centre – and extend them to young people in the local community.

The activities programme has several aims including, to facilitate and develop a broad range of interests and so educate the 'whole' child; to develop individual interests; to encourage multiple definitions of self; to develop social and teamwork skills; and to develop self confidence arising out of a sense of achievement. The 'outside' activities and clubs programme has the additional aim of promoting social confidence with hearing young people and integration into the hearing group.

Summary

Deaf pupils' personal and social development emerged as a major concern both in the questionnaires and in the case studies. We came across many schools and services where careful thought had been given to this.

Key findings in this section are summarised as follows:

- Concern with the personal and social development of deaf children is much in evidence with particular attention given to developing high self-esteem, independence, a positive sense of identity and appropriate social skills.

- Many see a strong link between the development of personal and social skills and academic achievement.

- Deaf adults and deaf peers play key roles in a range of contexts.

- Identity is a complex issue for deaf young people, families and educators.

4.10 Deaf children with disabilities

In seeking models of good practice for deaf children who have disabilities, one of the major challenges is a clear definition of what is meant and understood by this term. In a similar way to the discussions regarding medical and social models of deafness, there are medical, social and educational models of what may be considered to constitute a disability. In addition, the emphasis placed on the deafness affects service and school perceptions of the constitution of this group. The lack of agreement over terminology has implications for access to specialist services and for the development of expertise in this area.

Several schools and services were identified as displaying good practice with this group of children and young people. In visiting and recording such provision, it is apparent that many aspects of good practice identified by practitioners and parents as beneficial for deaf children and young people within the study, were mirrored in this specialist area. The statement that, 'Definitions typically reflect the current sociocultural standards of a given society, and are subject to constant change,' Shroyer (1982 p3)[1] underlines the difficulty in establishing a common base to compare and contrast models of practice.

Family perspectives

For all deaf children and young people the importance of meeting individual learning needs is clearly identified as a key feature of good practice. The availability of specialist support is highly valued by the families and carers of this group of learners.

> It was very hard because S was so poorly. She had a brain haemorrhage. She was so fragile I used to carry her all the time wearing a heart monitor. She had a tracheotomy tube. Any sudden movement she would stop breathing so I had to learn to resuscitate her. Because of all this she wasn't diagnosed [as deaf] until she was 3 years old. It was a shock, despair crept in, then A [the ToD] arrived. She was so full of confidence and gave me the courage to carry on'
>
> (parent, case study F).

The need for interdisciplinary working in such cases is clear but management of such a team can be problematic. Parents can feel overwhelmed and deskilled.

> 'When someone comes into your house, you welcome them, you expect some interest or follow up. The ToD would phone to check how things were going. She always made time to chat. We have had a number of life threatening situations

---

[1] Shroyer, E. (1982) Introduction, In D. Tweedie, E. Shroyer (eds). *The multi handicapped hearing impaired.* Washington DC: Gallaudet College Press.

with J. T [the ToD] was sensitive to the whole family. She has enormous confidence in J and so do we, even though things are going to be hard for the future. The others never even phoned to see if J was alright – we are just another "case" to them'

(parent, case study F).

Assessment

In services and schools where speech and language therapists (SLTs) were an integral part of the team, there was joint assessment and joint planning which was felt to be beneficial. In such cases, SLTs had had specialist training to work with deaf children. The advantage of this was reported to be 'shared language, common understanding and respect for each others specialism' (case study B). There was no evidence of the availability of multidisciplinary teams to assess and plan appropriate individualised programmes for deaf children with disabilities. Specific areas that were identified as inhibiting the possibility of holistic assessments were the lack of occupational and physiotherapists, specialist speech and language therapists, and educational psychologists who had specialist training in working with deaf children. In addition, the lack of routine visual assessment that goes beyond measurements of acuity was cited as problematic. ToDs were, in many cases, unclear of the exact nature of specialist support that the profession had to offer those with severe or profound learning disability. Many cited the provision of extra support or amount of support equal to that provided to other hearing impaired children, but the detail of the nature of such support remains unclear.

Whilst published assessments have a clear part to play, professional expertise is also an important feature of such assessments. The initial assessment of two to three days residential on-campus allows an in-depth look at skills. The assessment includes Non-Verbal Reasoning Test (Nelson/NFER), a communication strategies assessment, an assessment of sign language skills, the NATED assessment pack pro-forma and life skills in the residential setting (case study L). The Award Scheme Development and Accreditation Network, ASDAN, allows Care workers to set their own challenges for individual students rather than being prescriptive. This allows differentiation of tasks to suit individual students. The aim of each section is broken down into a set of personal objectives that can be negotiated with individual students as appropriate.

The academic and residential aspects were formerly separate, but we are very keen to work together, to promote a totally inclusive approach.

(case study L).

Support

The availability of support from a ToD for children who have disabilities is largely a matter of chance. Individual services have specific policies which may include all children with a degree of hearing loss or may concentrate on those where hearing loss is felt to be a central feature of a child's identified learning needs.

> The level of support offered to pupils with disabilities who have a degree of hearing loss is the same as that offered to any other hearing impaired child. ToDs support such pupils in mainstream and special schools.
>
> (case study K).

> The amount of support is needs-led rather than financially determined and the authority is in favour of inclusion. A request for 25 hours of auxiliary support was granted for C, a six year old boy with a moderate hearing loss, who also has cerebral palsy/hemiplegia and for whom the service considered a special school provision was inappropriate.
>
> (case study H).

> The challenge is to first sensitively assess those additional learning needs. This is a complex area. The compounding of needs make unpicking the specific areas for support challenging. Pupils with additional learning needs are identified through a range of assessments, although experience is also felt to play a large part.
>
> (case study C).

Specific needs

There is clear evidence that some very specific learning needs which may have been recognised informally by practising ToDs are now being identified and programmes are being devised to meet such needs. The specific areas identified have moved beyond the broad medical categories to educational areas. Special learning needs identified included:

- wordfinding and memory problems, central auditory processing disorder (case study E)

- mild learning disability, emotional and behavioural difficulties and dyspraxia (case study J)

- mild intellectual disabilities, Asperger's syndrome, mild to moderate physical disabilities, dual sensory impairment (case study L)

- poor auditory memory, mild dyspraxia, language integration difficulties, 'clumsy' speech, poor sequential memory and specific learning disability (dyslexia) (case study C).

Schools and services all felt that small group work and one-to-one tuition was important for deaf children with disabilities. 'All progress, however small, is recorded, expectations for all learners were high but realistic' (case study L). For children who have severe and profound learning disabilities the task can be more challenging. A recognition of the many specialist skills held by ToDs can enhance the approach to this group of learners. Such knowledge includes the development of pre-verbal communication, and play as well as the development of language, room acoustics and sensitive audiological management. The need to enhance learning and to further develop skills in areas such as fine and gross motor development, feeding skills, visual skills and alternative and augmentative communication options are important and recognised by services seeking additional training for their staff.

Services and schools identified as displaying good practice employed a variety of approaches to achieve effective support. These included provision of physical support and access, for example laptop computers, guidelines and controllable lighting for those with Usher's syndrome; LSA support; and in one case (L) a student with Usher's syndrome had been provided with relay sign support. In this case, the individual required sign interpretation, but was unable to understand the hearing interpreter. This was despite the fact that the interpreter has a good level of sign competence. The introduction of a deaf interpreter allowed access as this interpreter could be in close proximity to the student in a visually undemanding situation. The hearing interpreter stood near enough to the speaker to hear the lecture and relay the message to the deaf instructor who could then provide sign in very close proximity to allow access for the visually impaired deaf student. This is illustrated in the diagram below:

Lecturer ➤ **Hearing Interpreter** ➤ **Deaf Communicator** ➤ **Student**

speech near enough to hear | BSL | BSL near enough to be seen | reception

An approach adopted with secondary and FE students was to identify programmes that were felt to provide detailed and achievable objectives that enabled students to improve basic skills. The RSA certificate – National Lifeskills Profile and the Social Use of Language Programme – was used by case study X.

Summary

Schools and services gave individual examples of good practice. The specific group that was felt to be particularly challenging provision was the group of deaf children who have social and emotional difficulties. Only one case study directly referred to the needs of children with severe learning disabilities. This was surprising in view of the evidence of high incidence of hearing loss amongst this group (Yeates, 1995)[2]. The need to identify the detail of individual programmes, the lack of specific approach to the audiological needs of children with Down's syndrome together with the need for further training for ToDs clearly emerged during this review. In some services children received support if deafness was felt to be the main focus of need.

In view of the recognition of the compounding effect of deafness when it occurs with disabilities (Moores,1996)[3], it is hard to see where a child with disabilities can have those easily disentangled from the effects of hearing loss. The low incidence of hearing impairment together with the highly specialised training of ToDs suggest that one reasonable approach would be to ensure that at least one member of staff had specialist training and that other co-professionals have some specialist training in the needs of deaf children. In addition, close working between education, health and social service providers will be essential.

Key findings in this section are summarised as follows:

- A key worker is needed to coordinate services for deaf children with disabilities.
- Assessments should focus on the whole child and inform intervention.
- Very small steps in learning need to be recorded and built upon.
- Teachers and other professionals should have expectations which do not underestimate the child.
- All children with a degree of hearing loss which has implications for learning are entitled to sensitive support from a teacher of the deaf.

---

[2] Yeates, S. (1995) The incidence and importance of hearing loss in people with severe learning disability: the evolution of a service. *British Journal of Learning Disabilities,* 23, 79-84.

[3] Moores, D.F. (1996) *Educating the deaf: psychology, principles and practices.* Boston, Mass: Houghton Mifflin.

4.11 Work with families and young children

For many services, work with families by teachers of the deaf is recognised as a crucial element in their provision. As the policy and procedures of case study A states, 'The family is the most important and influential resource the child has. The more effective that family support is, the more beneficial it will be to the child'.

Information was gathered about working with families from a number of case studies. Eight of these were services and one was a nursery. Most also yielded valuable information about working with the very young. In addition, a primary day school for deaf children with a preschool support group was observed. Due to so many parents being interviewed, many useful insights were gained into the effectiveness of the work of the done. However, we were aware that at this vulnerable time, parents may be appreciative of intervention that later they may question. We also wanted to focus on good practice rather than the usual practice of most work with families. Thus we include here descriptions of more unusual features, examples of exceptionally good practice and the perceptions of parents about 'what worked for them'.

Work with very young children

The diagnosis

The period of time around the diagnosis of a child's deafness is seen as critical in working with families. In particular, early diagnosis is emphasised by some services as an important aspect of their provision.

> In one area visited (H), the service has come to expect all congenital severe and profound deafness to be identified by nine months with a diagnosis at eleven months being considered to be 'late'. The HoS, who is also the audiologist, meets with the ENT specialist and audiological scientist at the hospital once a week while the diagnostic clinics are in session. He is notified of cases which are not 'just glue ear' and is able to talk to parents as testing progresses. If there is a significant loss and amplification is needed, an immediate link with the service is formed through the HoS.

> In another case (K), the educational audiologist or a senior member of staff attends all diagnostic clinics. From the point of diagnosis the Service for the Hearing Impaired takes over management of the child. This policy has been agreed with health and the audiologist prescribes the hearing aids which are then purchased by health.

> Hearing impaired children are referred to the service at the moment of diagnosis. A member of staff of the service is present at the Hearing Clinic when the diagnosis is confirmed to the parents so that counselling and guidance can begin immediately. The age of diagnosis is now usually very early and the children can be diagnosed before they are one month old.
>
> (service handbook).

Neo-natal screening is available for at-risk children, but not yet routinely available for all babies. One parent described her experience of early diagnosis:

> Because my elder son was diagnosed at 5 months my second son was checked at 11 hours. Although it was still too early to confirm diagnosis, hearing aids were ordered and he was checked again at 6 weeks. He had his hearing aids at 7 weeks. At that time he was the youngest in the county.
>
> (parent, case study K).

The early diagnosis of hearing loss is generally regarded as an advantage and the introduction of neo-natal screening should be welcomed. However, for maximum benefits, a fast and reliable link must exist between health and education services.

Teachers of the deaf in different areas are very aware of the impact of late diagnosis and are frustrated by it. One teacher in H summed up the effect like this:

> Late diagnosis means lots of pressure because you're trying to get all of this information over which normally would have trickled over six months before the child becomes the focus... you're doing the same thing but can take it slower [i.e. when the child is diagnosed early].
>
> (ToD case study H).

Early visits

During the studies that we made many parents described their feelings at the news of their child's deafness. Many did not know what deafness would mean for the child's future life and many felt they did not know how to deal with the situation. The positive effect of the first visits by teachers of the deaf was reported by these parents. It was clear that these early visits were very important.

> It's quite devastating and you don't know where to turn. Without that we would have been just muddling through.

> You feel like giving up. She helped me through the bad times... I was lost for a long time. The teacher spent a lot of time letting me cry and just being there talking with me.
>
> It was a shock. Despair crept in. Then A [the ToD] arrived – full of confidence and gave me the courage to go on.
>
> [the ToD] was brilliant. You need the one person. She had been there before. It was lovely to speak to someone who understood. It wasn't just us affected – grandparents were affected and tried to be positive. It was an emotional time for us all. [the ToD] was a stranger which was quite nice. She was positive where we were very negative, thinking C would never speak, never get married... Everything was positive, whereas we were very negative and we needed that.
>
> G was diagnosed at the hospital at 2 pm. We got home at 4pm. By 5pm the ToD had phoned and came round that night and stayed all evening. We were incredibly tearful. He turned it round.
>
> (various case studies).

Phrases such as, 'being thrown a lifejacket', 'a weight lifted from our shoulders' and there was 'hope at the end of the tunnel' were frequently used to express the benefits of those initial visits.

Once a child has been diagnosed as having a significant loss, the child is assigned to a teacher's caseload. The aim then is to visit families as soon as possible. For at least one service (E) this means 'within the week' and is written into the proposed new working document. We were told of at least two services (B and E) which have 'on call' systems during the holidays, thereby enabling immediate support for families beyond term time. In another example (K), the service has a Quality Standard which states that a ToD will visit or contact the family by telephone within 48 hours of diagnosis. Good practice in that service was characterised by extension of support to as many relevant members of the family as possible, including grandparents. Evening visits are scheduled if necessary so that fathers can be there too.

For service D, care is taken by preschool support teachers from diagnosis onwards to be positive to parents about the potential and actual achievements of the child, but to emphasise that the child will always be deaf and will grow to be a deaf adult. There is a perceived need to 'break through' the medical model of disability and be quite clear that however good the quality of support or the hearing aids nothing will 'cure' the deafness.

Another team, A, presenting a similarly positive attitude to deafness recognise that there is an inherent tension for parents to which they must be sensitive:

> I think this can be an issue for parents because we give the impression of being really positive and sorted on deafness, and it's not a tragedy or disaster. That can be a problem if you're not careful, and I am not saying it is but we have to be conscious of it. It can de-skill parents because their feeling is that it's just the most awful thing that has happened. And they feel you get these really nice confident reassuring people who can do things you can't imagine yourself doing. And although we do it with the best of intentions, we must remind ourselves that if we were in that position and did not have the background we have working here, how would we feel?
>
> (HoS case study A).

Part of the role of the ToD at this time is to reassure and to stress potentially positive outcomes for the child. Several parents remembered the videos of deaf adults and children that the ToDs brought at this time to encourage them to see the progress that can be made. One parent (case study H) commented, 'To watch videos of teenagers who had good speech was brilliant.' Another said, ''It gave us a long term look. At first we thought it was kind of dire, but when you see adults it's not so bad' (case study E).

Telephone numbers are often exchanged so that parents requiring extra assistance can call a ToD at home. In some services this also applies to holiday periods. This continuous accessibility was particularly appreciated by many parents. One mother reported of this phase, 'She was always at the end of the phone'. A mother supported by the same service said that the greatest strength of the service was, 'The ease of getting hold of somebody. Right from the very first appointment I never had to look for someone. All the information was there... The ease with getting things done' (case study E).

Good practice during this phase appears to be characterised by an immediate home visit post-diagnosis, involvement of extended family, understanding of parents' feelings, sensitivity to parents' feelings, a confident and positive message and accessibility.

Continuing preschool support at home

After the initial period when, for one service (K) as many as two or three visits in a week may be made, a pattern of regular support is established. The same service sets out its objectives for regular home visits as 'to help and guide families, work with the children, assess linguistic development and carry out vital audiological management. At this early time, parents are counselled on a wide range of issues' (service handbook).

At this early stage, imparting relevant information at an appropriate pace was particularly appreciated. One mother said, 'Things were allowed to go with me, at my pace' while another explained, 'S [the ToD] brought videos and things, not in your face straightaway, only if you wanted to look at this or read this material'. Another said, ' I was drip fed with information slowly over the months. This was helpful.' Information typically centres around an explanation of the child's hearing loss, its implications and language development.

One service (F) in particular is compiling a resource bank of information leaflets for parents. Parents will have a loose-leaf folder to which information sheets will be added gradually. Leaflets will cover information relating to type of hearing loss, conversation, language, hearing aids and how to check personal FM systems. Each child's file will have a checklist so that dates can be recorded when sheets are added. Such a system seems appropriate in the light of parents' expressed appreciation of gradual dissemination of knowledge.

Parents seemed to be at their most confident when they felt that they were receiving consistent advice or instruction:

> If she [the ToD] tells me to do something then I know that she's asking me for a good reason and I'll try and try again.
>
> (case study F).

> It's also really good to have consistent advice rather than contradictions. Everyone I have met has given me similar advice, sung the same type of tune ... It makes you feel confident that they know what they are doing.
>
> (case study B).

These statements and others like them raise an interesting issue. The sense behind them is that these services have clear policies and philosophies which are upheld by members of the team. Indeed this is the case, particularly in relation to communication approach. However, it was not the case that parents only receive information about one particular communication approach. In fact, typically parents insisted that nothing was 'forced upon' them. However, strong beliefs about 'the best route' for a child's communication are held by these services and once parents have accepted that way for their child then specific guidance on the way to achieve this is given. To follow such an unequivocal route seems to give parents confidence and security, at least at this stage. However, this raises the issue of the relative merits of the 'consumer' model against the 'expert model'[1] and this will be returned to later in the discussion.

For some services, the concept of the empowerment of parents is an important one.

> A lot of the work is in empowering parents, facilitating their communication with their child all the time. It's difficult to do without being patronising. I don't know how I'd feel if people told me how to talk to my children.
>
> (case study H).

---

[1] Cunningham, C., Davis, H. (1985) *Working with parents: frameworks for collaboration.* Milton Keynes: OUP.

However, perhaps there is a less cause for concern by ToDs since as one parent supported by service D said :

> They're all very on the ball on how to put things without giving offence, and repeating it over and over when you forget or get it wrong.

Parents also spoke of the way that ToDs enable them to look for signs of progress in their child:

> The ToD taught me to look for little steps, small changes. She took lots and lots of video and it was really helpful. Both me and my husband played with her. She pointed out what was going on – not in a patronising way, just so we understood. It was really helpful to be able to watch it again and see other things for yourself too.
>
> M could pick out things I didn't see at all...then later I could see it. There were changes, progress but I needed M to point that out to me.
>
> (case studies B and F).

The use of videoing to monitor and demonstrate progress was mentioned in a number of places. Particularly useful to one service (F) was the availability of a technician to edit material.

In one authority (E) the ToDs accompany parents and their children on the first appointments for moulds and hearing aid fittings and in some cases for later assessments. The parents we spoke to viewed this positively. Great emphasis is placed in this service on 'getting the hearing aids right'. One teacher was particularly helpful in effecting a hearing aid change by making a strong case when it was needed. In another service, B, the ToD clearly suspected that the hearing aids were unsuitable for the child. The mother said, 'She kept details of everything and eventually after a year we got new aids. There was a noticeable difference straight away'. There is a clear implication here of a ToDs strong grounding in audiology. In both the services mentioned above, a number of ToDs have additional qualifications in audiology.

Early support in a sign bilingual setting

The early support in case study A, where there is a sign bilingual approach, is in some respects different from the other cases so far discussed. As soon as possible after diagnosis the family is visited by a support teacher. The aim is to provide a range of provision during this time to meet the individual needs of children and families.

The team does not feel it is possible at the very early stage to be sure about a child's likely preferred language. Sign language is presented as a positive option, but it is also recognised that spoken English maybe the preferred language. The implications of language choice are discussed with the parents at this stage.

The resources available for early support are:

- home visits by support teachers or deaf instructor
- sign language classes in the home for immediate and extended family, and friends (six weeks during the evening)
- family support group
- BSL playgroup which encourages development of BSL in playgroup setting
- developing English group where staff and parents work with children encouraging spoken English
- an Asian mothers support group

Home visits are carried out by a teacher of the deaf or a deaf instructor and take place either where a family does not attend any of the existing facilities, or when an issue arises for a family that is not easily dealt with within the context of a meeting.

Sign language courses are offered by the deaf instructor linked to the preschool programme. They take place at the family's request in the family's own homes. Although the focus is sign language, they often have a double function of introducing a deaf role model into the home who will discuss general deaf issues. Parents comment that this often helps them in trying to communicate with their friends and family about the implications of deafness.

A family support group is held once a week (described in the next section). At the same location a BSL playgroup takes place on a weekly basis. Here children play with deaf instructors in order to develop their BSL skills in a play environment. Parents can observe for the first half hour after which they meet together socially and can discuss any issues with the ToD.

There is a also a 'developing English' group which any parent and child can attend, the focus of which is developing children's English language skills. Children are encouraged to use their residual hearing and to develop listening skills. Parents are encouraged to join the group and develop their own interactive skills.

(case study A).

Parent support groups

The benefits which parents of deaf children derive from being with each other is appreciated and provided for in some services in the shape of the parent support groups. These groups are variously named across the country, for example Parent Support Group (B), Parent and toddler Group (K), and Family Support Group (A). Some are held during the day (B, K, A, P) some in the evening (M, H); some are held on a weekly basis (B, K, A, P), others less frequently.

Several parents spoke of their initial nervousness to meet other parents with deaf children. One backed out on the day of her first visit to the group because she was too upset by the thought of meeting a deaf person. Some expressed an inability to attend because they were in too much pain generally about their own child.

For those who do attend these groups the provision of transport, sometimes by the authority (K), and the extension of the invitation to siblings and other family members must be seen as positive features.

Although these groups have different management styles and approaches, they have a number of features in common. The major common feature between them all is the provision of an opportunity for parents to meet and share common experiences. The benefits of this were well documented by parents from different authorities.

> I go to the meetings religiously. With the other mums we have a good moan and a good laugh. We are all at different stages or ages; it gives you an idea of what you are heading for. L's mum had gone through all the same problems as I had with E. It's so good to feel you're not on your own out there.
>
> It takes about a week for you to come to the end of your tether. Then I think 'Oh thank goodness there's a meeting tomorrow'.
>
> If I didn't come here I would not know what to do.
>
> You talk to someone else at this group and they laugh about it because their child is past that and you know you'll be laughing eventually. It helps.
>
> (parents from various case studies).

Crèche facilities in one service (K) enable parents to talk more freely to one another. Tea and coffee are often provided, sometimes leaflets and books are available for people to take away.

In some cases (K and A), the technician or teacher of the deaf takes the opportunity to test the children's hearing aids, including through the testbox. Other audiological needs and queries can be met.

Members of the team – ToDs, deaf instructors – are on hand to answer questions and to give advice as required. The parents find this very helpful.

> There is so much information. We have had lots of people. They all simply say if you've got a problem bring it here. You can ask for anything – they are a source for so much. There is so much care; I am surrounded by this network. I am almost overwhelmed by how much all these people care for my little boy.
>
> (case study K).

Another key feature of some of the support groups is a programme of speakers and events. This programme is arranged in order that parents may be better informed about the implications of their child's deafness. The rationale for this approach was detailed by a service team leader (B), 'If you can help parents to feel relaxed, show them good practice and encourage them to get information for themselves you are half way there'.

An example of one such programme is described below from a service (B) where parents meet on a weekly basis.

> Parents have both formal and informal meetings, they attend workshops, discussion groups, share questions and offer mutual support. A termly programme is organised by the team leaders, mixing formal talks with a range of other activities. On the day of our visit parents were being asked to plan out and make resources for the next 'story bag' – 'Thomas the Tank Engine'. All the mums were gently encouraged to join in. One brought a sewing machine. Other resources were supplied by the team leader. Parents made the bag, finished games and planned other activities including songs that might be suitable to sing.
>
> (case study B).

In the primary day school for deaf children (P), a weekly session is held for preschool children and their parents. The prime function of the group appears to be for parents, grandparents and carers to meet and discuss. However, there is also an activity session for the children. On the day of the visit this was given over to the development of listening skills. Everyone was fully involved and encouraged to play with the children themselves. Activities were suggested which could be used at home.

Another specific example of such a group is that of case study H. This has a slightly different management style and ethos:

> There is a 'Parents in Partnership' group in the authority which meets a few times a year to discuss particular topics usually with the contribution of an outside speaker. The last meeting consisted of a speaker from the hospital on the subject of technical aids and two social workers for the deaf explained their role. The aim is partly to inform, but also an opportunity for parents to mix socially. The service helped set it up but parents now run it. Two ToDs are on the committee. Parents of

younger children are the most involved. One ToD suggested that one important purpose of the group is to further encourage all parents to feel fully involved in their child's education, not to leave it just to the 'experts', to reinforce the message that parents have control.

(case study H).

The evidence from the case studies is that parent support groups are important for families. The key to a successful group is arguably a balance between time to socialise and an opportunity to learn, and involving parents in the organisation and running of the group.

Other parent support links

As well as encouraging parents to attend the parent support meeting there was considerable report of the encouragement which parents were given to get in contact with other groups, particularly DELTA and the NDCS. One parent spoke of the difference such a group had made – 'My wife has been very depressed. DELTA gave her a chance to meet other people who knew exactly what she was going through.' In case study Q, a parent had been active in setting up a local branch of the NDCS. She saw part of her role as raising the awareness of the council in relation to their responsibility with deaf children. By this she believed that they had achieved a lot. In one instance by their 'vociferousness' they had been able to effect changes to the council's plans to decentralise the service and integrate more deaf children into local schools.

One service (H) circulates a newsletter to parents to keep them up to date with developments. It includes items on individual children. In the north of the same county there is a group for local parents which goes out for a meal a few times a year.

Working with school aged children and their parents

Choosing schools

Parents spoke of teachers' help in choosing schools and nurseries for their children. Characteristically, teachers will accompany parents to schools in which they are particularly interested. In some cases they will suggest to parents what to look out for and some questions which they might like to ask. Acoustics are often high on the priority list for consideration. For choice of school at secondary level, at least one service (E) had produced a handout to focus parents' thoughts on the suitability of the school for a child with special needs. It encourages parents to ask themselves (and others) a series of questions, for example 'Who will provide listening checks for hearing aids/radio aids in school and how will equipment failures be dealt with?' and 'Who should we go to with information or questions and who will deal with any problems?'

Although parents reported that in some authorities teachers would give an opinion as to which school they thought would be best for a child they never felt coerced into agreeing. At the end of the day it was their choice. One service (H), describing this process, uses phrases such as 'in full consultation' with parents while another (K) maintains a stance of 'respecting parents' wishes'.

Clearly this raises again the issue of the 'consumer' versus the 'expert' model (Cunningham, Davis, 1985 op cit). Many services around the country would not endorse a policy of giving advice in this situation, but rather assisting a parent to come to a decision with which they felt comfortable. Nevertheless, in several of these cases where 'work with parents' had been strongly nominated, parents appeared to feel more comfortable to receive direct advice.

Children coming into nurseries or schools for deaf children are invited to come in for days with their parents prior to school entry. At the nursery (case study M), parents are invited to listen to a hearing aid through a stetoclip and learn general maintenance techniques if they are unfamiliar to them. Thereafter, parents are always welcome to spend time in the nursery, experiencing and helping with the education of their child.

Continuing support

Once the child is at school or nursery, parents continue to be supported in well-established ways – by phone calls, notes in home-school notebooks and home visits. Some uses that we saw and heard about are worth recording and they appear below. In these examples it will be noted that many centre around the further development of language.

> The school and the peri coordinate the interaction between school and home. The basis of good practice is good communication. I get lots of feedback, both in person and through the home-school book. The home-school book allows me to take opportunities for language extension but also just to know what he's been up to all day.
>
> (parent case study B).

In case study M, notable achievements in a child's language and speech are recorded in the home-school book by teachers and parents for the children who attend the nursery. One entry in a home-school book read ' K said "thank you" very clearly today'. The mutual exchange of observations on language progress is helpful both to parents and teachers. Teachers also use the book to encourage parents to reinforce language introduced at school. For instance, a teacher wrote, 'We looked at square and circle things today. Perhaps you could point out to G some of the square and round things at home.' In addition, families are encouraged to make scrapbooks of their holidays and trips. These might simply consist of tickets and postcards but nevertheless form a valuable basis for discussion with the child. After Christmas and birthdays children are encouraged to cut out and stick pictures of their presents from catalogues for the same purpose. One service (K) has provided a Polaroid camera to a child to further facilitate dialogue between home and school.

One parent in case study E spoke of a ToD conveying similar observations about her child but by telephone, 'Sometimes she'll ring up after a visit (to school) and say, "Did you notice that X is doing that?" '

Some teachers continue to make home visits, often making themselves available both inside and out side working hours. One teacher of the deaf said:

> I have a system of visiting in holidays and evenings. Really this is essential if you are supporting a family. The head of service is sympathetic and knows that I have a family too, so it works both ways.
>
> (case study B).

In the same service one teacher said that she aimed to see all the parents of children on her main caseload once a week, often at the beginning or end of the day. If the child lives at a distance, a monthly visit is feasible. The teacher will make an appointment and make it clear what she intends the visit to be about. In addition, parents will have their own queries and concerns. These visits are seen to be highly important and useful for the insights they bring. The aim is to involve the whole family in the development of the child.

In another instance (K), the ToD, having planned the work with the classteacher, visits parents to go through the work to be covered in the next two weeks so that support can be given at home.

For case study H, decisions as to frequency with which family members would like to meet the ToD and location for the meetings rest with the parents.

> One family had chosen to meet the ToD in school for 45 minutes a week on a Monday afternoon. Dad would attend with mum if he was not on day shift. Such meetings centre around the IEP and the plan for the week. The parents have a diary where they note items such as words and topics. This enables them to introduce topic work and vocabulary at home if the child is happy to do it. This ToD also gives the parents copies of videos three or four times a year which document the child's progress. These parents were very clear as a result of such discussions about many different aspects of their child's education.
>
> (case study H).

Another example of support is included here to demonstrate a number of aspects all present in one case:

> In M's case the ToD said she makes a home visit at least every half term but also often gets telephone calls from mum at home. This ToD has initiated a scrapbook to provide a link between home and school. Mum is thereby able to continue the activities done in school. Mum also gets a copy of the IEP; she is in fact involved in compiling this. The final IEP is discussed with mum and she is shown how she can support the work done in school, for example regarding the target of recognising the written form of family names, she provided photos and played a game of family lotto at home. Also, in an attempt to encourage M to apply skills in different settings, Mum will continue activities done in school. Mum also brings the weekend news into school every Monday; M himself can't tell people, 'Parents have to be involved in every single thing [at this stage]'.
>
> (M's ToD, case study H).

Another aspect of the continuing support which ToDs offer is in the role of advocate. One parent expressed the importance of professionals who, 'Really understand deaf children and fight for the best service for your child'. When problems arise in school, for example when a mainstream teacher is known not to be wearing the radio aid transmitter, parents are grateful for ToDs' interventions, 'They will fight the battles if parents can't or won't'. Another example of this kind might be helping a non-English speaking parent to have a textphone installed and to obtain access to other speakers of her own language (D). In one authority (K), if deaf children want to join the Cubs or Scouts or Tumble Tots the ToDs will go and meet the leaders and talk to them. One ToD (H) had offered to attend swimming lessons out of school time with a child.

It is worth considering here that in some of these outstanding cases of support for parents, the ToDs involved have relatively few children on their caseloads. In two cases quoted above, members of the service are concerned about oversupporting the pupils rather than undersupporting them. The implication of aiming to see all the parents of children on one's main caseload once a week (see above) must be that one has around 10 children on a main caseload. This raises issues around the management of caseloads and how caseloads are kept within reasonable proportions.

Parents, IEPs and Annual Reviews

Good practice is characterised in these case studies by involvement with parents in the creation of the IEP. This is happening on a termly basis. In practice this appears to mean that parents receive a draft and have an opportunity to discuss it with the ToD and to make amendments based on discussion. In some cases they are also asked to write a statement to reflect their perceptions of the progress of their child.

Team members were invited to attend one termly review whilst engaging in case study B and it is described below.

Both parents were invited, but only the mother was able to attend. The mother appeared to be at ease in the resource base and had brought a prepared sheet with her to discuss with the ToDs. Her secondary aged daughter did not attend the review, but had previously recorded her contribution on video. Her parents had been provided with a copy of the video two weeks before the review. Initially the mother expressed her concerns about her daughter's lack of friends, the amount of time spent working in the evenings and attending speech and language therapy in the holidays. The teachers, who clearly have a long-established relationship with this parent, listened and negotiated on the points she raised. The teachers have a clear view on what is needed for success but were prepared to consider alternatives, 'I'm taking in what you're saying... We've always been flexible, all of us, all the time... I know, we're piling things on'. The advice that was given, however was clear-cut, for example that 'notes must be read after homework is completed, leave the homework if the child is too exhausted and stop the child from de-voicing'. The mother was advised that 'closing the language gap' should be a long-term target rather than a termly one. She was advised to, 'Give her a bit of a break ... don't take it all too seriously'. At the end of the meeting the mother's accolade was, 'I didn't imagine A would cope as well as she has done and it's all down to your support'.

(case study B).

There seem to be a number of elements within this description which could be held up as good practice, including the parent's preparation for the meeting in the form of a prepared sheet and the video recording given to parents in good time on which comments can be based. The mother was very positive about the benefits of using the video, 'She was so relaxed, able to concentrate for all that time on conversation. It was really thrilling for me to see it'.

Summary

Teachers of the deaf are very clear about the importance of their work with parents and the benefit that families derive from the earliest days by the support of the ToD is clear from their comments.

Key findings in this section are summarised as follows:

* Many services we visited stress the need for very early visiting after diagnosis with a target time written into policy.

- Regular support and advice during preschool years with provision for school holidays is seen as vital.

- Schools and services should make a number of resources and opportunities available to parents including the opportunity for visits, information packs, parent groups, signing classes, audiological support and links with national organisations.

- There should be a continuing partnership between schools and services and families during the school years.

- Good practice is also characterised by the constructive use of Individual Education Plans (IEPs), annual reviews and advice on provision in working with parents.

4.12 Work with children and families from minority ethnic backgrounds

Work with pupils and families from minority ethnic backgrounds was explored mainly in two case studies, A and Q. In both areas, there was a significant percentage of pupils from minority ethnic backgrounds. In one instance this accounted for approximately 75% of hearing impaired pupils. In both cases it was seen as essential to make some special arrangements in order adequately to cater for these groups of pupils and their families. While other areas might not regard it as appropriate to make such distinct arrangements, aspects of this provision would translate into other settings.

Several of the case studies were in areas where there were very few pupils in the school population from minority ethnic backgrounds and therefore, had either no pupils or very few pupils from minority ethnic backgrounds. Some examples of work with individual pupils was observed in other case studies apart from the two main ones.

Support for families

Support was offered to families from minority ethnic backgrounds which was additional to that offered to other families. There was a group which met regularly to offer support and signing skills predominantly to mothers in both areas, and in one there was also an English class. Similar issues arose from both settings.

Contact with families

It was necessary to make very regular contact with families. There were different ways of achieving this.

> The development worker telephones each family on Sunday evenings as the meetings are held on Monday mornings. She checks whether there are any problems and whether the mother will be attending the group the following day.
>
> (case study Q).

> The support worker spends the first part of the morning phoning round to all the families to find out whether anyone is coming to the group.
>
> (case study A).

This also afforded an opportunity to pick up any concerns from the family. There was a feeling that such concerns needed to be dealt with quickly in order to ensure that the family continued to have confidence in the support workers and the service.

Transport

It was considered essential to provide transport to enable families, particularly mothers, to attend the group. The women are often closely supervised, going out very little unless escorted by their husbands. One HoS says they soon realised that if any groups were to succeed they would have to provide transport as husbands and fathers would only allow wives and daughters to attend if convinced that they would be taken directly to the centre and home again. Other groups had failed in the past, possibly because they had not addressed this issue. Funding was obtained to finance this transport.

Signing

Part of the function of the groups was to teach the mothers to sign in order to communicate with their children. In both instances the nature of the signing tuition offered was not formally structured and the emphasis was on communication. This was seen as a strength rather than a weakness.

> One lesson observed arose from a request from the group, all of whom were Muslim, that they learn signs in order to teach their children about Islam. This was a major concern with the group in general and there was a feeling that not enough was done in school to support them in this very important part of their culture. The deaf person running the group had read up on the topic and introduced some language they would need to talk about the books of the Quran. There were a number of discussions such as whether Jesus was a prophet, and the relationship between Christianity and Islam. The tutor also raised discussion about Asian women, such as whether they could wear jewellery, and the group were happy to answer these questions. Although much of the communication was not strictly BSL the interest they had in the topics meant that they exploited all possible forms of communication that they could which in the long term must have positive effects on the interaction with their children.
>
> (case study A).

> The other signing instructor stressed the need to establish all possible channels of communication for the deaf children who sign as she considered that they were trying to cope with five cultures; the culture of home and school, deaf culture and the culture of the hearing world and British culture. The instructor says that the class also gives the mothers the opportunity to talk about their children and about issues they have never talked about before. She finds it difficult to accommodate the different ability levels within the class but tries to get in more advanced signers to act as advocates for the others. When the class began some fathers attended. More mothers were drawn in and now the group is exclusively female. The development worker explained that in Bangladeshi culture men and women cannot mix easily and do not usually sit together which makes it difficult to cater for both mothers and fathers.
>
> (case study Q).

In both instances the signing instructor provided a deaf role model for the mothers. This was seen as particularly helpful in one area where some mothers may not have seen many deaf adults in a professional role.

Behaviour

The question of managing their children's behaviour had emerged as an important one with both groups. Being equipped with the relevant signs for managing behaviour was seen as very beneficial and one group had additionally been offered a course in behaviour management strategies.

English

The need to improve their spoken English skills was an issue in both groups. Indeed, some mothers had passed CACDP Stage 1, but were being held back in achieving Stage 2 by their lack of knowledge of English, although a number of them commented that, through attending the sign language classes, their spoken English had improved. This need to improve their English was addressed in case study Q by the provision of an English class solely for these women. This class was held on another morning and so raised the same issues concerning the necessity to provide free transport. One mother summed up the difference that the group had made to her life:

A has two boys who are deaf. There is a history of hearing impairment in the family. Her husband was born in Britain but A came over from Pakistan to marry him. Her elder son was diagnosed at the six-month check up. She was 'very scared about it'. The service began visits to her home twice a week 'to teach me how to talk and play with him.' The younger one was diagnosed at a few weeks old. She says that the HoS and Development worker 'pushed me to come to the English class'. At the time she spoke no English. She also started the signing class, but has given this up as her children do not sign and she has concentrated on improving her English. The service also found her an English class at the local college. She became a voluntary worker at her son's school to practise her English on the advice of a friend. Her English is now very good and she is obviously proud of what she has achieved. These developments have made a big change in her life. 'I go everywhere with my children. Before I didn't go out. Now I can go by myself on the bus or the tube.' Her husband has been supportive and is proud of her. She relates his surprise when she was able to speak to the teachers at a school meeting. She appreciates the help she has received such as adaptations for the telephone and television. 'My children are speaking well and understanding very well.'

(case study Q).

Social contact

Both groups were seen by all involved with them as serving a strong social function for many of these women, as is exemplified by the example just given. One HoS told us that for some women this group is the most exciting part of their life. When they first started it, some of the mothers had rarely left their homes.

Meeting place

The meeting place where the group was held was viewed as needing careful consideration. It was seen as vital that both the mothers themselves who would attend and other members of their family should find the place acceptable. In one instance this was solved by meeting in the local Pakistani Centre and in the other by meeting in the learning support base where several other groups also met and many of the professionals were based. A previous attempt at running a group had failed partly because the venue was not seen as acceptable.

Support/development workers

The role of the support or development worker was seen as essential to the success of work with families from minority ethnic backgrounds. One service is able to employ their own support workers whilst the other secured funding for the post for a fixed period under a Social Regeneration Project. These workers are seen as the vital link between families and the service.

Individual support for pupils

Support for a deaf pupil from a minority ethnic background was observed in a mainstream school in another case study.

We have made individual arrangements for M. She was supported in class by an LSA who is a native speaker of her home language. This gave support to the pupil and helped her make the transition to English. The LSA also acted as interpreter when the teacher of the deaf and I went to visit the home. M has a group of friends who speak the same language, but none of them are deaf. She also has a friend in another deaf girl in the school and gets on well with the hearing children in her class.

'Now M is still supported for some of the time by the same LSA but she also works with another LSA whose first language is English. M prefers to speak English in school now.'

(SENCO, case study E).

Summary

Key findings in this section are summarised as follows:

- It is vital that support for families should include a native speaker of their own language.

- Families from minority ethnic backgrounds, particularly mothers, derive great benefit from a support group. This can help with developing children's language and communication and managing their behaviour.

- Schools and services need to facilitate access to a range of services such as providing free transport to parent support groups.

4.13 Further education

The FE provision which was the subject of research in this project was provided by specialist schools/colleges for the deaf (case studies C, J and L), and so the following discussion relates solely to that type of provision. All the students were attending local mainstream FE or tertiary colleges, but receiving support from the specialist college where they were enrolled. Some students were 'staying on' after their secondary education in the same specialist school, others were transferring from other provision, either specialist or mainstream. Reasons for opting for a specialist college varied according to each student's individual situation in terms of curriculum and communication requirements.

In case study C, the post-16 department leaflet states that the school aims to provide 'the best of both worlds [to FE students] ... the breadth of curriculum and opportunities of mainstream colleges supported by the expertise and experience of a national school for the deaf'.

College L's mission statement is: 'To provide young deaf people with access to the range of educational opportunities, on and off campus, available to all young people; to enable them to develop their own identity and self-confidence and gain esteem from a supportive community of peers and staff; and to assist them to become more independent and self-reliant in their social and emotional development'.

While these are specialist provisions, the importance of the notion that students were being prepared to take a part in the wider world was clear.

> We have always believed in inclusion, it underpins all the work we do, but we will have to change the mission statement simply because the word inclusion is not there. It will not alter what we do...We like the inclusive approach, they're out in the mainstream sector, but we're matching it with 100% support. We do not want segregated provision. We get young people ready for life and life is in the hearing community with links with the deaf community. Students will be living and working within the hearing community. That is the real world. We need to offer very good and very clear support in the real world.
>
> (head of college, case study L).

Advice and information on courses and careers

Young people and their families need good quality information and advice in order to make a choice of college, course and career in which they can be successful. Careers advice now has to begin earlier (in year 10), mainly in response to funding arrangements. However, this must also be a positive feature in helping schools and colleges to foster high aspirations whilst encouraging carefully considered choices.

The head of post-16 in case study C aims to make pupils aware of their choices and will talk to parents, but will also stress the need to be realistic and have clear expectations. 'It won't work if their parents are forcing them to be here. The major thing is they have got to want to be here and to work.'

> 'Sometimes you find it's something someone's suggested to them rather than what they really want to do. Students are told "You couldn't possibly look after children because you're deaf", when we have had very able students go through those courses. Deaf students with proper support, technical support can access a whole variety of courses ... When students visit the college during the assessment we talk to them about the course, get other students to talk to them, maybe sit in on some lectures. They are interviewed by Student Services. we explain the 'highs and lows' of the course. Try and get what they really want. [We]need to get [to] what they feel rather than what they think is expected of them.'
>
> (Communication Support Workers Team leader, case study L).

In one setting, there was particular focus on the preparation for college phase. Parents are asked to attend a meeting with careers advisors and representatives from industry and parents and students are encouraged to visit different colleges. Higher year tutors well-versed in the range and content of GNVQ courses available at the school established a transition plan for each student in the autumn term of year 11 (case study J).

Case study L used a three-day residential assessment programme before entry to the college. Students are individually assessed both academically, in communicative competence and in the social/residential situation. The NATED assessment pack is used as a 'trigger to look at everything' – communication skills, basic skills, support needs, career options and aspirations. The student's primary mode of communication or what is likely to be their primary mode is ascertained.

Case study C was strong in its career advice and support. This included a careers education room and displays in the post-16 group accommodation illustrating the wide variety of employment possibilities and opportunity for year 11 students to spend a week living in the post-16 accommodation and to go into college. Work experience was provided for students including in the school itself. For example, a student wanting to do an NNEB course worked in the primary department and one interested in catering worked in the kitchens. Good contacts with many course tutors have been established by the head of post-16 who will try to contact the relevant tutors when students are making choices about courses to follow and before they are interviewed.

Students have one a day a week on work experience which is supervised by school staff and one day a week at the local college fully supported by school staff. One of the students spoke to us enthusiastically about the course that had taken her into a well-known cosmetics shop where she had clearly excelled herself. A project on the course had been to develop a small business venture. She and student friends had designed greeting cards, packaged and priced them and were now 'marketing' them. Such real life experiences had given her the confidence to succeed and it was expected that she would return the following year to pursue a GNVQ at Intermediate Level in Retail Management.

(case study C).

Language and communication

Two of the case studies visited use an oral/aural approach, while in case study L, English and BSL are given equal status. The principal stated, 'We have a very open communication policy. We don't reject anyone on grounds of communication. Although we are predominantly a signing community, we have people with English as their first language of communication. Forty five percent of students come from oral schools. We have to match the needs of the students and choose the most appropriate method for use in the classroom, whether notetaking or BSL'.

Because the development of language and other skills may be delayed in deaf students, all the case study locations provided various ways of 'bridging' between the Key Stage 4 curriculum and FE courses.

Where appropriate, students are encouraged to take an 'extra' year to prepare them better for FE. Not all students need it and not all LEAs will fund it, but out of 30 year 11 students, 23 have applied for the school's FE foundation course. This offers a GNVQ Foundation course 'Skillpower' which focuses on the development of confidence in literacy skills and the opportunity for work experience in between three and six different types of occupation.

(case study J).

Specialist provision is also able to offer additional types of support on-campus. All three case studies provided the expertise of audiologists and speech language therapists as well as courses aimed at improving communication skills.

> The English department runs the RSA Communicative English Skills for year 12, which 'keeps their English ticking over and also gives them a certificate at the end' (English teacher). There are four possible modules; Speaking and Listening, Reading and Writing, and Receptive Language and Interactive Communication. One teacher expressed disappointment that this qualification is being discontinued by the RSA as it provides something 'different from school English', particularly with its use of environmental print which is helpful for their future lives.
>
> (case study C).

> On-campus speech and language therapy support was reported to be a very popular option with students. Students were very aware that speech is an important aspect of communication and to be useful must be intelligible. There is also a course in communication strategies which is targeted at all 16 to 17 year olds with additional difficulties. This is tutored by an SLT and a deaf teacher/BSL user.
>
> (case study L).

Communication and tutorial support

The wide range of courses and the individual needs of students demand considerable time and skill from the coordinators or heads of department who organise the support programme.

> When timetables become available the head of post-16 will discuss support needs – where support is needed for induction week or for the first half-term and where 'to pull out'. She then devises support timetables for herself and the teachers and notetakers. 'It is important to have support in all classes where it is needed and to shift it flexibly, as and when necessary.' After three or four weeks these arrangements are reviewed by a checklist (a simplified version of the NATED assessment document) and 'tweaked as appropriate'.
>
> (case study C).

According to needs notetaking, lipspeaking and signing is provided by Communication Support Workers (CSWs). The role, however, goes beyond simple communication support. A CSW (case study L) pointed out:

> You need a reasonable understanding of the subject. From the student point of view, understanding their needs so that if they're oral their needs will be different

> from the profoundly deaf. You need to ascertain whether they're fully comprehending what the lecture is about. Sometimes they don't fully grasp it but don't want to show that they don't. You have to break down what the lecturer is saying – Do they want more visual explanation? Are they happy with the language? You've got to know the student to do that effectively.

The team leader in this case study was also concerned about other needs that students might have.

> We're here to communicate, but if they have additional needs you try to facilitate their needs as well ... try to make sure the student is accessing the course appropriately and their behaviour is integrated within the group. Sometimes they need extra support with emotional or social needs.
>
> (team leader, case study L).

Sometimes this means 'overlapping into educational support' (principal of college). Education Support Workers (ESWs) provided more specific language and educational support for students needing extra help. However, the role is not a teaching one, and students need to become independent and take responsibility for their own learning. 'Sometimes it means encouraging them to ask questions. I'm very conscious that I'm not the teacher. I don't want to tell him my concept of what's needed' (CSW).

Two particular examples of support we came across were:

> A relay system of support was used with a student who had Usher's syndrome. Despite excellent signing skills, the student found accessing the interpreter very problematic. The introduction of a third communicator overcame this problem.
>
> Lecturer ➢ Hearing interpreter ➢ Deaf communicator ➢ Student
>
> NNEB students were having difficulty with listening to tapes of children's talk for studying language development. A video and a transcript were provided so the deaf students could access this part of the course.
>
> (case study L).

More general educational tutorial support may be directly related to the course or provide skills to enhance participation in the courses at students' request. Topics for group tutorials last year included; Sign Language, Art, Wordpower, Engineering Maths and IT, Speech Therapy, English Enhancement, GCSE Maths and English, Study Skills, and Health Education. Driving Theory has also been introduced. These are taught by ToDs, deaf tutors or lecturers with the aid of a CSW where necessary. There are also one-to-one tutorials in college course subjects given by subject specialists. The level of support is based on the assessment procedure, but at least three hours a week. It is negotiated with the student by the Principal, Tutorial Support Manager and Student Support Manager. Most students want extra maths and English. One college had a policy of matching the interests and expertise of CSWs to meet the needs of students, for example, a retired engineer working with an Engineering student. Another insisted on control over who is doing the tutorials even when tutors have to be paid through their own mainstream college invoicing system.

There needs to be a programme of deaf awareness training available for mainstream staff and students. At L, either during induction week or in Personal Tutor time, the team leader will try to talk to the other students on the courses where there are deaf students. Sometimes the students feel the deaf students are being unfairly helped and the CSWs have to explain that they are allowing the student to access the course.

All the locations visited provided INSET training for mainstream tutors in some form, from an hour and a half session to an accredited course on four Saturdays during the year. In one case this will be delivered by two deaf members of staff. There were also booklets and information packs which they had devised and 'A summary of terminology and supporting information' which explains relevant terms and gives information on the college's support strategies and programmes.

Personal, social and emotional development

In all three case studies the personal social and emotional development of students was a focus. This focus was endorsed by the questionnaire responses. Describing how case study L celebrated all achievement, whether they were academic or social, a respondent wrote:

> The college has a positive approach/work towards trying to create an environment where children/students, deaf adults and hearing adults can work and develop together in the aim of sending out a whole Deaf child/adult/young person to another chapter of their book of life! There is the recognition also that there is still much work to be done, but the continued working effort in this respect is positive.
>
> To recognise initially they are "Deaf" and will always be deaf – to create an environment where their identity is always recognised positively, then education, social, personal developments can build up and they individually succeed at their own level whether it be to get to University or "have a dry bed".

The head of the college pointed out:

> We ensure success, encourage independence, provide enough information for students to make decisions, treat all students the same – success for one student in life skills is as important as success in exams.

As part of their guidance for good practice in this area, case L produced a booklet, *Your future starts here,* which was jointly devised by staff and students. It set out rules, regulations and expectations of behaviour in relation to study or work experience and on the school premises. Students sign an agreement to abide by these rules.

There was also the option of choosing a member of staff as a personal counsellor, a weekly meeting with the head of post-16 and other staff and a care officer assigned to each student on entry to college. Particularly appreciated is the deaf counsellor who is available for students who need this service, though on the permanent roll the counsellor is 'independent' of all other staff structures and mechanisms. In addition, there was a policy of ensuring that as many deaf people are employed as possible at all levels within the college (case study L).

As these colleges were residential, living accommodation and independent living was an issue. For students in residential accommodation, there can be difficulties with maintaining a balance between the level of supervision and control necessary to allow staff to ensure safety and care whilst acting *in loco parentis* and the need for allowing young people freedom to grow and develop. All three locations differentiated their post-16 provision from the accommodation for younger pupils, even where this was on the same campus. In case study L, there was a clear progression route from fully supervised accommodation to a halfway house, partially supervised students being responsible for cooking to moving off campus to the local university with discreet supervision and increased responsibility for food. The university accommodation is better quality, for example Internet access, textphone, and 'provides an excellent carrot for the students' (principal). At J, a new hostel is planned in the town centre away from the school campus.

Students are encouraged to become independent learners and self-sufficient in the wider, hearing world.

> The head of post-16 'gradually tries to make them take more responsibility, to make them think of solutions themselves', for example, when appropriate, directing the students to seek help from college tutors themselves in the normal way. 'You see them become more independent.' Although the students receive a lot of individual attention, one teacher says 'the role is more supportive than a

teaching role', and is a gradual change which starts to develop as teachers see the students through their GCSE examinations in year 11. Inevitably some students may, at least initially, take advantage of the freedom that college provides but 'the head of post-16 is good at getting the balance between chivvying them and giving them the responsibility'.

(case study C).

Care plans are used with pupils until Year 10. Years 11 and FE students are monitored via a 'Supervision model'. The format in this case is a meeting to which care staff and the young person attend. The young person is then encouraged to reflect upon his/her progress in different areas of personal and social development and so identify new targets for the forthcoming period. The member of care staff in charge of the year 11 boys spoke of how a questionnaire given to the boys had helped to pinpoint areas in which they felt less confident to operate independently. These responses were borne in mind when thought has been given to the areas in which students should be proficient. By the end of year 11, the aim is that the young person should be entirely responsible for their own care.

(case study J).

Professional development of staff

In one case study, the professional development of staff was given priority. A training and development manager had been appointed two years previously to 'coordinate the training needs of college staff and also to take advantage of the skill and expertise available to provide external courses' (annual report, case study L). He himself commented 'Specialist colleges have to keep up with what's happening in the rest of the sector'.

This case study made the following provisions for staff development:

- CSWs with qualifications in notetaking and/or sign at minimum level CACDP2. Many with level 3.

- Sign Language International (SLI) training for Level 3 BSL 'ensuring quality of our communicators' (Training and Development Manager).

- Professional Development Award: Communication Support Worker for deaf people.

- Part-time tutors offered free training on an accredited course 'Working with Deaf People'.

- The new FEFC 'Inclusive Learning Quality Initiative' resource pack, rated as an 'excellent resource which helps colleges to move towards more inclusive practice. The best staff development materials' for which the Principal is a trained facilitator.

- Creation of a post of Training and Development Manager 'to coordinate the training needs of college staff and also to take advantage of the skills and expertise available to provide external courses'.

- NVQ team for training residential staff – Caring for children and Young People.
- Appraisal system introduced and Appraisal training for managers.
- Working towards Investors in People accreditation.
- Deaf awareness training for all staff.

Summary

Key findings in this section are summarised as follows:

- Information on courses and careers is important for students and their families.
- The provision of adequate support in lectures requires careful initial assessment and the monitoring of provision.
- Professional development of staff is a key feature of provision.

Chapter 5

Language and communication approaches to the education of deaf children

Language and communication approaches to the education of deaf children

5.1 Issues around the language and mode of communication

One of the four main aims of the research study is to 'provide clear definitions and description of system and approaches used in the education of deaf children in the UK'. This has long been a controversial area in deaf education and there are debates around the best language and mode to use in the education of deaf children. This is further confounded by the lack of a consistent terminology to describe the various approaches. In a recent report to the DfEE [1], discussing approaches to the education of deaf children, it is suggested that 'In the absence of any agreed terminology and usage, care must be taken in interpreting the literature in terms of the description of the approach use'. (Powers, Gregory and Thoutenhoofd 1998, p140). It is also noted in the conclusion to the DfEE report that 'while we would not want to minimise the importance of language and language use in the education of deaf children, we consider the energy that has been put into debates on this topic has, in the past, drawn attention away from the content of the curriculum, and this has been to the detriment of the education of deaf pupils' (Powers *et al,* op cit p177).

It should however be pointed out at the outset that, as will already be apparent, we did not present our findings on good practice classified by the language and communication approaches used. This was for a number of reasons. Firstly, it would not have been easy to categorise all the case studies in term of approach to language and communication approach unless very crude categories were used or a large number of categories were introduced. Many categories could have led to the creation of distinctions and divisions that were not apparent from the data. Secondly, most of the categories that we examined went across language and communication mode; it was not a useful distinction. Thirdly, we also held the view that a dominant focus on differences rather than similarities in deaf education has been counter-productive and distorted discussion about the best way to educate deaf children.

It will become clear from this discussion that this is a complex area. It seems that apparently equivalent practices may be known by different names, while the same name

---

[1] Powers, S., Gregory, S., Thoutenhoofd, E.D. (1998) *The Educational Achievements of Deaf Children: Research Report RR65.* London: DfEE.

may apply to practices that appear to be different. Thus, the case studies did provide an opportunity to examine the various language and communication approaches used in the case studies and the terminology associated with them. This allows us to review the consensus or lack of consensus in this area. We supplement this discussion with the information that we received from the deaf organisations to see how they delineate the various approaches.

However, before going on to describe and discuss the various language and communication approaches used in the case studies, some distinctions may be useful. There are two main languages that may be used in deaf education, the spoken language of the hearing community and the sign language of the deaf community. In the UK this is English and British Sign Language (BSL), though there are other issues to address for children whose first language is not English or BSL.

As well as the distinction between languages, there can be a distinction between modes. For children being educated in English, the mode of the language may be its spoken and written form, but it may also be presented in a signed form which takes the signs from BSL but uses them in conjunction with English, following English grammar. This is variously known as bi-modal, Sign Supported English (SSE), Signed English (SE) or Manually Coded English (MCE) though the last term is more often used in the USA.

Thus, there are two possible distinctions to make in deaf education, between monolingual and bilingual approaches, and between approaches using sign and approaches which do not include signs. The first is a language distinction, the second is a mode/language distinction. Although it may seem most appropriate to make the distinctions based on language, very often the distinction is based on mode, on whether or not signs are used.

A further option is to make a three-way classification, between spoken English only, English plus signs (bi-modal or Sign Supported English) and a sign bilingual approach. For convenience in the discussion below, the first of these is termed oral/aural, the second SSE and the third sign bilingual. This does not imply any special status for these particular terms other than their convenience for this discussion.

The case studies

If we consider the approach of case studies, eight describe themselves using predominantly oral/aural terminology. Four of these describe themselves as natural aural, with a further two using the term natural aural but also using other terms, in one instance auditory oral, in another, oral/aural. In practice it would seem that these six all have a similar approach, usually described as natural aural.

The natural aural approach is based on:

> ... the belief that if children learn to use their residual hearing effectively, and are offered normal interaction they can acquire their mother tongue naturally. It is believed that the development of speech and language is dependent on the use of residual hearing and auditory discrimination. This is achieved through natural experience rather than by direct teaching.
>
> (policy document, case study B).

The county follows a natural aural approach to the development of spoken language. Since within this approach the primary sense through which language is acquired is hearing, the philosophy is based on maximising the use of residual hearing. Great emphasis is therefore placed on building good audiological foundations. Parents are encouraged to provide a stimulating environment for their child, appropriate to their age, which will offer 'a full range of sounds, spoken language and learning experiences which are available to the normally hearing child' (service handbook). During home visits, ToDs discuss the importance of interaction and meaningful conversation. All advice is based on the premise that 'almost all hearing impaired children have useful residual hearing which can be reached by modern hearing aid technology' (service handbook, case study K).

Of the other two oral/aural based approaches, one specifically rejects the term natural aural and prefers auditory oral, and the other one describes itself as oral. In the first (case study H), the term auditory oral is preferred to natural aural, which the head of service suggested had a philosophy that every child could be successful in an oral approach. This is not the position of his service which serves a small number of children in signing programmes in special schools for children with learning difficulties, using either Makaton or BSL.

They (the service) adopt a very natural, non-structured, conversational approach to developing language skills. However, they are currently reviewing their approach to developing speech skills, with the possibility of introducing more structure. They won't do anything different without any evidence that it works – 'it's a very light hand on the tiller'.

The service is developing its speech work and feels it can be more challenging and at quite an early age. They always take an informal approach, believing that audition is the crucial thing (case study H). It is not clear the extent to which this differs from the approach usually described as natural aural, except the seeking of a more structured approach may indicate an implicit emphasis on the structured use if languages.

The school that describes itself as making oral provision, case study C, does this in conjunction with the maternal reflective method (MRM), and thus has a more structured approach than natural auralism. The school is an oral school and uses the maternal reflective method (MRM) to develop spoken language skills (see section on spoken language). All pupils are encouraged to use speech all the time, in and out of class. The document on Oral Policy states 'oral language gives the option in adult life to be part of the hearing community and to maintain independence'.

The policy is to encourage the use of spoken language and speech and to discourage sign, but much more emphasis is given to encouraging pupils to use their voices than on stopping them signing. Most pupils are discouraged from signing in class, depending on their communication skills, and some pupils are also discouraged from signing out of class. Teachers do not sign to the pupils. The school recognises that as adults some of their pupils will use sign as their main method of communication but it aims to equip all its pupils with as much skill in speech as possible, in order, in their view, to maximise choice and opportunity. The school is 'pro-choice in the long term' (senior teacher, case study C).

The essential features of the oral/aural approach are discussed in more detail in the section on specific approaches which follows.

The other seven studies are more difficult to classify. Of the three describing themselves as having a specific approach, one describes itself as sign bilingual and two as Total Communication. A further two describe themselves as offering two approaches, the first, oral and Total Communication, and the second oral and sign bilingual. The other two have eclectic approaches using a variety of languages and communication modes and do not label themselves in any particular way.

For the service that has a sign bilingual policy, the introductory sentence to the Language and Communication policy of the service is:

> The service has a sign bilingual policy in which the place of British Sign Language and Deaf people is recognised.

The policy also states that:

> Methods of communication used with each child are based on his or her needs as appropriately assessed.

This range of methods includes those based on English (spoken, sign supported and written) and those based on British Sign Language. A key point of this policy is that it:

> actively encourages the acquisition and development of two or more languages.
> Sign bilingualism recognises the sociolinguistic and cultural identity and
> affiliations of Deaf people whilst ensuring that the potentially disabling effects of
> a hearing loss are overcome, for example through attention to the development of
> majority language skills.
>
> (policy document case study A).

A more detailed description of the sign bilingual approach, relating to good practice in sign bilingual approaches is included later in this chapter.

The two cases which described their approach as Total Communication differed radically in their interpretation of the term Total Communication. The school with a Total Communication approach interprets it in the original meaning of the term, that the use of language and communication is flexible and the intention is to meet the individual communication needs of each child. This means that English, Sign Supported English and BSL are all used; the choice depends on the context and the children involved. The head believes this gives the staff flexibility and is the best way to meet the needs of individual children

> Our first priority is the child and to have clear communication which is
> comfortable, through which the child is able to learn freely but which will take
> that child to a position where they have equal access to both deaf and hearing
> society and to widen their choices in the world of work.
>
> We let the child determine what we do. Its not up to you to decide for the child
> where they are going to fit in.
>
> (head teacher, case study G).

However, the resource base that also describes itself as having a Total Communication approach, case study N, uses a bi-modal or Sign Supported English approach, where signs are only used in conjunction with spoken language. The Policy Document states 'The Resource Base operates under the system of Total Communication'. In practice the approach taken is a Sign Supported English (SSE) one where signs are used to a greater or lesser extent according to the individual child or group. 'We're using SSE as appropriate' (acting head of unit). It is considered that some groups do not need the use of signs. Currently some consideration is being given to introducing a more complete form of sign support (that is Signed English) in some situations. The acting head of unit told us 'A main aim with all children is to promote spoken language and speech skills' and an important part of the approach is to use residual hearing to the maximum.

This use of the term Total Communication to mean Sign Supported English was also the usage of the two case studies where Total Communication was used in conjunction with another oral/aural approach. Thus for these three case studies it was clear that Total Communication was not seen as an umbrella term covering every possible means of communication, but specifically to mean SSE.

The issue arises due to the way the use of the term Total Communication has developed. In its original use, it was as a philosophy of education where all possible forms of language and communication were used. The term was originally adopted by Denton in 1968 to describe the philosophy of his school. He described it as 'the full spectrum of language modes, child devised gesture, the language of signs, speech reading, finger spelling, reading and writing... the development of residual hearing for the enhancement of speech and speech reading skills' (Denton 1976[2]). However, more recently it has been increasingly used to describe the practice of Sign Supported English.

The choice of terminology could be political as well as language based, because of decisions about how a school or service wished to be perceived. Two heads in our case studies, one of a school in one of a service, discussed their decision about the use of the term in interviews with us, although they arrived at different conclusions.

The service, case study A, has defined its philosophy as that of Total Communication – a needs based, equal opportunities philosophy in which the methods of communication used with each individual are based on his/her needs and the requirements of each teaching communication situation. However, this term is so often inappropriately used, it is better to refer to the above in term of equal opportunities and sign bilingualism (from the service policy statement). The head of service described it thus:

> The pressure really came from this Total Communication thing... I was happy and have been happy until recently with the use of the term as a philosophy, ... had it been agreed that we are talking about philosophy and not methodology, then we could have done more within that umbrella without having to make things as explicit as we had to. So it was because of the issues around Total Communication. that we had to start looking at something that has ended up being called Sign Bilingualism.
>
> What emerged as a sign bilingual policy we did in order to say that not all children in X were being taught in two languages, sign language and English, but in order for those that needed it to have it we had to have a policy in place that meant that

---

[2] Denton, D. (1976) The philosophy of total communication. *Supplement to British Deaf News*. Carlisle: BDA.

> we could legitimately employ deaf people and Communication Support Workers and have a large sign language programme and so on ...
>
> (case study A).

The school, case study G, prefers to describe itself as having a Total Communication policy. The head believes this gives the staff flexibility and is the best way to meet the needs of individual children. One of the concerns of the head is not to be drawn into debates about language and terminology, which she sees as unproductive.

> I don't think terminology matters. I think the area is a mess and I don't like playing politics ... I don't like the children to think 'this is BSL' and 'this is English'. I want them (the two languages) to help one another, for the two languages to work together, with equal respect. This is the kind of ethos that I am trying to create here.
>
> (headteacher, case study G).

A further issue arises with respect to all the case studies where BSL is used as a separate language. The question arises as to whether these are similar in approach regardless of terminology or are they different. There are three instances to consider, a service with a sign bilingual policy, a service with a sign bilingual policy alongside an oral policy and school with a Total Communication policy which includes BSL.

The evidence from the case studies would suggest that all three are different. The service describes itself as give equal status to BSL and English and this pervades all their policies and work. English and BSL are treated as separate languages and are used systematically and distinctively in their educational provision. Thus an explicit distinction is made between the two languages in the way in which they are used.

The service where the approach is one of two possible choices, inevitably because of the few children involved, can only make a more limited provision. The sign bilingual approach is only used for children who have failed under the oral system or whose parents request it. The emphasis is on the communication rather than the specific language used. However, the approach is seen as having a role for a particular group of children and 'progress through sign is pleasing'.

In the Total Communication approach that includes BSL, there was a flexible approach to language, rather than the systematic use of English and BSL as in the sign bilingual approach reported above, the emphasis was on the flexibility and interchangeability of the languages. The use of each language was not matter of policy decision, but of responding to the needs of each individual child at all opportunities.

A further legitimate question to ask relates to services that offer a single approach. It concerns the way in which the needs of those deaf children who require a different approach are met. This question does not apply to schools and resource bases that were included in the study as these were usually part of a continuum of provision and thus other options were likely to be available.

Five authorities offered oral/aural approaches. Two of these offered unit provision using sign support. In one authority there were two units, one of which was for children with special needs. The provision was for children for whom a different approach was deemed more suitable or whose parents wanted them to be educated using sign, or children with additional special needs. The second offered special programmes for a small number of children in signing programmes in a special school for children with learning difficulties.

The other three all recognised there would be some (a small minority of children) for whom their approach was not suitable. However, it was less clear what the alternative provision would be. One said an 'interactive conversational approach'. A second said that 'it is recognised that there will be some children for whom this is not the approach of choice, either on account of parental preference or the individual needs of the child, and alternative provision will be made when required'. The third pointed out there could be difficulties:

> We must try to cater for the needs of all children, be flexible but accept that there are problems in rural areas. If we have a deaf family, we naturally accept what the parents require. We always try to meet parents' needs, but can't provide everything for everyone.

The service with a sign bilingual approach had about one quarter of the children in bilingual setting, and the others were all in mainstream schools, being educated through English. However, their preference was to subsume all this under the title sign bilingualism to recognise that each language had equivalent status and both were seen as appropriate choices for the deaf children.

It is clear from this discussion of the approaches used to language and communication in the case studies that it was very varied. Approaches with the same label could differ from each other, while some case studies chose different labels for approaches that seem essentially similar. It would not be possible to arrive at a consistent and coherent terminology based on these, and in addition there is evidence that there might be resistance should anyone make the attempt.

The deaf organisations

To explore this issue further we also looked at the responses and policy documents from the deaf organisations as they related to approaches to language and communication in deaf education.

A distinction needs to be made between those organisations that cover a wide range such as BATOD, representing teachers and the NDCS, representing parents and children and those organisations that have grown up because of their advocacy of a particular position. The former recognises a range of approaches whereas the others focus on a particular view which they elaborate upon. Often their policy statements are more keen to emphasise their differences from other viewpoints rather than to examine similarities.

In discussing language and communication, both the NDCS and BATOD stress the importance on the development of language and recognise a range of options.

NDCS

- Deaf children need to develop fluent language skills in order to understand and influence the world around them, by whatever means is the most appropriate to the individual.

- Deaf children do not acquire or gain access to language in the same way as hearing children. It is therefore of the utmost importance to ensure that the means are available for deaf children to acquire the appropriate level of linguistic competence.

- Deaf children and their families should be able to participate positively in the shared experience of deafness. To assist this process, they should have access to the widest range of deaf people. This includes Deaf people in the sign language-using community, deaf people who use spoken language, as well as those who use both.

- Deaf children should have the appropriate technology, resources and support so that they have full and equal access to the languages and cultures of the wider hearing community.

BATOD

All children and young people have the right to a developed communication system which enables them to communicate effectively in a variety of settings and for a variety of purposes.

Philosophy underlying the development of language in deaf children
The desire to communicate must be fostered in order for language to develop. The methods of communication used with a child should be based on his or her needs, as assessed by all concerned with the child's development.

For the majority of children and young people, the range of methods offered is based on English, the majority language of the UK; many will use a sign system in order to access English. Some children, especially those whose first language is British Sign Language (BSL), may use this as the main medium for their education, while also developing literacy skills.

BATOD recognises the difficulty in describing approaches and states: 'It was decided not to provide further detail about the various approaches and methodologies in use as there is much variety in interpretation and practice'. However, they do provide brief descriptions; the distinction they make is based on mode rather than language.

The smaller organisations have a different focus (note as before the BDA is included here because of its identification with a particular approach). Because these organisations came into existence through of their commitment to a particular approach, often their statements about approach tend to stress differences rather than similarities. The following comments with respect to approaches is drawn from the policy statements:

BDA

- Bilingual education is the most appropriate form of education for the majority of deaf children and should be offered from the start.

- Some children will be monolingual in either BSL or English, and this is acceptable if it is in the child's best interests in the view of the parents, LEA and the Deaf Community.

- Many deaf children have BSL as their first language and foundation for acquisition of English.

DELTA

- The approach recognises that the hearing impaired child is capable of acquiring language in a normal way out of his/her communication experiences, deducing the rules of the language in a similar manner to that of hearing children.

- Through optimum use of personal hearing aids, including cochlear implants and other ancillary equipment, from the earliest possible age, children can be enabled to use their hearing to acquire spoken language and access the broad educational curriculum.

- Educational provision needs to take place in an environment where spoken language is the routine means of communication.

- The approach does not use any formalised signs and asserts its belief that the introduction of sign language or sign-assisted communication into the experience of hearing impaired children before spoken language is well established will seriously interfere with the development of speech and language.

DEX

There are growing signs that all deaf children benefit from having sign language as a first or second language in order to access the host language of education For some deaf children, BSL will be their first language and the foundation for their acquisition of English. The transfer of skills from BSL to English, and vice versa, is positive and does not create permanent interference.

LASER

LASER describes the method of sign bilingualism as:

> an approach to the education of deaf children in which the language of the Deaf community (British Sign Language) and the language of the hearing community (English) are used. In the case of children from minority ethnic groups it is more appropriate to use the term 'sign multilingualism' in order to recognise the position of home languages other than English.
>
> LASER, Sign bilingualism: a model (1998)

- BSL and English should both be used for instruction and taught as subjects using first and second/foreign language curricula and teaching approaches.

- Both languages should be used in live and written forms, but kept separate and used in teaching, learning and assessment according to the needs of the child and the learning objectives.

- Both languages should be used in learning, social and communicative contexts with varying balance of languages and modalities across most of the BSL -dominant/ English-dominant continuum.

Conclusion

The whole issue of approaches to language and communication in deaf education is a complex one. While there may be some consensus on the aims of deaf education, there are differences in people's views as to how best these aims are realised. These differences lead to different approaches, particularly in the area of language and communication. Some approaches differ from each other in major and significant ways, while other differences seem to be variations on a theme. The problems are confounded by the lack of clarity about definitions. The choice of terminology to describe an approach has linguistic, social, historical and political roots.

However, such differences make describing and commenting on the situation in deaf education all the more difficult. Specific issues arise in particular areas and just two examples are given here. Giving parents full and appropriate information and advising about language and communication is a difficult task. It can only be made more confusing and complex by the lack of agreed terminology. Comparing results of research studies is also more difficult if it is not clear as to the way in which the children were educated, and how priorities were established. Differences can arise not because of the situation itself, but due to the way it is described. There is thus a strong and pervasive argument that some consensus should be reached.

The next two sections explore and describe key features of two approaches in some detail based on information from the Good Practice Review. We consider the oral aural and sign bilingual approach. Total Communication is not discussed here as at present the term serves as an umbrella term to include different practices.

Summary

Key findings in this section are summarised as follows:

- The issue of approaches to language and communication in deaf education is a complex one.

- While there may be some consensus on the aims of deaf education, there are differences in people's views on how best these aims are realised.

- Different priorities in deaf education have led to different approaches, particularly in the area of language and communication, some of which differ from each other in major and significant ways, while others seem to be variations on a theme.

- Issues in approaches are confounded by the lack of clarity about definitions.

- The choice of terminology to describe the approaches has linguistic, social, historical and political roots.

5.2   The oral/aural approach

It is difficult to give a single definition of the oral/aural approach since there are several approaches which could be described under this heading. These approaches have some aspects in common and some essential differences. In eight case studies the communication approach used was described as oral/aural, although the precise terminology varied. In a further case study, the predominant approach was oral/aural.

Target language

The target is spoken language with the promotion of literacy skills building on a foundation of spoken language. In services committed to this approach, it is generally acknowledged that there is a minority of children for whom an oral/aural approach will not be the chosen route.

> It is recognised that there will be some children for whom this (oral/aural approach) is not the approach of choice, either on account of parental preference or the individual needs of the child.
>
> (HoS case study K).

> Although the policy includes a discussion about other communication options within the county for particular children, the great majority of children are educated by oral/auditory means 'the county has a broadly oral/aural approach to communication for deaf children' (policy document). The policy further states that the specific method adopted by the service is a natural aural approach. This was also the clear understanding of the staff.
>
> (case study E).

Fundamental principles

Fundamental to all oral/aural approaches is the belief that residual hearing should be exploited to the full. Since 'the philosophy is based on maximising the use of residual hearing, great emphasis is therefore placed on building good audiological foundations' (Ho/S case study K). This has implications for resources and staffing.

> 'An essential part of their role is to provide the best audiological support possible. This means that:
>
> 1.   hearing aids, ATUs and FM systems are maintained at peak efficiency by regular checks including electro-acoustic checks.

2. spare hearing aids and FM systems are available when repairs are taking place.

3. advice on checking aids is given to schools, teachers and parents to ensure continuity of management.'

(case study F).

The good audiological foundations extend to ensuring favourable acoustic conditions in classrooms as well as the provision of personal hearing aids and radio aids.

Classroom FM Systems

The service recognised the possible benefits of fitting classrooms containing a hearing impaired pupil with a soundfield system. A few systems have now been purchased to set up in classes on a trial basis. It is hoped that when the benefits which they offer to all pupils, hearing as well as hearing-impaired, become apparent the schools will decide to purchase a system from their own funds and this has already happened in the case of one special school.

Some personal soundfield FM systems are also being trialled to decide which pupils these will benefit.

(case study E).

There is more variation in the way that spoken language development is promoted. Whilst there is agreement that the basis is conversational interaction, this may be seen as the primary means of promoting spoken language, or it may be supplemented with additional strategies. Natural auralism espouses the former view

It is believed that the development of speech and language is dependent on the use of residual hearing and auditory discrimination. This is achieved through natural experience rather than direct teaching.

(HoS case study B).

Straight away the teacher begins to encourage the parents to stimulate language development in their child through play. One teacher stressed that she was:

> not there to teach the child, but to empower the parent and to play with the child in such a way that language develops.

For the same reason another teacher said that when she plays with the child, she also encourages family members to play too.

> Teachers concentrate on listening skills, conversation skills and vocabulary development. They may also show parents videos of deaf children with developing spoken language in order to give parents a clearer picture of the steps that their child might take towards spoken language.
>
> (case study E).

The maternal reflective method (MRM), however, although starting from the same basis of conversational exchange, would build on this 'deposit' by turning it into a text for analysis.

> Texts are written with certain features in mind, for example pronouns, embedded meaning. Usually one text is produced each week and the aim is to produce one that is not only new, but exciting.
>
> Reflection on language is going on all the time, not just on a prepared text. An important feature of the approach is to teach pupils to understand and use the proper linguistic terms (for example, subject, pronoun, idiom, syllable, homonym). This approach is applied consistently and across all situations.
>
> Another essential element of the approach is that the language should come from the child. The teacher is guided by the language produced by the class when deciding what features of language to reflect on. There is no set order of, for example, grammatical features to work on. A lot comes down to the experience of the teacher knowing when the pupils have had sufficient experience of a particular feature of language before they can reflect on it and see where the rules are operating. The pupils must have come across a large number of examples in ordinary conversation before they are asked to reflect on a feature.
>
> (case study C).

Other case studies described their approach using their own terminology, as is discussed in the earlier section of this chapter, with one teacher even referring to 'structured natural auralism'.

There is general agreement that, in order to promote spoken language development, early diagnosis is highly desirable. Diagnosis should include an accurate assessment of hearing thresholds and other essential parameters, for example uncomfortable loudness levels, followed by the fitting of the most appropriate hearing aids immediately.

> Hearing impaired children are referred to the service at the moment of diagnosis. A member of staff of the service is present at the hearing clinic when the diagnosis is confirmed to the parents so that counselling and guidance can begin immediately. The age of diagnosis is now usually very early and the children can be diagnosed before they are one month old.
>
> (case study K).

Emphasis is then laid on regular assessments of hearing levels, maintaining the hearing aids at optimal performance, ensuring that they are worn consistently and then promoting the development of listening skills by managing the acoustic environment and providing the child with interesting auditory input which will stimulate the child to listen. In some case studies (for example E), this was seen as a 24-hour approach to listening and a structured listening programme was not seen as necessary, whilst staff in other case studies included a structured listening programme as well.

> The service has a specific listening programme that is used with all children and monitored carefully as part of the overall process of assessment.
>
> (case study B).

> Each class follows on from the other in terms of approach, in terms of the emphasis on good audiological support and the development of listening skills. Also, little things are important, for example teachers do not touch the pupils to gain attention but rather say the child's name, and there is no flashing of lights or banging of desks to gain attention. 'I would put my life on it that you would never see that' (senior SLT).
>
> The senior SLT has developed a programme based on a hierarchy of skills in listening. This uses material coming from the pupils themselves and is therefore age appropriate.
>
> (case study C).

Since the aim is the development of spoken language as the main means of communication, speech intelligibility is seen as important, although of secondary importance to communication. Within natural auralism there is the assumption that speech intelligibility will follow from the maximum use of residual hearing and the promotion of listening skills, with encouragement to listen to the way that sounds are articulated being the main facet of any speech teaching. However, some case studies where this was the approach used mentioned the inclusion of some speech intervention work, with the emphasis on a phonological/contrastive approach. This was seen as following in the wake of the development of spoken language (for example, case studies B and H).

> There is an appreciation amongst all professionals, ToDs and SLTs, that there must be fluency of speech before intervention can occur. In real terms this means that a child must be producing phrases before 'treatment' can occur. Before this time, advice and modelling would centre around listening skills. There is a schedule for the development of these skills.
>
> (case study B).

Implications of oral/aural approaches

For all settings using an oral/aural approach there are implications of the approach with respect to staffing and resources. There are also implications for teaching. Where the approach is implemented in a service, there are additionally implications for organisation and management of the service.

Staffing

Staffing implications relate firstly to ensuring 'good audiological foundations' (case study H). Responsibility for this will be shared with colleagues in the health service. The appointment of an educational audiologist (or more than one) will usually be seen as essential to work the interface between health and education, although the precise nature of the post will vary as is discussed under the theme of audiological management. A technician may also be considered highly desirable in order to maintain equipment.

There will need to be sufficient teachers of the deaf working directly or indirectly with deaf pupils to ensure that pupils receive the desired level of interaction. Frequently teachers of the deaf will act as facilitators by enabling parents, LSAs and other professionals to work in an appropriate way to stimulate language development. Since much of this early interaction needs to be on a one-to-one basis, this will require a high level of staffing, both in terms of LSAs and teachers of the deaf.

Resources

The main resource implications relate to ensuring that deaf children are enabled to use their residual hearing. Thus there will be a necessity to provide a great deal of audiological equipment. While health will bear the responsibility for the cost of personal hearing aids, other equipment will be provided by the school or service. This is considered under the theme of audiological management and the cost implications should not be under-estimated.

Implications for service organisation

There are several key implications for service organisation.

1. INSET

All staff will need INSET related to the approach. Training in use and maintenance of hearing aids and audiological equipment will be essential for all staff. Teachers of the deaf and LSAs can take responsibility for basic checking of hearing aids, radio aids and other amplification equipment, including regular electro-acoustic testing. Educational audiologists can be used to update the skills of other staff and introduce new technology. This will require them to continually keep abreast of new developments in the field.

All staff will also need to keep abreast of developments in understanding of language acquisition in hearing children since the approach suggests that the language acquisition of deaf children will follow a similar pattern. They will need to reflect on the implications of research into work with hearing children for their work with deaf children. Where teachers of the deaf are expected to carry out some speech intervention work, they will need to maintain and extend their expertise in this area and keep up-to-date.

Similarly, since the approach to literacy is based on work with hearing children, teachers of the deaf need to understand the implications for work with deaf pupils of approaches to literacy with hearing children.

Since so much of the approach is based on an understanding of work with hearing children and its appropriate application to deaf pupils, the implications will be that teachers of the deaf will need to access training offered to mainstream staff, for example in relation to literacy or aspects of the national curriculum. They will then need their own discrete INSET on the application of these areas to deaf pupils.

2. Preschool

In order to promote spoken language development from as early an age as possible, there are implications for organisation. This can take different forms.

- Twice weekly visits from a teacher of the deaf
- Weekly parent and toddler group with talks for parents and organised activities for children
- Technician tests all aids on test box weekly at parent and toddler group

Children offered place in support nursery staffed by teachers of the deaf and LSAs, or supported by a teacher of the deaf in mainstream nursery.

(case study K).

Depending on the child's language development the service aims to find them a place in normal nursery provision, believing that they need exposure to the language level of their peers. At this stage they will be working with nursery staff and assistants but also keeping up the home visits.

(case study F).

3. Primary/secondary phases

Many deaf pupils in oral/aural programmes will be educated in their mainstream school or in a resourced school, with the exception of the minority who attend a special school. Since the pupils will be surrounded by spoken language in the mainstream school, this is seen as a facilitating environment. As the HoS in case study B said, 'Children will construct language from the natural environment'.

> Many deaf pupils will require a high level of mainstream support; this can be in-class support, in one-to-one withdrawal sessions or as 'reverse integration'. There was seen to be a challenge in finding the balance between offering sufficient support to allow the pupil to access the curriculum while encouraging the pupil also to develop independent learning skills. There were seen to be implications for the way in which support is targeted and organised and this was a matter for reflection, for example it was under discussion in case study K.
>
> Levels of support are decided according to levels of hearing loss: five times a week for profoundly deaf pupils, three times for severely and once for moderately deaf. These are maximum levels of support and may be reduced in consultation with mainstream staff.
>
> (case study K).

At the secondary stage, support for some pupils took the form of tutorials at which they discussed any difficulties with the teacher of the deaf. An example of this was seen in case study K, where a sixth form pupil appreciated the weekly tutorials and would ask for more support if necessary. The concern of teachers of the deaf in some case studies was 'to give pupils the language to cope in a mainstream class' (case study H). The underlying premise is that if pupils are given the tools of well-developed spoken language and literacy skills, then they will be able to access the curriculum alongside hearing peers, although it is accepted that many pupils will continue to benefit from support and pre-tutoring throughout their school career.

4. INSET for mainstream staff:

The necessity to give INSET to mainstream staff was mentioned in several case studies. There were examples (B and E) where the service had developed packs for delivery of INSET to mainstream schools. In case study B, all teachers of the deaf were expected to deliver INSET to mainstream schools, and the mainstream schools were expected to allocate time during their training days for staff to attend.

> The service provides a two-day INSET course annually for mainstream teachers and SSAs working with hearing impaired pupils. The service used to have money for 20 teachers and supply cover, now schools have to pay out of own INSET budget. Teachers and SSAs mentioned how useful they had found this course.
>
> (case study K).

> When a new child with a significant hearing impairment is about to enter the school, substantial INSET for staff takes place. In two cases that I was made aware of, INSET for the staff occurred over two days. On one day a basic training was given to all staff, including playground supervisors. On the next, the teachers who would actually be teaching that child were given more advanced training.
>
> (case study B).

Summary

Oral/aural approaches require high levels of resourcing and staffing, the implications of which need to be borne in mind. Pupils in mainstream classes may require a great deal of support in order to access the curriculum, but there is a need to ensure that this support is offered in such a way as to also promote the development of independent learning skills.

Key findings in this section are summarised as follows:

- The target in all oral/aural approaches is the promotion of spoken language.
- Fundamental to all oral/aural approaches is the belief that residual hearing should be exploited to the full.
- Early diagnosis is seen as highly desirable, followed as soon as possible by hearing aid fitting and the promotion of listening skills.
- Spoken language is promoted through conversational interaction. In natural aural approaches this is seen as the primary means, but other oral approaches may supplement this with more structured language teaching.
- Speech intelligibility is given priority in oral/aural approaches. This is promoted through the use of residual hearing, supplemented in some approaches by speech intervention work.

5.3   The sign bilingual approach

This account of the sign bilingual approach aims to provide a definition of the approach and examine those elements which are critical to it. It is based on only one case study (case study A), which is seen as an exemplar of the approach. However, this is an example of a whole service provision based on resourced mainstream schools. Although similar issues arise, the provision will differ some ways from that provided in schools where there is a sign bilingual approach.

Defining sign bilingualism

'Sign bilingualism' has been defined as an approach to the education of deaf children in which the language of the Deaf community (British Sign Language) and the language of the hearing community (English) are used. In the case of children from minority ethnic groups it is more appropriate to us the term 'sign multilingualism' in order to recognise the position of home languages other than English' (Pickersgill and Gregory 1998 [1]).

An evolving approach

Sign bilingualism is a relatively new approach in deaf education, the first programme using this approach was only introduced in the UK in 1989. Thus it is an evolving system, and it has changed and developed since it was first implemented.

The head of service in case study A pointed out some of the ways in which it has changed.

> What you see now in the classroom is totally different from what we started off with partly because people's skills are light years away from where they were there and their knowledge is light years away but also because the education system is totally different at X now than it was in '86. Schools are different, there was no such thing as the National Curriculum. So the sign bilingual work has emerged along with the work on the National Curriculum and assessment and they've been mutually supportive of each other.

She mentioned in particular the ways in which deaf people have gained experience of working in the education system and now bring their unique insights to bear on areas such as teaching children literacy skills and strategies for communication with hearing people. Thus this account should be seen as a description of an evolving approach.

---

[1] Pickersgill, M., Gregory, S. (1998) *Sign Bilingualism*

The use of two languages

A critical and essential feature of the sign bilingual approach is the use of two languages. It 'actively encourages the acquisition and development of two or more languages' (policy document case study A). This has a number of features. The languages are seen as of equal status and both legitimate in the education of deaf children. In particular, sign language is not seen as the less desirable option for those children who fail to develop spoken language.

> We set out from the start not putting children, parents and staff into positions of making decisions that were too exclusive of each other and the way we got round that, which is quite unusual, is by making sure that children start off by accessing two languages and then as a result of that we're able to identify children who are essentially monolingual in English ... and require an auditory/oral approach and those children who are sign bilingual and require access to two languages.
>
> We didn't want sign ever to be a last resort ... it wasn't going to be failure, it was going to be that decisions we made about children are going to be based on children's strengths, not on failure and if there's failure, it's our failure and not that of the child. So, that's put a lot of pressure on us to get our early years work sorted.
>
> (HoS, case study A).

This means that there will be children for whom the main language of education will be BSL, and others for whom it will be English, although this may be different for a child at different stages of education. The head of service in case study A saw positive effects of this.

> As we have progressed we've identified a far greater range of children who benefit from a two language programme than we expected.

Initially, work was based on children acquiring BSL as a first language but they have also found that there significant numbers of children who have English as a first language, but also benefit from the use of BSL.

> We are looking at children who are dominant or have a preference for English which is quite a challenge because our bilingual programme is based on sign language as the first language or the preferred language and English as a foreign language. Because of the early work in the nursery and parents wanting children, who would traditionally have gone onto peri caseload... those children are staying in the programme, but they are different children. They have different learning needs from the sign language dominant children so we're having to develop, within the sign language programme, ways of meeting the needs of children who are learning through English. They may be learning BSL as a second language ...
>
> (HoS, case study A).

Implications for staffing

Deaf instructors

A major requirement of sign bilingualism is the involvement of deaf people in all aspects of the provision. The head of service suggested that the need to involve numbers of deaf people had a major impact on the way in which the early policy documents were developed.

> The policy emerged from a need to be absolutely clear about who was going to work for the service, where we were going to have children placed, how we were going to move on in terms of professional development, what the issues were around curriculum and assessment. So the policy issues emerged that way.
>
> What emerged as a sign bilingual policy we did in order to say that not all children in X were being taught in two languages, sign language and English, but in order for those that needed it to have it we had to have a policy in place that meant that we could legitimately employ deaf people and communication support workers and have a large sign language programme and so on...

In case study A, deaf instructors are employed with separate and distinctive terms and conditions of service who fulfil a number of roles including:

- Teaching alongside hearing teachers of the deaf
- Teaching a class, but with the teacher of the deaf retaining responsibility for the lesson
- Teaching deaf studies to deaf and hearing children
- Working with parents of young children
- Working in the BSL playgroup and nursery
- Teaching sign language
- Assessment of children's BSL
- Working with deaf children on aspects of discipline and behaviour
- Contributing to training within the service
- Contributing to overall service development

Communication support workers

A sign bilingual provision also requires people to work in mainstream classrooms alongside children who have BSL as a first language or who cannot access English in the classroom situation. In case study A, this role is mainly fulfilled by communication support workers (CSWs) although deaf instructors and teachers of the deaf may also have a role in this. Although part of their work is interpreting the mainstream teachers, CSWs make a careful distinction between their role and that of an interpreter. Their responsibility goes beyond interpreting the lesson into sign language as they have a responsibility to facilitate the pupils access to the curriculum. They need to check what the child is understanding, and where difficulties lie. Such support is complex. The pupil has to know when to attend to the class teacher, the CSW or other aspects of the situation, such as visually presented teaching material. The skills of both pupils and CSWs in managing this effectively are considerable.

CSWs do not teach themselves, but if there are problems they would discuss these with the class teacher. They may also take notes, and check the pupils know what homework is expected. CSWs also keep records of vocabulary use in lessons and discuss specific terms and ways of signing them. This work is carried out in collaboration with deaf instructors.

Implication for service organisation

1. Sign language tuition

A major implication for the service is that it has to ensure that sign language tuition is provided for pupils, staff and parents. For staff and pupils there must also be the means in place to assess sign language development. The various provisions are described in the appropriate sections.

This raises significant issues as, compared with English, little is known about BSL development in children and how it is facilitated. Assessment of BSL development is a new field, and while the new BSL scale should begin to help here there is still an issue as to how problems in BSL development can be recognised and acted on appropriately. Also, although there is general sign language tuition available in the community, the special needs of teachers and parents, particularly those of young children, are not addressed by this and require specific provision.

2. Preschool provision

From diagnosis onwards, there needs to be ways of facilitating and developing both BSL and English. There must be a recognition that, for families, the sign bilingual approach is not a simple option. It requires the acquisition of sign language, a new language for most families and language which is not likely to be used in the extended family or by friends. In case study A, the necessary support is provided in a number of ways:

- Home visits by support teachers or deaf instructors
- Sign language classes in the home for immediate and extended family, and friends (six weeks during the evening)

- Family support group
- BSL playgroup which encourages development of BSL in playgroup setting
- Developing English group where staff and parents work with children encouraging spoken English
- Families from minority ethnic groups may also attend the Asian mothers support group
- Nursery provision offering both BSL and English

The nursery is open everyday, and children attend either the BSL group or the English group in the morning and are integrated into the mainstream nursery, on the same site, in the afternoons. All children have an opportunity to access the other language on a Friday when they attend the other language group.

The decision about which group is made in conjunction with parents. If it is not clear the child may attend both groups until a preference emerges. Where parents are in disagreement, for example, where a parent particularly wants an oral/aural approach, their wishes are respected and the child will attend that group, although if the staff have concerns these are expressed to parents.

3. Primary and secondary

In case study A, the provision for school age children is in resourced bases, that is a mainstream school that is staffed in order that it can meet the needs of sign bilingual children. There are three resource bases at primary level and one at secondary level. At primary, staffing is predominately teachers of the deaf and deaf instructors who support the pupils in the mainstream classes and withdraw them for individual work. At secondary stage, the majority of the support in classrooms is by communication support workers, with some withdrawal and support work being carried out by teachers of the deaf.

At secondary stage, all teachers have a pastoral responsibility for a group of pupils and also responsibility for particular curriculum area. The curriculum for deaf students included deaf awareness and sign languages.

It was explained that teachers based in mainstream schools feel it important that they contribute to the life of the school as whole and take a share of general school responsibilities. If they are working in a class they may take responsibility for some of the preparation of material or some of the teaching. In the ideal situation there is time before the lesson for consultation between teacher and teacher of the deaf, which allows responsibilities to be shared and for effective differentiation. This involvement with the school can involve extra work as they attend both meetings the school plus the meetings of the service itself.

The head of the secondary school said he was delighted that it was a resourced school and that having the deaf pupils added to the life of the school and the quality of school experience for everyone.

4. Audiology

Sign bilingualism has been criticised for a lack of commitment to good audiological provision. However the policy is based on two languages and thus attention should be given to both. In case study A, the service policy states that:

> The service encourages all children for whom hearing aids are prescribed to wear them at all times. Staff are expected to ensure that aids are in optimum working order. All deaf and hearing impaired children are entitled to the best possible amplification of their residual hearing, in order that they might maximise the auditory potential for the development of spoken language.

5. Resources

Such requirements clearly have resource implications. Because sign bilingualism recognises the diverse needs of pupils, it also recognises the range of provision that is required, both in terms of language support for sign language and bilingualism, and audiological support. Sign bilingualism requires the active involvement of deaf people and communication support workers. In order to achieve effective implementation of such an approach, these issues must be considered.

Implications for teaching

Sign language development of pupils

In a sign bilingual programme, it is necessary for pupils to be exposed to good models of BSL, and to see deaf people in communication with each other, overseen (cf. overheard) communication which can be considered of particular importance. In case study A, the role of deaf instructor is important here, but also general signing levels of staff.

Children's competency in must be assessed and in case study A, it is measured against a framework. It was described as being 'like the National Curriculum' with attainment targets and level descriptors. Children's signing skills are assessed through the use of video analysis and moderated by deaf instructors across the authority. From these assessments, termly IEP targets are set.

The provision has been limited by the fact that until recently there were no established and standardised means available to adequately assess sign language development. However, in case study A they are fully involved in the development of the new BSL scale at City University and the senior deaf instructor is member of that research team.

Live English

'Live English' is the term used to define a whole range of strategies for deaf people to use in communication for hearing people. In using the word 'live' the purpose is to discriminate it from written forms of communication (although it is recognised that writing may be a strategy) and to suggest face-to-face interaction.

Deaf awareness

There is a sense in which it seems inappropriate to talk of deaf awareness within this sign bilingual provision as it is intrinsic to the whole situation and not, in any sense, added on. Deaf awareness comes from the presence of deaf people. In case study A, deaf instructors were involved in every part of the service with clearly defined roles which utilise their experiences as deaf people but also demand other skills.

Implications for training

In case study A, the service put a high priority on professional development, due to first, the challenge facing those in education and second, the cutting edge nature of the work. Also, due to the particular nature of the work of this service, not all staff may come with the range of experience and relevant qualifications for their post. Due to the innovative nature of the service, for some staff members, some of their training needs relate to the particular demand of their post.

Good signing skills of all staff must be an essential feature of a sign bilingual approach. In case study A, the development of signing skills in all staff both deaf and hearing is given priority. All attend a signing session, once a week, after work. People work in different groups depending on their level of signing competence, and different formats and strategies are employed within the group.

Summary

Key findings in this section are summarised as follows:

- Crucial to sign bilingualism is the systematic and separate use of two languages, British Sign Language (BSL) and English.
- The use of BSL requires tuition and assessment of sign language for all involved – children, parents, teachers and other staff.
- The approach has implications for staffing including the increased participation of deaf people and communication support workers.
- Sign bilingualism is a relatively new approach to the education of deaf children and thus is evolving.

Chapter 6

Conclusions

Conclusions

General points

The question of what constitutes good practice within the field of deaf education is complex and multifaceted. No simple answers can be found to represent the views of families, ToDs, deaf adults, support workers and other interested parties. There are nevertheless important features that can be identified across the full range of deaf education which unite all aspects of work with deaf children. These features can be viewed as central to all good practice with deaf children and many are features of good practice in general education. This chapter identifies a number of key themes that have emerged in this study.

As stated in the DfEE literature review (Powers *et al.*, 1998 op cit) there is an obvious and urgent need to monitor the progress of pupils nationally to provide value added measures of pupil achievement to help identify and learn from effective practice. However, this research project was not designed to address this issue.

The aims of the study were threefold:

1   to gather evidence from a broad constituency of those involved with deaf education as a basis for a consideration of what constitutes good practice

2.   to identify the common threads in the reported examples of good practice

3.   to provide clear definitions and descriptions of systems and approaches used in the education of deaf children in the UK.

While clear descriptions of some systems and approaches used in the education of deaf children were possible, there were also some considerable difficulties encountered. Lack of agreement over terminology and use of approaches broadly classified as 'Total Communication' within the profession made it impossible to provide a consensus view. This in itself is seen as problematic, presenting difficulties to parents, practitioners and researchers.

The research team was impressed by the varied, innovative and interesting practice they were able to see. The fifteen case studies, whilst only a small sample, provided clear evidence of good practice in deaf education within the UK. The team was in a unique and privileged position in having the time to visit a range of practice and to ask a range of questions outside the more usual Ofsted framework. Additionally, the opportunity to talk to practitioners, parents and deaf children/young people provided the opportunity to reflect on a range of perceptions and views. This not only provided a rich source of information but also promoted discussion. A number of practitioners and parents noted the importance of having such an opportunity to talk in some depth about the issues raised.

For some the feeling of isolation, together with the complexity of many areas of deaf education meant such an opportunity was highly valued. In some cases there is evidence that practice has been changed as a direct result of our visits. The team feels there is particular value in being able to contrast the different ways in which some challenges are being met in different situations, and the opportunity for ToDs to visit and talk in-depth with a range of service providers would be likely to offer considerable benefits to the profession.

The shared view of the practitioners and the families of deaf children involved in this study was that effective education of deaf children is a broad concept incorporating self-esteem, independence, a positive sense of identity and appropriate social skills as well as academic achievement. This report reflects that perspective.

Leadership and management

Good leadership and management was repeatedly identified as central to good practice, although one clear weakness in some contexts is the strong reliance on an individual head of service or school. In order to ensure that such reliance does not have a negative effect on provision for deaf children there is a need to ensure positive teamwork. Strong leadership, accompanied by clear detailed documentation that outlines a shared vision, together with a philosophy translated into a consistent approach emerged as important factors in promoting cohesion and a sense of team spirit. There was evidence that a clear philosophy consistently applied is often associated with good practice. However, clear philosophy consistently applied does not necessarily lead to good practice.

Continuing professional development

Specialist training was repeatedly reported to be a key feature of good practice. Such training is important not only for ToDs, but also for all other professionals working with deaf children, including educational audiologists, learning support assistants, communication support workers, educational support workers, deaf instructors and speech and language therapists. Good practice is characterised by qualified ToDs who view their initial training as a specialist teacher as the starting point for continued professional development. This view was not linked to a specific methodology or type of provision, but was a general feature of good practice as it was reported to the research team.

Preschool support

The importance of preschool support being flexible, child and family centred, easily accessible and open to negotiation is stressed by families and professionals. Parents value early identification if this is associated with immediate access to educational services for deaf children. The nature and type of support, together with the long-term impact this has on the individual child and on family dynamics, are central to any concept of effective practice. All the families involved in this study place very high value on the support received. Families express a preference for a clear, well-defined approach which provides a focus on methodology. The parents of young deaf children involved in this study reject a 'consumer model' in which a range of options is discussed with them, rather they are looking for consistency, commitment and a high level of professional expertise. There is no evidence available from this study about whether parental preferences change over time. In addition, it is clear that it is impracticable to offer all options to all families and maintain quality of provision. This in turn is likely to mean that the needs of all deaf children are unlikely to be met in any single setting as they are presently organised.

Empowerment

Empowerment is a central feature of this review, permeating all areas of practice. The stated aims of participating schools and services are all related to empowering deaf children and young people by enabling them to achieve their full potential both educationally and socially. Similarly, ToDs seek to empower families to make informed decisions rather than controlling and dominating.

The strong move to inclusion also demands that ToDs empower mainstream teachers to provide sensitive support for the individual child and ensure curricular access. This is the main area of the work of peripatetic ToDs. In addition to supporting individual deaf children directly, ToDs place great emphasis on the importance of liaising with mainstream teachers, a task they see as essential but one that demands time within the busy school day. Demands of delivering the National Curriculum put all pupil contact time at a premium, and teachers have to give up non-contact time, lunch-time, time after school or even at weekends to ensure such information as necessary is discussed. This places considerable demands on all concerned and threatens to make unfair demands on those class or subject teachers who have deaf children in their teaching groups. It is, however, interesting to note that mainstream teachers found many teaching strategies suggested for deaf pupils benefited their teaching group as a whole. Rather than seeking to work in isolation, ToDs were seen to be genuinely seeking a partnership.

ToDs work collaboratively, sharing responsibility for deaf pupils with mainstream teachers and LSAs. ToDs were identified as playing an significant role in overall school improvement and in promoting whole-school policies. The long tradition of ToDs working in mainstream contexts has allowed effective strategies to develop, including well-planned INSET for both mainstream teachers and LSAs. Inclusion was reported in this sample of case studies to provide a positive framework for deaf children and their families. The common goal is for deaf children to grow as equal partners in society. The goal of inclusion is viewed as being central to all approaches, encompassing both mainstream and specialist provision, and involving linguistic, cognitive, social and cultural concerns.

Different priorities in deaf education have led to different approaches, particularly in the areas of language and communication, some of which differ from each other in significant ways. All aim for literacy competence, all demand highly trained, skilled and committed staff who have access to continued professional development. A common feature of service/school support, whatever its nature, is detailed planning and evaluation, a clear view of the importance of the work being undertaken and of the need to define outcomes in a clear and accessible way. While this is a common feature of all educational practice, those involved in deaf education focus specifically on the development of communication and literacy skills, not only as goals in themselves but also to enable the individual child to access education and the wider community. Additionally, there is evidence that ToDs seek to ensure the personal growth of the individual child, including awareness of their deafness. For the majority of deaf children individually placed within mainstream education this is seen as an important aspect of effective practice.

There is an increasingly recognised role for deaf adults in deaf education. Their expertise in a range of settings is identified as a positive step towards inclusion and equal opportunities. This is identified as a central feature of good practice within a sign bilingual setting, but is also increasingly recognised as a key feature contributing to the personal and social education of deaf pupils in all settings.

Professional standards

In all settings we visited, ToDs achieve high professional standards. One aspect noted in school and home settings was that staff are commonly expected to work above and beyond what might be reasonably expected. Parents particularly value access to ToDs in the evenings, at weekends and in the school holidays. Similarly the workloads and level of professional competence demanded in some services make very considerable demands on individual staff. This suggests that additional staffing of services is needed to maintain high standards at the same time as ensuring reasonable working conditions.

In the majority of schools and services studied, audiological competence was viewed as a key feature of both preschool and school age provision. Good practice in this area features strong links with health service providers, positive and immediate follow up by education services following identification of hearing loss, appropriate aids, and on-going proactive management by all those involved, including the deaf children themselves. In a number of cases, audiological management was considered to be a key feature underpinning successful inclusion. Effective and positive audiological management was seen as central to success in spoken English. Correspondingly, for those children in sign bilingual programmes a clear and defined approach that incorporates the skills of deaf adults proficient in BSL is central to good practice.

Resources

The issue of funding and resources was identified as a potentially important area given recent changes in government funding and the high cost of effective support necessary for individual deaf children, whatever the setting. In our case studies the individual heads of services and schools ensured that sufficient funds were available to provide high quality services. Funding came from the LEA, the local health service provider or from fund raising activities by ToDs, families and local branches of the NDCS. In all cases funds were obtained as a result of skilful negotiation and hard work and were not there as a right. The lack of established funding mechanisms to ensure equality of provision for all deaf children, irrespective of their geographical location, suggests that some deaf children and their families will be disadvantaged. A national funding policy providing equal access to technological and educational support for all deaf children would clearly have advantages over the present system.

In reviewing practice and views on what constitutes 'good practice', it is interesting to note that the main aspects identified in this review of deaf education has identified many of the same areas highlighted in the DfEE Green Paper 'Excellence for all Children'[1] (Table 6.1).

---

[1] DfEE (1998) *Excellence for all children: meeting special educational needs.* London: The Stationery Office.

Table 6.1
Themes from the Green Paper 'Excellence for All Children' compared with features of good practice identified in this study

Themes from the Green Paper	Features of good practice according to the study
1. Policies for excellence	- early identification of deafness, including neo-natal screening - emphasis on preschool work - curricular access via liaison between ToDs and mainstream staff and INSET to mainstream staff
2. Work with parents	- parents say that very early intervention and access to a ToD is essential - importance given to this work by ToDs
3. Framework for provision	- importance given by ToDs to detailed joint planning with mainstream staff, LSAs, families and pupils - IEPs are used to good effect
4. Inclusion	- a universal concern with the goals of inclusion by both mainstream and special school providers - the role of deaf adults in promoting inclusion - inclusion seen as linguistic, cognitive, social and cultural rather than locational
5. Developing skills	- continuing professional development for ToDs, LSAs, deaf instructors - INSET for mainstream staff, other professionals and families
6. Working together	- services for deaf children seen as depending on the skills of schools and services to work across professional barriers in order to ensure optimum services for deaf children and their families
7. Regionalisation	- the challenge of providing a range of options locally for deaf children and their families is seen as constrained by demographic and geographical factors; regional coordination potentially offers benefits

Diverse needs/diverse options

High expectations and aspirations for deaf children are a key feature in a changing educational climate. Such change is a feature of general education and more specifically a feature of deaf education where innovative changes in technology and knowledge and understanding of sign language are making further demands on ToDs. Notions of good practice change over time, between cultures, between educationalists, families and many others. The concept of only one type of good practice within this complex field of education is flawed. Families and their deaf children are diverse and have many needs and aspirations. There are clearly some aspects of practice that are poor or contra-indicated, but 'good' takes many forms. A clear vision of objectives, combined with a detailed plan of how these can be met, respect for the individual needs of children and the wishes of parents, monitoring and evaluation are features of any good practice. Diversity of need is best met by informed reflective practice that incorporates societal, educational and legislative change and is informed by research evidence. Whatever the approach or setting, rigour was a key feature of the successful practice we observed. Parents comment that central to all this are the skilled ToDs and their co-professionals who advocate high quality access for all deaf children.

Finally, research reports such as this are expected to end by identifying further areas for investigation. While this can appear little more than a gesture of self-interest on the part of the researchers, it serves the important purpose of acknowledging gaps in the study. In chapter 2 we have already mentioned two of these. The first gap is that this report has not addressed the particular needs of children with mild deafness, but rather has focused on those with more severe deafness. This is a result of how the research was conducted and the role that ToDs are asked to perform. The second gap concerns two areas of work, work with deaf children from minority ethnic backgrounds and work with deaf children with disabilities. The team was disappointed that these two areas, identified as important aspects of the study, yielded very little data. It is possible that, despite the effort to achieve wide circulation of questionnaires, we were unable to access relevant groups. These gaps in the present study clearly constitute important areas for further investigation.

Glossary

Glossary

ATU	auditory training unit
BATOD	British Association of Teachers of the Deaf
BDA	British Deaf Association
BPVS	British Picture Vocabulary Scale
BSER	brain stem evoked response (audiometry)
BSL	British Sign Language
CACDP	Council for the Advancement of Communication with Deaf People
CSW	Communication Support Worker
dB	decibel
DELTA	Deaf Education through Listening and Talking
DEX	Deaf Ex-mainstreamers Group
DfE	Department for Education
DfEE	Department for Education and Employment
DI	Deaf instructor
ENT	Ear Nose and Throat (consultant/department)
FTE	full-time equivalent
FE	further education
HoS	Head of Service
ICT	Information and Communication Technology
IEP	Individual Education Plan
INSET	inservice training
KS	Key Stage
LARSP	Language Assessment Remediation and Screening Programme
LASER	Language of Sign as an Educational Resource
LEA	Local Education Authority
LSA	Learning Support Assistant
NATED	National Association for Tertiary Education for Deaf People
NDCS	National Deaf Children's Society
PSE	personal and social education
QToD	qualified teacher of the deaf
RNID	Royal National Institute for Deaf People
SATs	Standard Assessment Tests/tasks
SEN	Special Educational Needs
SENCO	Special Educational Needs Coordinator
SENSA	Special Educational Needs Support Assistant
SLT	Speech and Language Therapist
SNA	Special Needs Assistant

STAP	South Tyneside Assessment of Phonology
STASS	South Tyneside Assessment of Syntactic Structure
TC	Total Communication
ToD	Teacher of the Deaf
TROG	Test of the Receptive Use of Grammar
VToD	visiting Teacher of the Deaf

Further Reading

Further Reading

A selection of relevant texts relating to the themes in chapters 4 and 5 are presented here. First some general texts are listed, then texts under the thematic headings. There are some themes where our search of the literature did not reveal any material we would wish to specifically recommend here.

General texts

Gregory, S., Knight, P., McCracken, W., Powers, S. and Watson, L. (eds) (1998) *Issues in Deaf Education.* London: David Fulton Press.

This book recognises the changing context and practice of deaf education. It provides an accessible and comprehensive account of current issues in deaf education, including educational policy, the development of deaf children and young people, language and communication, curriculum issues and audiological management. Contributors are all specialists in these areas.

Luetke-Stahlman, B., Luckner, J. (1991) *Effectively educating children with hearing impairments.* London: Longman.

This book published in the US is written for teachers working in all types of educational setting and is full of practical suggestions many of which are directly applicable or can be modified for use by teachers in the UK. There are three main sections:

1. Preparing for Instruction

2. Language, Speech, Audition, and Speechreading: Assessment and Intervention Strategies

3. Effective Strategies for Teaching Academics to Students with Hearing Impairments

Luterman, D., Kurtzer-White, E., Seewald, R. (1999) *The Young Deaf Child.* York Press: Baltimore.

A key text in relation to support of the young child and his/her family. It is written in the context of changing technology, in particular, neo-natal screening, and deals with the many important implications of detecting hearing loss in babies. When do we tell parents? What do we know about the development of hearing and speech discrimination in the first year of life? How can we make best use of ever-advancing hearing aid technology? How do we tackle the issue of communication approach with parents of newly diagnosed deaf babies? How do we develop interaction between parent and child in the first few months? How do we ensure 'appropriate amplification'? What do we mean by 'appropriate amplification'? All these questions and more are addressed with a wealth of information, knowledge based on research and invaluable practical suggestions.

McCracken, W., Laoide-Kemp, S. (Eds) (1997) *Audiology in Education*. London: Whurr Publishers.

This book, which is informed by recent research, provides practical information on audiological management for teachers and others working with deaf children. It covers the role of teachers, diagnosis, communication options and conditions for the optimum development of listening, language and learning skill in deaf children.

Moores, D. F. (1996) *Educating the deaf: psychology, principles and practices.* 4th edition. Boston: Houghton Mifflin.

This is a comprehensive source book for teachers of deaf children which covers a wide range of topics including, an historical perspective on deafness and deaf education, deafness and the family, teaching speech, teaching deaf children with additional difficulties, literacy and deafness; and mental health. It was first published in 1978 and is now in its fourth edition. In the US it is a key text.

Powers, S., Gregory, S. and Thoutenhoofd, E. D. (1998) *The educational achievements of deaf children.* DfEE Research Report RR65. London: DfEE

This report is a major review of the literature on research on the educational achievement of deaf children and young people. It identifies both factors of educational achievement and factors affecting educational achievement. Taking as its starting point the work of Conrad, it reviews studies since that time. It discusses the present understanding in this area and also gaps in the information available.

Webster, A. (1986) *Deafness development and literacy.* London: Methuen.

This is a key text although it is over fifteen years old. The chapter on 'The basic facts of hearing impairment' describes different types of deafness and how hearing loss is measured; 'Understanding and appraising reading' looks at different models of reading and how reading skills are assessed including the difficulties of using some tests with deaf children; 'Reading writing and thinking' considers different explanations of the difficulty that many deaf children experience in acquiring skills in reading and writing; and 'Teaching strategies' suggests a number of approaches to teaching literacy skills to deaf children.

Webster, A., Wood, D. (1989) *Children with hearing difficulties.* London: Cassell.

This text is firmly set within a particular theoretical approach to the nature of learning. It is primarily written for mainstream teachers, but is more than an introductory text and will be useful for teachers of the deaf in training. The book provides basic information on hearing and hearing aids including a list of points for checking personal and radio aids; there is a checklist for assessing preverbal stages of language development with accompanying suggestions for intervention, a list of suggestions for promoting conversation, and useful ideas for developing reading and writing skills. There is very little discussion on signing approaches.

Wood, D., Wood, H., Grifiths, A., Howarth, I. (1986) *Teaching and talking with deaf children.* Chichester: John Wiley.

This book is still widely regarded as one of the key texts in the education of deaf children, even though it is now over fifteen years old. The book is based on several years research. It takes as its main focus processes of communication and language rather than a consideration of particular modes of communication, that is it is not concerned with issues around the use of spoken versus sign language. Its particular focus is on the styles of interaction of parents and teachers and centres its discussion around notions of contingency, conversational control and repair. There are many transcriptions of conversations between deaf children and adults which are used to illustrate how interactional features of language can be analysed.

Other reading

4.1 Leadership and management

Foulkes, A. M. (1992) Coping with a Conductive Caseload.
Journal of the British Association of Teachers of the Deaf, (16), 1, 3-16.

Garner, M. (1985) The Conductively Deaf Child – Our Problem?
Journal of the British Association of Teachers of the Deaf, (9), 4, 95-100.

Rayner, S. (1999) *Headteachers and Leadership in Special Education.* London: Cassell.

4.2 Ethos

Scottish Office Education Department (1992) *Using Ethos Indicators in Primary School Self Evaluation: Taking Account of Views of Pupils, Parents and Teachers.*
School Development Planning Support Materials.

4.4 Inclusion

Ainscow, M. (1997) Towards inclusive schooling. *British Journal of Special Education,* 24, 1, 3-6.

Dyson, A. (1994) Towards a collaborative learning model for responding to student diversity. *Support for Learning,* 9, 2, 53-60.

Powers, S. (1996) Inclusion is an attitude not a place: Parts 1 and 2.
Journal of British Association of Teachers of the Deaf, 20, 2, 35-41 and 20, 3, 65-69.

Thomas, G. (1992) *Effective Classroom Teamwork: Support or Intrusion.*
London: Routledge.

4.5 Support in mainstream

Edgar, G. (1990) The role of the Peripatetic Teacher of the Deaf.
British Association of Teachers of the Deaf Magazine, September 1990, 2-4.

Lynas, W. (in press) Supporting the deaf child in the mainstream: is there a best way?
Support for Learning.

Monkman, H., Baskind, S. (1998) Are assistants effectively supporting hearing-impaired children in mainstream schools? *Deafness and Education,* 22, 1, 15-22.

Watson, L. (1992) Supporting hearing-impaired pupils in mainstream classes.
Support for Learning, 7, 2, 82-87.

Watson, L., Parsons, J. (1998) Supporting deaf pupils in mainstream settings.
In S. Gregory, P. Knight, W. McCracken, S. Powers, L. Watson (eds)
Issues in Deaf Education. London: David Fulton.

4.6 Audiological management

Richards, S., Smith, M. (1990) Some essential aspects of an effective adiological management programme for school age hearing impaired children.
Journal of the British Association of Teachers of the Deaf, (14), 4, 104-113.

Ross M. (ed) (1992) *FM Auditory training systems. Maryland:*York Press

4.7 Spoken language development

Bonsor, P. (1994) Fostering the Development of Oral Language through the Use of Multimedia Software. *Journal of the British Association of Teachers of the Deaf Magazine,* September 1994, 5-7.

Gallaway, C., Richards, B. J. (Eds) (1994) *Input and Interaction in Language Acquisition,* Cambridge: Cambridge University Press
Lewis, S. and Richards, S. (1988) *The early stages of language development - a natural aural approach,* Journal of the British Association of Teachers of the Deaf, (12) 2, 33-38

Mogford, K. (1989) Oral language acquisition in the prelingually deaf, In D. Bishop and K. Mogford (eds). *Language Development in Exceptional Circumstances.* Edinburgh: Churchill Livingstone

4.8 Literacy

Banks, J., Fraser, P., Fyfe, R., Grant, J., Gray, C., Macauley, M., Williams, S. (1989) Teaching Deaf Children to Read. A Pilot Study of a Method. *Journal of the British Association of Teachers of the Deaf,* (13), 5, 129-141.

Fahy, W. (1988) Reading Groups at St John's Catholic School for Hearing-Impaired Children, Boston Spa. *British Association of Teachers of the Deaf Magazine,*
March 1988, 6-7.

Lewis, S. (1996) The Reading Achievements of a Group of Severely and Profoundly Hearing Impaired School Leavers Educated within a Natural Aural Approach. *Journal of the British Association of Teachers of the Deaf,* (20), 1, 1-7.

Lewis, S. (1998) Reading and writing within an oral/aural approach, In, S. Gregory, P. Knight, W. McCracken, S. Powers and L. Watson (eds) *Issues in Deaf Education.* London: David Fulton.

Swanwick, R. (1993) The use of DARTs to develop deaf children's literacy skills within a bilingual context, *Deafness and Development,* (3) 2, 4-9

Watson, L. M. (1994) The Use of a Developmental Approach to Teaching Writing. *Journal of the British Association of Teachers of the Deaf,* (18), 1, 18-29.

Watson, L. M. (1999) Literacy and deafness: the challenge continues, *Deafness and Education International,* (1) 2, 96-107.

4.9 Personal and social development

Clark, P, Fulwood, L. (1994) Social skills activities to use with hearing impaired children. *Journal of British Association of Teachers of the Deaf,* 18, 3.

Rustin, L., Kuhr, A. (1989) *Social skills and the speech impaired.* London: Taylor Francis.

Spence, S. (1980) *Social skills training with children and adolescents.*

4.10 Deaf children with disabilities

Bond, D. E. (1986) Psychological Assessment of Hearing Impaired and Multi-handicapped Deaf. In D. Ellis, (Ed.) *Sensory Impairements in Mentally Handicapped People.* Croom Helm.

Clark, P. (1994) Access to the National Curriculum for Hearing Impaired Children with Additional Handicaps. *Journal of the British Association of Teachers of the Deaf,* (18), 2, 61-71.

Jones, J. (1986) Hearing Impaired Children with an Additional Visual Problem. *British Association of Teachers of the Deaf Magazine,* March 1986, 5-6.

McCracken, W. (1994) Deaf Children with Complex Needs: a Piece in the Puzzle. *Journal of the British Association of Teachers of the Deaf,* (18), 2, 54-60.

Morgan, L. R. (1994) The National Curriculum and Multi-sensory Deprived Children. *Journal of the British Association of Teachers of the Deaf,* (18), 2, 41-44.

Murdoch, H. (1990) Deaf and Visually-Impaired: A Support Service for Deaf Visually Impaired Children Educated alongside Sighted Deaf Peers. *Journal of the British Association of Teachers of the Deaf,* (14), 4, 93-103.

4.11 Work with families and young children

Evans, D. M. (1980) Some Aspects of Parent Counselling in Schools for the Deaf. *Journal of the British Association of Teachers of the Deaf,* (4), 3, 81-83.

Hunter, N. (1995) You are Never too Young. *British Association of Teachers of the Deaf Magazine,* May 1995, 20-21.

Robson, M, Wilders, T. (1980) Parents in Partnership. *Journal of the British Association of Teachers of the Deaf,* (4), 5, 142-147.

Ruggles, T. G. (1980) Counselling and Guidance available to the Hearing Impaired Child, his Family, and those Concerned with his Welfare. Primary Age. *Journal of the British Association of Teachers of the Deaf,* (4), 3, 84-85.

Taylor, B. (1980) The Guidance of Parents of Hearing Impaired Children. *Journal of the British Association of Teachers of the Deaf,* (4), 3, 76-78.

Watson, L. M., Lewis, S. (1997) Working with parents: setting the parameters. *Deafness and Education,* (21), 2, 32-40.

4.12 Deaf children from minority ethnic backgrounds

Ahmad W, Darr, A. Jones, L., Nisar, G (1998) *Deafness and ethnicity: Services, policy and practices.* Bristol: Policy Press.

Ahmad, W. I. U. (1993) *'Race' and health in contemporary Britain,* Milton Keynes: Open University Press.

Chamba, R. Ahmad, W., Jones, L. (1998) *Improving services for Asian deaf children: Parents and professional perspectives.* Bristol, Policy Press.

Duffy, A. (1993) *A Capital Service? A Review of Educational services for Deaf Children in Inner London.* London: RNID.

Turner, S. (1996) Meeting the needs of children under five with sensori-neural hearing loss from ethnic minority families. *Journal of the British Association of Teachers of the Deaf,* (20), 4, 91-100.

4.13 Further education

Greenwood, P. (1982) Further Education – The Need for a Coherent National Policy. *British Association of Teachers of the Deaf Magazine,* May 1982, 9-11.

Kell, M. D. (1980) FE for the Hearing Impaired – theoretical basis and practical implications. *Journal of the British Association of Teachers of the Deaf,* (4), 4, 130-136.

Luterman, D. (1987) *Deafness in the family.* Boston: Little: Brown and Company.

McLoughlaine, G. (1983) Establishing and FE Service. *British Association of Teachers of the Deaf Magazine,* January 1983, 9-10.

Nield, E. (1987) Preparing Vth Year Pupils for Further Education. *British Association of Teachers of the Deaf Magazine,* (11), 3, 75-79.

Sutton, J. (1980) Counselling the Post-16 Hearing Impaired. *Journal of the British Association of Teachers of the Deaf,* (4), 3, 89-92.

5.2 The oral aural approach

Andrews, E. M. (1988) The relationship between natural auralism and the maternal reflective way of working, *Journal of the British Association of Teachers of the Deaf,* (12), 3, 49-56

Matthews, Sr. C. (1988) The maternal reflective method (MRM) in an English setting, In, I. G. Taylor, (Ed) *The Education of the Deaf: Current Perspectives,* London: Croom Helm

Watson, L. M. (1998) Oralism – current policy and practice, In S. Gregory, P. Knight, W. McCracken, S. Powers and L. Watson, (Eds) *Issues in Deaf Education,* London: David Fulton.

5.3 Sign bilingualism

Ahlgren, I., Hytenstam, K.(Eds) (1994) *Bilingualism in deaf education.* Hamburg: Signum-Verl.

Deafness and Education (1997) Special Focus Edition. Sign bilingualism in the education of deaf children. (21) 3

Dowe, S. (1990) The Contribution of Deaf Adults to the Education of the Deaf in Bedfordshire. *British Association of Teachers of the Deaf Magazine,* May 1990, 7-8.

Knight, P., Swanwick, R. (Eds) *Bilingualism and the education of deaf children.* Leeds, ADEDC School of Education.

Llewellyn-Jones, M. (1986) An Example of the Application of a Bilingual Approach to the Education of Deaf Children. *British Association of Teachers of the Deaf Magazine,* September 1986, 7-11.

Malhshie, S. (1995) *Educating Children Bilingually.* Washington DC, Gallaudet University Press.

A review of good practice in deaf education

Appendix 1

Questionnaire

**THE UNIVERSITY
OF BIRMINGHAM**

THE UNIVERSITY
of MANCHESTER

Good practice in the education of deaf children

What is good practice? If you have an interest in the education of deaf [1] children we need to know what you think.

The Royal National Institute for Deaf People is funding research by the Universities of Birmingham and Manchester into good practice in the education of deaf children and young people. We want to collect examples of good educational practice as reported by parents, teachers and deaf children and young people.

We need to know the names of schools, services or individual teachers. Once we have collected your ideas of examples of good practice, some will be selected for case study. The information you give will be treated confidentially. Do get in touch. This is an opportunity to have your voice heard!

You are asked to complete *EITHER* Part 1 *OR* Part 2 *OR* BOTH PARTS of this questionnaire.

First of all

If you are completing any part of this questionnaire please state if you are a

parent of a deaf child	☐	*tick one or more boxes*
teacher of the deaf	☐	
deaf adult	☐	
other (please specify)	☐	

---

[1] The term 'deaf' is used here to cover all degrees of hearing loss.

Questionnaire part 1

1   Please state here your suggestion of an example of good practice

Name of school, service, college or teacher   **Their address**

_____

_____

_____

_____

_____

_____

2 If possible please indicate the areas in which, in your opinion, this school, service, college or individual teacher is particularly good

(you can tick as few or as many items as you like)

Teaching reading and writing	☐	Working with parents	☐
The use of hearing aids	☐	The language/communication approach used	☐
The choice of schools for parents	☐	Exam results of deaf children	☐
The work of classroom assistants	☐	Developing children's signing skills	☐
Supporting deaf pupils in ordinary schools	☐	Developing children's spoken language skills	☐
In-service training for teachers of the deaf	☐	Helping children develop independence	☐
Helping children develop their identity	☐	Work with deaf children with disabilities	☐
Work with very young children	☐	Further education	☐

Other (please specify) _____

3. If you wish you can add further comment in the box below about what you think is particularly good about the school, service, college or individual teacher you have named

Questionnaire part 2

(you can ignore this part of the questionnaire if you wish)

There are different views about aims and what constitutes good practice in deaf education. For example, different approaches to the education of deaf children place different emphasis on the importance of language and communication, literacy, access to the curriculum and the development of self-esteem and identity. We would welcome your views on these matters.

1. What in your view are the most important aims of deaf education?

> huh?

2. What do you think most helps deaf children and young people develop their full potential?

> nowt.

3. What in your view are the main obstacles to deaf children and young people achieving their full potential?

> nowt

4. Please state here any further comments you would like to add concerning your views on what constitutes good practice in deaf education.

Finally

If you would be happy to discuss your comments with us further please add your name and address here.

It would be useful for us to know where you obtained this questionnaire. Please state this here.

Thank your for completing this questionnaire.

Please return to:

Mrs J Little, University of Birmingham, School of Education, Edgbaston, Birmingham, B15 2TT.

Appendix 2

Deaf Organisations

Deaf Organisations

The following organisations were contacted as part of the Good Practice Review and we express our thanks to them for responding to our request for information.

BATOD (British Association of Teachers of the Deaf)
The professional association for teachers of the deaf.
> BATOD, Paul A Simpson, 21 The HayStacks, High Wycombe,
> Buckinghamshire, HP13 6PY
> batodsec@compuserve.com

BDA (British Deaf Association)
> BDA, 1-3 Worship Street, London EC2A 2AB

DELTA (Deaf Education through Listening and Talking)
An association of young deaf adults, teachers and parents of deaf children to promote the natural aural approach to the education of deaf children.
> DELTA, PO Box 20, Haverhill, Suffolk CB9 7BD

DEX (Deaf Ex-Mainstreamers' Group)
Deaf adults who have attended hearing mainstream schools, and deaf and hearing supporters who consider mainstreaming has not been successful and want to ensure that 'inclusive' education is true integration of both deaf and hearing pupils.
> Jill Jones (Chair of DEX)
> PO Box 3, Ryhill, Wakefield WF4 2AE

THE EWING FOUNDATION
A charitable foundation which supports parents, teachers and other professionals in their work with hearing impaired children with the aim of fostering the maximal use of residual hearing and the promotion of spoken language competence.
> The Ewing Foundation, 40 Bernard Street, London, WC1N 1LG

FYD (Friends for Young Deaf People)
> East Court Mansion, College Lane, East Grinstead, West Sussex RH19 3LT

LASER (The Language of Sign as an Educational Resource)
An alliance of educators, researchers and parents from deaf and hearing communities which promotes the use and role of BSL in the education of deaf children.
> LASER, 8 Church Lane, Kimpton, Hitchin, Herts SG4 8RP

NATED (National Association for Tertiary Education for Deaf People)
An association for all those interested in the participation of, and access for, deaf and hard
of hearing students and trainees in tertiary education
    NATED, 54 Cavendish Road, Harringay, London N4 1RS

NDCS (National Deaf Children's Society)
An organisation of families, parents and carers which exists to enable deaf children and
young people to maximise their skills and abilities.
    NDCS, 15 Dufferin Street, London EC1Y 8UR

SENSE (The National Deafblind and Rubella Association)
An organisation supporting and campaigning for people who are deafblind, their families,
carers and professionals who work with them.
    SENSE, 11-13 Clifton Terrace, London N4 3SR

Documents

The following documents and publications were referred to in the process of compiling
our report:

BATOD (1994)	*The organisation and management of LEA educational services*
	for hearing impaired pupils and young people in England and Wales
(1995)	*Towards a national policy in the education of deaf children and young people*
(1998)	*Communication modes currently in use in the education of deaf children and young people in the UK*
BDA (1996)	*The right to be equal. Education policy statement*
DEX	*Responses to the government Green Paper*
DELTA (1997)	*The right to hear and be heard. Education policy*
	The natural aural approach: a statement of principles
	The natural aural approach to the education of deaf children: a definition
LASER (1998)	*Pickersgill, M., Gregory, S. Sign bilingualism: a model*
NATED (1998)	*Response to the government Green Paper: Excellence for All*
	Response to the government Green Paper: The Learning Age
NDCS (1994)	*NDCS policy on communication*
(1995)	*Inspection for schools with deaf pupils*
	Charter for parental partnership in education
Sense (1998)	*The education of deafblind/MSI children*